France on Foot

France on Foot

Village to Village, Hotel to Hotel:
How to Walk the French Trail System
on Your Own

Bruce LeFavour

1999; Attis Press
Saint Helena, California

Publisher's Cataloging-in-Publication *(Provided by Quality Books, Inc.)*

LeFavour, Bruce.
France on foot : village to village, hotel to hotel : how to walk the French trail
system on your own / Bruce LeFavour — 1st ed.
p. cm.
Includes bibliographical references and index.
Preassigned LCCN: 98-85117
ISBN: 0-9663448-0-4

1. Hiking—France. 2. France—Guidebooks.   I. Title.

GV199.44.F7L55 1999   796.5'1'0944
                             QBI98-612

First Edition, January 1999

10 9 8 7 6 5 4 3 2 1

Attis Press
1247 Hudson, Avenue, PO Box 209
Saint Helena, CA 94574-0209

with love,
for four extraordinary individuals:
Faith
Sidney
Nicole
Cree

Acknowledgements

FIRST AND FOREMOST I want to thank my primary editor, Naiomi Cutner, whose sharp eye and incisive comments honed and focused this book. Her knowledge of France and the French language was invaluable. I am also greatly indebted to Anne Fox whose edit at the end helped find the errors that I had introduced during the revision process. Her comments were leavened with a large dose of kindness and encouragement. While the design of the interior of this book is entirely my responsibility, San Francisco designer Sandy McHenry unselfishly offered both the names of essential resources and gentle suggestions concerning my efforts.

Among the many readers, Jim Shrupp, who tackled the book when it was nearly complete, contributed a fresh and helpful perspective. No less influential were the early readers: John and Catherine Smith, Sidney LeFavour, Susan Kraus and Nicole LeFavour. Having walked in France, readers Dwight Garner, Cree LeFavour and Jerry and Angela Foster gave detailed critiques from a knowledgeable point of view. All of you who braved the unedited wilds of my manuscript will see the results of your corrections, questions and comments in the book. Thank you.

Initially, three magical chefs, Cindy Pawlcyn, Barbara Tropp and Margaret Fox, gave me sound advice and much-needed encouragement from their perspective as successful cookbook authors. Later in the process, author Susan Costner shared her time and knowledge generously. Dwight Garner, book editor of the online magazine *Salon*, has helped continuously with specific and useful advice that, as far as I'm concerned, goes far, far beyond any pro forma obligation he may have as a son-in-law. Thank you all.

So many people have helped in so many ways that it will be impossible to remember them all, but the following individuals come immediately to mind. Thanks to Camilla Turnbull for the important connections; to Brigitta House at Michelin, to Roger Perrier and Béatrice Youmbi at the FFRP and to Catherine Dupré at the IGN for timely aid in getting the necessary permissions; to Trön Bykle, Agathe Bennich, Sarah Forni and Tony Cartlidge for their perspectives on walking in France and, to Tony, for the loan of out-of-print books; to Herb McGrew for early inspiration; to Benedicte Denizet for a French woman's take on walking and for critical help with the key man; to Tim and Stephanie Johnston for information and wine (not necessarily in that order); to Herb and Ann Young for understanding and sustenance at the beach in Maine; and specially to Alta Tingle, Colin Smith, Bill Noonan, Carl Duncan and Lisa Holland for unquestioning support and encouragement.

Putting one word after another is not easy for me; to compound that problem I immerse myself completely in any project I take on. As a result, the writing of this book was a long, intense affair, which, for unreasonable periods of time, diverted me from the routines and pleasures of life at home. My wife, Faith Echtermeyer, suffered these "absences" with good humor, patience and almost constant understanding. Thank you, Faith!

Credits

Though modified by the author, the two detailed maps of France in this book, which appear on pages 42 and 44, were based on maps created by Mountain High Maps, Digital Wisdom, Inc., PO Box 2070, Tappahannock, VA 22560, and are reproduced here under license.

    Mountain High Maps ® copyright © 1993 Digital Wisdom, Inc.

The small sections of map 903 and map 1710 E, which appear on page 86, have been reproduced with the permission of French Institut Géographique National or IGN, Départements Grands Clients, 2–4 Avenue Pasteur, 94165 Sainte–Mande Cedex.

    carte n° 903 © IGN PARIS 1996, © FFRP 1996
    carte n° 1710 E © IGN PARIS 1988
    Autorisation n° 90-8011

The small section of Michelin map 231, which appears on page 80, has been reproduced with the kind permission Michelin Travel Publications, Michelin North America, Greenville, South Carolina 29602.

    © MICHELIN, Carte No. 231 France Normandie (1995 édition)
    Autorisation No. 9804210

Throughout this book written and pictorial references are made to blazes and trail marks. I reproduce these marks with the kind permission of the Fédération Française de la Randonnée Pédestre or FFRP, 14, rue Riquet, 75019 Paris.

    Sentiers de Grande Randonnée, GR, GR *de pays* and PR, as well as the GR path patterns: white/red and yellow/red, are registered trademarks of the FFRP. They cannot be used, reproduced or transcribed, in any form or by any means, without the prior written permission of the FFRP.

The list of regional tourist offices starting on page 221 comes from several sources, but the primary reference was the *Guide Pratique du Randonneur*, © 1993 by the FFRP.

All products or brand names mentioned in this book—such as Gore-Tex®, Magic Marker®,Tampax®, Vibram® and Kelty®—are trademarks, registered or otherwise, of their respective owners.

Summary of Contents

Table of Contents

A note on money

Lately, the value of the *franc français* or French franc
(FF) has fluctuated widely. Almost two years ago, one
dollar would buy only 4.90 FF, but in August 1997, one
dollar would have bought 6.35 FF. As I write, the dollar
is back down to 6.00 FF. This volatility has made it
difficult for me to give you, the reader, a firm idea of
how much purchases—hotels, maps or meals—will
cost while you are walking in France. My solution has
been to give all prices in francs and to leave the conversion up to you. Inconvenient, perhaps, but at least you
will not be misled. I have included as sidebars some
rough dollar to franc conversion rates; you can find
yesterday's actual rate in the financial sections of many
newspapers. All prices quoted in this book were current in 1998.

The euro is scheduled to replace the franc (at the rate
of 7 francs to 1 euro) on 1 January 1999, but even if the
changeover occurs on schedule, French francs will
continue to circulate alongside the euro for three years,
that is until 1 January 2002.

I'd rather...
ride on Shanks's mare.

– Samuel Bishop, 1795

France on Foot

Why Walk?

Your vacation on foot

Walking through the French countryside on your vacation is like lingering over a leisurely feast, the equivalent of the best meal of your life. In contrast, driving through France is a ten-minute gobble in a fast-food joint, speedy but not very satisfying.

Everyone has a personal vision of the ideal vacation. Before I knew better, mine included traveling in France by car, but after three years of vehicle-centered leaves and passes from the army while I was stationed there during the early 1960s, I came to dislike such holidays. After only two or three days on the road, I'd find myself bloated from a combination of too much rich food and no exercise, bored with kilometer after kilometer of driving and annoyed that much of what was important—the small villages, the people—was going by too fast, a blur on the bug-splotched windshield.

Once free of Uncle Sam, my solution was to bicycle through France whenever I could take time off from my career as a chef. This slower method of transportation was far superior to the automobile because—bingo!—it introduced me to the fact that exercise could be combined with self-indulgence. I didn't camp out. Instead I stayed in hotels. I drank my share of wine. I ate well and, when I could afford it, very well. And most important, I was exposing myself to the details—people, smells, sounds—of what lay *between* my destinations.

The man who walks takes title to the world.
– American proverb

Ultimately, however, bicycling itself became unsatisfactory. I was covering only thirty to seventy miles a day, but that was still too fast. Also, as France prospered over the years, traffic, even on the secondary roads, increased dramatically, and pedaling became more and more dangerous. That's when I discovered that it was possible to walk, and when I did, I made sure to port over the proper attitude. No camping gear, no cooking out. I was still in France to enjoy what that culture had to offer and now, walking, I was just doing it a bit more slowly and a bit more thoroughly than before. By necessity I was paying even *more* attention to the details and I found the experience delightful.

All fine and good, but here you could be forgiven some confusion and a question: *How is it possible to spend a vacation walking in France?*

It's easy enough to imagine the English out on a long-distance walk, clomping along in heavy leather hiking boots, wearing tweed over bulky wool sweaters and carrying droopy old-fashioned canvas packs. This is simply a crude caricature of what we picture the English to be. But the French? Walking? Such an idea doesn't fit our stereotype at all. But as unlikely as it may seem, France even more than England is a walker's paradise: France, only three times England's size, has more than eight times the mileage of public footpaths. These are not just secondary roads cobbled together and called trails but real paths, dirt tracks passing through forests, vineyards, gardens and fields, that are well marked, well mapped and open to anyone who has both the knowledge and the determination to use them.

France on Foot will give you the necessary knowledge, all the how-to details you will need to plan a walking vacation and then travel from village to village, hotel to hotel and restaurant to restaurant on foot for a few days, a few weeks or a month.

In the following chapters you'll find a detailed description of the vast French trail system, my recommendations for the equipment needed to make every day in France a comfortable one and an explanation of the various maps that will prove helpful before and during your walk. There are critiques of the guides needed to locate a meal and a bed at the end of the day. There's a

Facing page:

Walking in France is pleasurable and leisurely. The pace allows you to absorb the details of the forests, fields and villages—as here— you will pass through.

portable walker's vocabulary that will help the non-French speaker to communicate. Sources for maps and books are given. The cost of a walking vacation for both the retired executive and the student with a limited number of francs in his pocket is spelled out. The only element lacking is the determination, and after you've read the book it's possible you'll find even that.

And once you decide to walk in France you'll do it on your own. Many people dislike joining a group to travel, but at the same time they are at a loss about how to plan and then take a trip independently, particularly when it involves more than just driving around the countryside in that moving isolation booth, a car. There are some activities—trekking in Bhutan, scuba diving in the Solomon Islands, visiting Antarctica—that, if you are to do them at all, absolutely require that you use an adventure travel company, but setting off with a few friends or with your family to walk cross-country in France is not one of them.

Armed with the information in this book, you won't walk with a tour guide and a group of strangers but on your own with the people *you* choose. Instead of paying someone else thousands of dollars to plan and organize your trip, your "fee" will consist—as I explain later—of four to ten hours spent at home extracting and organizing hotel and restaurant information from guidebooks, an enjoyable task since it allows you to imagine and visualize your trip in advance.

But first, here at the beginning, let's get one thing straight. As I have already hinted, walking in France is *not* backpacking in France. Walking, as I define it, means sleeping in a hotel bed, not in a sleeping bag on the ground. Walking means dining in restaurants, not downing freeze-dried dinners around a smoky fire. Walking means stopping in a sidewalk café for a cold draft beer, not drinking tepid water from a canteen. Yes, like a backpacker you will carry a pack with all your clothes, your books and whatever else you need to live comfortably, but unlike that backpacker you will not carry food, cooking pots or camping gear. And by carefully following the guidelines I'll spell out, you can reduce the weight of your pack to a very comfortable minimum yet still carry everything you'll need for even weeks of independent travel.

Walking is to backpacking as strolling on the beach is to running a marathon; both involve physical exercise, but the one is a leisurely, often social experience while the other is a punishing personal challenge, individual and intense. Put another way, walking in France is a glass of good wine while backpacking is a tumbler of ice water. Cold water is good for you and all that, but in this book we are definitely talking wine. After all, it is your vacation.

There are other reasons to walk in France beside the desire to experience the countryside more slowly.

Though some might be embarrassed to acknowledge the fact, the most basic is that the very idea of walking cross-country from one town to the next and then on to another is romantic and enthralling. At some very primitive level transporting oneself over long distances on foot—a return to much simpler times—appeals to an important part of our psyche. To walk from Paris to Avignon is a dream of mine that may never be realized. Yet, whenever I envision that adventure, the picture in my head unfailingly sets fire to my imagination and, as dreams do, sustains my spirit.

More practically, my wife Faith, whose successful career as a photographer demands that she spend a great deal of time on the phone and on the road, says that the main reasons to take a walking vacation can be put very simply: "No phone, no FAX, no car!"

But even though these other reasons are compelling, the *best* reason to walk is still the fact that doing so makes the traveler slow down. This was forcefully brought home to me by a young Australian bicyclist whom my wife and I met in 1989 as we were setting off on a day hike up the Fillière Valley near Annecy in the French Alps. We and the bicyclist were outside the same small grocery store packing away picnics— *reblochon* cheese, ham and bread—when, hearing our English, he initiated a conversation.

It turned out that he was on his way around the world and had already been on the road for a year and a half. During that time he'd pedaled as much as was physically and politically possible from Australia through Southeast Asia, the Middle East and into Europe. After I remarked enviously what an interesting experience

The slow pace of a walk allows you to notice the details. Here a dead crow strung up by a farmer in his newly planted field serves as a very real scarecrow.

his trip must have been, he agreed that it had been that and more but then added that he had one regret, that he was not walking.

"Traveling by bicycle is just too fast," he said. Walking, he believed, dictates just the right pace, a pace that allows the traveler to become intimately involved with the country and, not incidentally, to meet more of the local people along the way.

"If only I had the time!" was his lament.

A walk in France *is* slow, and that is its glory. The pace forces the person on foot to notice not just the broad outlines but also the details: the formality and weed-free neatness of the backyard vegetable plots with leeks and carrots spaced just so, the bewildering variety of wildflowers in the fields, the eerie stillness of rural villages at midday and the newly planted field with a dead crow strung by its feet from the top of a pole as a warning to its brothers (a *real* scarecrow). You hear the joyful chaos of sound from a schoolyard at recess time and you not only see the color but also smell the knock-you-down perfume from a blooming hedge of lilacs. The foot traveler is not an isolated spectator but a participant, sensually as well as intellectually involved in the events of the moment.

Village cafés are not just drinking establishments. They are also social centers where you will be as welcome as the locals.

Arriving at five in the afternoon in a small village that on the surface seems almost lifeless, the person on foot doesn't have the option of speeding onward in a car to another perhaps more exciting town or city. Instead, the walker must settle in and make do.

But those who remain open and curious will, more

often than not, find hidden delights. Perhaps a huge, almost swimmable claw-foot bathtub in the bathroom off a spacious and comfortable room up under the eaves, the walls decorated with blue and white toile but somehow right in spite of that fact. Or a friendly café with an intense, *pastis*-fueled *pétanque* game in the dirt outside the front door. Or a small Romanesque

church on the village square with primitive but moving wood carvings and a nicely proportioned apse. Maybe even the surprise of a simple but well-prepared meal in a rustic dining room that, if the truth were told, was better than the expensive but disappointing dinner eaten at a fancy restaurant the night before.

Long spring evenings are conducive to serious but good-natured pétanque games.

The leisurely pace of a walk in France doesn't permit the foot traveler to bounce frenetically like the traditional visitor from monument to monument, restaurant to restaurant and sight to site. Because you are circumscribed physically by the limited number of miles you can cover in a day, you are liberated from the dictatorial must-dos, must-sees and must-eats of the guidebooks.

With only a tentative itinerary and a schedule at the mercy of the weather, you have only one decision to make each morning: how far do you wish to walk? All the rest, all the other happenings of your day flow naturally and inevitably from that, leaving you free to appreciate and absorb whatever comes your way. You are carefree.

Paradoxically then, to walk in France is to relax in the true sense of the word.

Marchons!

The Footpaths
110,000 miles of trail

CLODS OF MUD stuck to the soles of our sneakers and then peeled off suddenly and unpredictably—an incredible lightness of being—as my wife Faith and I slogged up the path bordering the vineyard.

Fog dimmed nearby landmarks and obscured the vineyards, woodlots and low hills in the distance leaving us as though isolated on an ever-changing island. Hinting at the sun just above, the fog smothered color but at the same time made the terrain shine with a luminous monotone of grey. Faith, ever the photographer, remarked on the strange beauty of the light.

At the corner of the vineyard the path we were following took a sharp right turn to pass through a break in the low stone wall that marked the boundary of cultivation. There nature reasserted itself and the path deteriorated immediately, disappeared into a dense thicket of head-high, very wet willow shoots. Despite the fog, the drops of moisture sparkled on the new spring leaves. I hesitated. To Faith, who had stopped behind me, I said, pointing to the obvious, "This is the way." She shrugged in reply. Enthusiastic, patient but just the slightest bit dubious from the start, she didn't complain.

After another glance at the map in my hand to assure myself there were no alternatives, I tentatively and then forcefully led the way into and through the dense

Randonnée n. fem. (old French randir, to run rapidly) 1. A journey over an extended period of time on foot, bicycle, horseback, skis, etc.. Sentier de Grande Randonnée (abbr.: GR): a specially marked trail which makes possible long-distance trips...

– Petit Larousse Illustré, *1990*

copse, crossing my fingers that the road marked on that map was as close on the other side as it was supposed to be. After only thirty seconds of thrashing, my "water-repellent" windbreaker soaked through, and my chino pants felt as if they had absorbed more than their weight in water. The willows, bruised by our indelicate passage, smelled curiously sweet.

This was the inauspicious start of my first "walk" in France and, as you can tell, it was not exactly enjoyable. Faith and I had arrived the day before for a week's stay at a farmhouse in Chaintré, a small town in the Mâconnais region north of Lyon. We had come to this quiet area to spend our vacation strolling the countryside on foot.

Back home in the United States I would never have attempted to walk cross-country where the land is owned by anyone other than the State or Federal government. There are no public trails through private land where I live, and the local landowners would take a dim view of my crossing their property without permission. I'm sure if I were ever to walk off-road from my home to the neighboring town only eight miles away, I would be arrested by an indignant sheriff— *what the* hell *are you doing?*—before I got halfway there.

Walking paths in France pass through private forests and vineyards. Here walkers approach the hill at Solutré.

But the previous autumn I'd read a short article in a travel magazine that assured the reader the situation in France was different: many trails there crossed private land and were open to anyone. It was, the author stated, easy and enjoyable to walk off-road in France. So, even though the article was long on enthusiasm but short on detail, we—innocents abroad—had bought a map of the local area at a bookstore in the nearby city of Mâcon and, with not a clue as to what we were doing, had then set out to walk around the local wine country, places like Pouilly and Fuissé.

On that first walk, we did finally reach our destination, the small town of Fuissé, and, after a hot grog followed by a filling lunch, we dried and recuperated enough to enjoy, since the fog had burned off, a sunny return that took us over back roads rather than evanescent trails. As our week progressed, we ventured off pavement again, choosing routes more carefully. Eventually during our wanderings, just west of the town of Solutré with its dramatic hill and many prehistoric artifacts, we ran across white and red blazes on a trail that was wider and much better groomed than any we had seen up to that point. Curious, we followed the path for a mile before returning to Chaintré.

The next day I went back to the bookstore in Mâcon to ask questions. After I described the trail we had seen, a friendly clerk patiently explained that what we had stumbled across was just a tiny part of a system of maintained walking paths called *sentiers de grande randonnée* (long-distance trails). They went everywhere, he said.

What I had not understood when we started our vacation was that France had not only paths but an extensive *system* of paths that the clerk claimed would be easy to use once we learned how. *These* were the trails that the article I had read was apparently attempting, however vaguely, to describe.

A trail system in France?

At first I found it hard to believe that a system existed. After all, I had lived in France for three years and later, over a thirty-year period, had traveled at least a dozen times by car or bicycle to almost every part of every region of the country and yet I had never heard one word about official walking trails. Yes, I had hiked in the Alps, and yes, I had walked a few canal tow paths, but what I was hearing about now was different from anything I could have imagined. Even after the clerk in the bookstore explained that the blazes and the fine trail we had seen outside Solutré were part of something larger, I still thought this "system" must be a new, half-realized project that might prove to be superb in places like Solutré but incomplete and therefore unusable elsewhere. But then, just before we returned to the United States, I happened on a map that convinced me the system was not only real but also far more extensive than even the clerk had been able to convey.

This map is called *France Grande Randonnée* or France Long Distance Walking Paths, and once it's completely unfolded, the most convenient way to look at it is to spread it on the floor—it's too big for all but the largest kitchen table. At first glance you assume you're looking at a road map that indicates highways with red lines,

Map 903 presents an overview of the French trail system

but on closer examination you find that all the red lines aren't roads but the routes of numbered footpaths as they snake their way everywhere. The map is number 903, published by the Institut géographique national or IGN, the French equivalent of the United States Geological Survey. It presents you with a grand overview of the French trail system, and what a view it is.

During our wanderings in the Mâconnais we had walked on only a small segment of one national trail, the GR 76A, but once we became familiar with map 903 we realized that what we had seen near Solutré was not, as I had continued to suspect, an anomaly but was just what the bookstore clerk had claimed—the norm. Looking at the map, you can see plainly that every region—Provence, the Loire, Normandy, the Dordogne, Brittany, the Alps—has a whole complex of numbered off-road trails and that each of these complexes is in turn joined to those in adjoining regions. The whole forms a web that makes it possible to choose, for example, five or six obvious routes, each one of which would allow you to walk, if you had the time and energy, across France from the English Channel to the Mediterranean.

Almost 37,500 miles of trails are traced on map 903, more than one and a half times the distance around the world at the equator.

Who established the system?

The existence of a complex and vast system of trails in a culture that, on the surface, seems urbane and sedentary was so surprising to me that I immediately began to wonder what individual or group established the system.

The Fédération française de la randonnée pédestre, a big mouthful of French that translates into the French Long Distance Walking Federation or FFRP for short, established and continues to maintain all the French walking paths. Its origins lie in the 1930s before the Second World War, when a small group of hikers and climbers began to mark trails in certain regions, particularly the Alps. These activists were concerned because the paths, which up until that time had been open to all, were in decline, even then increasingly lost to the automobile or swallowed by the ever-larger farms of modern agriculture.

In 1947 other individuals and organizations joined the preservation effort, and under the vigorous leadership of guidebook writer and activist Jean Loiseau, they formed a quasi-governmental organization that had official backing and was able to influence national policy. Today that organization is known as the FFRP.

The French delight in bureaucracies with layers and layers of organization: local to departmental to regional to, always, national, which, when translated into real terms, means to Paris. And in typical French fashion the FFRP is organized into just such a hierarchal structure. It extends linearly from each one of its one hundred thousand individual members in more than sixteen hundred local walking clubs up through departmental and then regional associations to the national headquarters and, finally, to Jacques Dumont, president (in 1996) of the association. Ultimately, Paris runs the show, but a group of six thousand volunteers from the membership do the grunt work on the paths.

Origins

Originally, most of the trails in the agricultural areas of France like the Loire, Normandy, Picardy, Lorraine, much of Brittany and all the wine regions were rights-of-way from the villages to the fields surrounding those villages. In medieval times the French peasant was threatened regularly by robbers, marauding armies, imaginary ghosts and all-too-real wolves, so to protect himself and his family, he retreated with others into the relative security of villages near but not next to his fields. During the day the family ventured out to their fields warily on foot or horseback, using a warren of muddy paths. At night they scuttled back to the village over those same tracks. Since *all* the villagers needed to walk the paths, they were public, not private. Those that are left today remain so.

In areas less suited to agriculture—the Alps, the Pyrénées, the Massif Central, Corsica, the Jura and the high-country areas of Provence and Languedoc—the walking trails follow the old tracks that for centuries have linked valley to valley and region to region. These are the routes used in medieval times by itinerant tinkers, monks, armies and shepherds moving their cows or sheep to and from high summer pasture. Many of these paths pass through substantial forests, ownership of which was transferred—to put it mildly—from the Church and the nobility to the neighboring *communes* (townships) during the French revolution. Again, most of the trails through these areas are public.

The Roman Empire left behind an enduring legacy of paved roads, which, through the middle ages, made up the core of the sparse infrastructure of long-distance paths and ways. Most of these ancient Roman routes are now under the pavement of modern French highways, but some, still cobbled, form parts of today's long-distance walking system. And one path that runs all the way from le Puy on the eastern edge of the Massif Central to the Spanish border in the western Pyrénées, follows as faithfully as possible the pilgrims' trail that, in the Middle Ages and earlier, linked France to the Spanish religious shrine at Santiago de Compostela or, as the French put it, Saint-Jacques-de-Compostelle.

The origin of the vast majority of French paths lies, then, in the Middle Ages and before. And it is a minuscule portion of the original web—principally the rights-of-way but also the interregional trails and, here and there, the Roman roads and pilgrimage routes—that the early activists like Loiseau preserved and joined together into the basic network that now forms the core of the system. However diminished, these remnants of different times are still glorious for, instead of isolating the walker on the periphery, they plunge the person on foot directly into the flow of daily life.

GR trail sign indicating a right turn

Trail clasification

There are four kinds of trail in France. The differences between them are significant, and it is important for your understanding of much of the information that follows to know and understand the distinctions. I'll try to be clear and brief.

National trails: First, there are the national trails, which I have already mentioned. These are the 37,500 miles of long-distance *sentiers de grande randonnée**, called GR trails for short. It was a GR, blazed as they all are with white and then red, that my wife and I ran across outside Solutré, and it's the GR trails in the main that are represented by all those red lines on IGN map 903. Each of these trails is numbered—GR 7, GR 52, GR 13B, etc. What distinguishes the national trails is that they go somewhere, that is, they connect one place to another rather than take a closed, circular path. For example, the GR 3 runs from the mouth of the Loire for almost a thousand kilometers to a point near the river's source in the hills between Le Puy and Valence. Another long trail is the GR 5, which traces a path from Luxembourg through the Vosges, Jura and Alp mountains all the way to the Mediterranean near Nice. It is these trails—or more likely sections of these trails—that you will use when you walk from point to point in France.

Regional trails: The second type of trail is the *sentier de grande randonnée de pays** (regional long distance path or GRP). These generally cover one region thoroughly, often in a circuit. Though only regional in scope, they can be quite long; the GRP that traces a circular route within the Morvan Regional Natural Park (a heavily forested area west of Dijon and just south of Vézelay) is 134 miles long and could easily take a whole vacation to walk. The regional trails are blazed in yellow and red, not white and red. These paths, because they cover considerable territory, often join the national trails, so even if you are walking a national trail, you may see regional yellow and white blazes. All 25,000 miles of these trails are just as well maintained and marked as GR trails; some but far from all are shown on map 903.

Local trails: The third type of trail, the *sentier de promenade et randonnée** (trail for strolling and walking or PR for short), is purely local in nature. These trails radiate out from towns and villages all over France, and to walk one or another of them takes only hours or, at most, one day. They often lead to places that the members of the local walking club consider beautiful or interesting from an historical point of view. The blazes for the local trails are single yellow stripes, but when many different ones connect and cross, other colors—blue, green, purple—may be used to avoid confusion.

A GRP or regional trail sign

---

* *Sentiers de Grande Randonnée,* GR, GR *de pays* and PR, as well as the GR path patterns: white/red and yellow/red, are registered trademarks of the FFRP. They cannot be used, reproduced or transcribed, in any form or by any means, without the prior written permission of the FFRP.

Officially, there are 50,000 miles of local trails, but one walking publication states that France has 500,000 miles of trails, which, if true, would mean that there are hundreds of thousands of miles of local trails! But no matter how many miles there are, local trails will unfortunately prove of little use to the long-distance walker because when they are encountered—and you will encounter them everywhere—you will have only a vague idea where they actually go. These trails are of real use only to residents or visitors who are armed with a map from the local walking club. No local trails are marked on map 903.

International trails: The fourth type of trail you may encounter is the *itinéraire européen* (European long-distance footpath). These trails are the continuation in France of paths that also cross other countries and have been designated as international long-distance paths by the governments involved. Like the French national paths, the GRs, they are numbered—E 1, E 5, E 9, etc. In France international trails always follow French paths as an overlay rather than as independent trails in their own right. In other words, the international trails quite logically use the trail system of the host country, and this means that when you are walking in France, any E signs you encounter—they are rare—will mean little. It is the white and red GR or the yellow and red regional signs you will use.

Though the European trails will not be of any real importance to you while you walk in France, the fact that an international network of long-distance trails exists in Europe is fascinating. The E 9, for instance, starts in the Baltics and ends at the tip of Brittany. For the dedicated walker, this is truly the stuff of dreams. E trails are marked with red/green lines on map 903.

International, national, regional and local trails. An alphabet soup of E, GR, PR and GRPS. It's a confusing mix, but the important fact to remember is that, though each label represents a different type of walking path, all the trails are well marked, open to all and offer the person on foot an incredible variety of choice.

What are the paths like?

French GR and regional trails only rarely follow busy roads, and when they must join the highway, they do so

Trail markers

Some foresters as well as some public utilities use red and white marks on trees, walls and buildings, a practice that can—if you're not attentive—lead to confusion. Be sure the mark you follow is white over red, not red over white.

for as short a time as possible on the road with the least amount of vehicular traffic. Of course you will walk on streets and even sidewalks as you approach and pass through cities, towns and villages, but long traverses on busy highways, anything more than a few kilometers, are rare, usually the result of the footpath passing through extremely rugged terrain or through a fenced military base that restricts all travel, vehicular as well as foot, to the one highway.

In very mountainous country, the high Alps and along the spine of the Pyrénées, the footpaths resemble trails in our Rocky Mountains, though in France the paths in rough terrain are more numerous, well worn and served by many more huts and refuges than the walker would find in the United States. Walking in these less inhabited regions is naturally more demanding than in flatter, more rural areas, but at the same time the rewards in spectacular scenery—an isolated hill town at sunset, a small avalanche cascading off an alp onto a glacier high above, a thousand sheep descending in a wedge down a long open slope, their bells clanking— can more than make up for the extra effort.

In France many farm lanes, only one vehicle wide and used infrequently, are nevertheless paved, and you will walk on many of these. But the vast majority of trails follow not pavement but dirt. The French prefer that their trails avoid cement, tar and civilization, so at times a path will climb the hill above a town rather than stay in the valley and pass through that town. As a result, the person on foot will often find himself walking the ridges above all the hustle and bustle.

But civilization is sometimes hard to avoid, and when the paths traverse areas that support a healthy agricultural economy, the walker using them will pass through hamlet after hamlet following obscure streets and meandering through, not around, vineyards, wood lots, orchards, fields and gardens. On these trails you will skirt backyards and laundry lines, sties and gardens, homes and shops so closely that sometimes the conversation of the inhabitants is embarrassingly audible. Chickens will scurry from under your boots, dogs will bark behind fences, children will play, laugh and cry only a few feet away. In the inhabited areas you will experience all the mundane details of French life in a way that is simply impossible to duplicate when

---

How safe is a walk?

Some of my friends have asked me how safe it is to walk the French countryside. My answer has always been that I have never encountered a situation in which I felt at all threatened and, though I have seldom done so, that I would not hesitate to walk alone anywhere except, perhaps, in the suburbs of the largest cities.

Faith and I do have a French friend, an athletic young woman who often walks by herself, and she does take her large dog on the trail with her for security. A single woman should plan to walk with a companion or, if that proves impossible, she should walk in areas such as the Loire, where the presence of many people would afford some security.

Having said this, I have to add that my own (male) experience has been that the vast majority of the people I have met on the trail have been friendly. None have appeared in the least bit dangerous.

traveling in a vehicle. And as an added bonus, you will observe a countryside that has been tamed and then burnished by hundreds, even thousands, of years of human use and is often achingly beautiful.

When you walk you will sometimes, as here, enter villages not on the road but from the surrounding woods and fields.

To summarize, then, the French maintain 110,000 miles of marked walking paths that are open to the public, to anyone, foreigner or Frenchman, with the gumption and the time to use them. Over 60,000 miles of these are long-distance trails that will lead the vacationer on foot from town to town, from region to region and always to the rural heart of a country that sometimes annoys but always fascinates and surprises the visitor.

Day walks

My purpose is to show you that it is possible to walk the vast French trail system cross-country from point to point on your own. Consequently, day walks, walks that start from and return to a fixed base each day, are not strictly within the purview of this book. However, since the French themselves are more often than not day walkers, and since anyone walking in France during the months of July or August may by necessity be forced by the crowds of vacationers to find and maintain a home base, I will cover briefly some of the details that will be helpful for those planning to settle in a hotel or bed-and-breakfast and from this base take walks each day into the surrounding countryside.

In the chapters that follow, I discuss the equipment, maps and guides needed by the long-distance walker.

Much of the material there will serve the day walker equally well, and I urge anyone considering day walks to read the rest of this book, particularly chapters 4, 5, 7, 8 and 9.

GR trail

Any area of France that has particularly attractive walking country—the regional parks, the Alps, Provence, the Vosges, the Cévennes, etc.—is sure to have active walking clubs in its larger towns, and these clubs will have established, marked, maintained and, most important, mapped the local trails. These same towns will also support an office called the Syndicat d'Initiative, a combination Chamber of Commerce and Tourist Office, which will distribute, for a small fee or free, these sometimes rough but informative maps. The local maps, when combined with an accurate and detailed IGN *blue map (see chapter 5), will most likely lay out at least a week's worth of fine walks for anyone staying in the village.*

Regional trail: turn

GR trail: wrong way

After arriving in your chosen area, I suggest that you also peruse the stock of guides in the local librarie *(bookstore),* tabac *(tobacco shop)* or marchand des journaux *(newspaper store). If the area is at all popular as a walking center, you may find a regionally produced guidebook that will map in some detail the local walking trails. Again, these books are sometimes roughly produced with maps that are no more than line drawings but when used with a blue* IGN *map they can be very useful.*

Many French walkers who live and work in a particular area will, on a Saturday or Sunday, drive into the countryside—ten miles, fifty miles—where they will park their cars at the base of a particular trail or somewhere along a trail loop. They then walk for half a day or a day. If you have rented a car for your stay in France, you can imitate the French and greatly expand the "local" area where you can take day walks.

But if you prefer to skip the expense and hassle of an automobile, you can take a bus from your base out into the countryside—as again many local and vacationing French walkers do—where you could stroll for a day before hopping an evening bus back to your lodging. The bus system is extensive, and comfortable long-distance buses called cars *run regularly to surrounding towns and cities, serving at the same time the smaller*

villages in between. If the circumstances are right, you might even, after a bus ride out into the country, spend the day walking back into "your" town from another village five, ten or fifteen miles out.

Day walks are even more relaxing and laid-back than cross-country walks. By spending, say, a week in one town, you will become much more familiar with the restaurants, the shops and the people than the long-distance walker who would usually spend only one night in that same town before walking on to the next village. You will settle in and become not only familiar with *but also familiar* to *the inhabitants. You will become in some small way a "local."*

Day walking is, I suppose, the next step down from cross-country walking in that chain that extends from guided bus tour to independent auto trip to bicycle trip to cross-country walk to day walk. Each method of getting around France is slower than the one before, and each forces the traveler to concentrate his or her attention on a smaller and smaller portion of that country until, when you day walk, you limit yourself to an area only twenty miles in diameter.

I myself prefer the stimulation and the sense of accomplishment that comes from cross-country walking, but someday I might slow down enough to prefer day walks. Someday...

What It's Like

A taste of paradise

IMAGINE THIS.

A day on the trail

It's nine-twenty in the morning. The sky is a limpid blue, and the air is still night-cool as you and your companion exit the hotel onto the sidewalk outside. You each carry a pack awkwardly by the straps, and once you're clear of the steps, you lean your burdens against the wall of the building.

In payment for your hotel bill—the meal the night before, a modest but spacious room and a filling breakfast—*Madame*, the blond, svelte and fashion-conscious proprietress, has just processed your VISA card at the counter inside. Now, impeccable, more representative of *Vogue* than *Country Living*, she stands in the open door watching as the two of you rub in sunblock, don hats and then reach down to take up the packs. As usual, the load seems heavy as you swing it up from the cement onto your shoulders. Shrugging upward, almost jumping, you cinch the waist band to transfer the pressure of the twenty pounds to your hips where habituated muscles make the pack's bulk a part of you. The weight eases.

"Bonne route," *Madame* says. Have a good trip. With an arch, bemused smile she takes a backward step into the hotel and closes the heavy door.

But to walk in France is no solitary experience. No people are as insistently welcoming, I have found, than the people of the French countryside. Their readiness to communicate and their lack of indifference should put the English to shame. No one here will accept unquestionably, as Englishmen do, that you have just walked five days to meet them. You will constantly be shaken by the hand and told of your courage, *a word that is endlessly repeated and works marvels for a drooping ego.*

– Adam Nicholson,
Long Walks in France

Splotches of sunshine reach the pavement. The heavy smell of night's damp coolness is already yielding to the dry odor of stones and straw; the bright spring day ahead will be another warm one. You glance at your map and then, with a nod to your companion, stride off down the village's main street.

On your way out of town, you pass the grocery, where outside on a wooden counter a young clerk is arranging a sparse but beautiful display of produce—shallow baskets of wild strawberries, small new potatoes, the season's first Burlat cherries and bunched, stubby carrots with the greens attached. The strawberries are so fragrant that you smell them as you pass. The store is very busy as the women of the village are out in full force to shop for the noon meal. Ordinary, even frumpy in their nondescript dresses, they seem to be from a different planet than *Madame* at the hotel.

"Bonjour, mesdames."

"Bonjour, monsieur. Bonjour, madame."

"Bonjour," with the usual nod, *"Bonjour."*

Further down, a tractor putts out of a side street and turns on its way to the fields. Its fumes, acrid diesel, mix with the penetrating scent of cinnamon from a white climbing rose that sprawls in the sunshine over the façade of an east-facing house.

The overall direction of your trip is from north to south. The GR trail you left the evening before that you now want to rejoin is up above to the left on a wooded ridge. Your detailed map shows a short track leading from the road at the south edge of town up to the trail, and just after the last house, right where it is supposed to be, you find the narrow dirt path.

Leaving the pavement, you walk between two vineyards, then climb the short hill to the top of the ridge where the path ends abruptly at a dirt forestry road. Panting a bit—why does every day seem to start with a climb?—you turn right to head south along the height of land. Only a minute later you spot, painted neatly on the trunk of a tree next to the trail, a white and red blaze, the mark of the French national trail system. It confirms what you already knew from your map: you're back on your route, the familiar GR.

After ten minutes of walking you pause, dropping your pack in order to take off and stow away your sweater. The air is still cool under the shade of the trees, but the exercise has made you warm.

For another hour you walk easily on the straight-forward path that offers no confusing options. The infrequent white and red trail markers seem unnecessary but reassure nonetheless. The way, a one-lane fire road through forest, sometimes rises and falls gently but is mostly level. In the freshness of the morning you

Trails are well marked in France.

easily cover more than five kilometers, three miles, during the first hour. You're loose, and the walking feels good.

Under the forest cover, now exclusively pines, you stride along on springy duff, The smell of rotting pine needles reminds you of other walks in other woods at home, but there are differences. Here there are few flowers or, for that matter, much undergrowth of any kind in the shade of the mature trees. French foresters manage their woods by keeping brush and the under-growth cleared away, and their thoroughness results in an open parklike aspect which, while pleasing, is strange to the American eye so used to the extravagant blowsiness of the forests at home. The trees, where possible, have even been planted in rows; there is little Nature with a capital N here. It's only where the ridge has been recently logged and where the newly planted seedlings are still small and low that out-of-control explosions of wild flowers burst forth in the sun. These fragrant outposts of yolk-yellow scotch broom, tall clumps of white daisies and invasive splashes of red fireweed are welcome islands of chaos.

Now, crossing one of these logged areas, you notice that the ridge has narrowed and the view has opened up to reveal higher wooded hills across a ravine to the left and, on the plain below to the right, a mix of pastures, wheat fields, vineyards and wood lots. From your vantage point, the few villages visible on the plain are compact units, each huddled into a tight protective clump as if to ward off an enemy. Grey, almost black, they appear anonymous and shy as if they wished to avoid notice. The fields, in contrast, are a mosaic of different shades of vibrant spring green.

You know from your map that a short way ahead the GR wil drop off the ridge and descend to a village, which is hidden from view, tucked up against the hill at the edge of the plain, and soon you come upon the white and red turn marker painted prominently on a large tree.

The trail down to the village is steep and much narrower than the dirt road you've quit, but it is easy enough to follow since there are no alternatives. The slope has been logged sometime during the past few years, and the sides of the path are overgrown with deciduous bushes and small trees so that, when a covey of grouse flushes with an startling explosion of noise from the brush off to one side, the low-flying birds are hidden by the foliage.

Strange. Though these neat French forests are highly "managed," there still seems to be a surprising amount of wildlife. Just this morning in some dried mud along the trail you walked over the tracks of some *chevreuil,* the small European deer, and the patch of torn-up ground in the recently lumbered area up above looked very much like the work of rooting wild boar.

Here on the shaded west side of the hill the branches of the bushes and small trees, even now at almost eleven o'clock, bend toward the trail under the weight of last night's dew. No one else has passed here today so, your pant legs get wetter and wetter as you lead the way down the hill, whacking the branches ahead with your walking stick to dislodge at least some of the moisture. It is still cool here, and the smell is of damp and decomposing leaves. At the bottom you finally emerge out of the brush onto an open dirt track that leads through closely planted grapevines into the village ahead. In the sudden sunshine the moisture on your pants immediately begins to evaporate, cooling your

... t to you, is closed and quiet, all ... ndows. From outside there ... ut. You pause, strain to hear a ... shake your head. You are thirsty, ... own is big enough to have a café. ... picnic.

... e vineyard between two buildings, ... inted discreetly on the wall where ... the paved street, a GR trail sign ... center of the village. When you ... urn, another sign on the other side ... *n Marius – Vins du Pays* (The ... Country Wines), juts out from a ... rm on the corner. The gate in the ... *aison Marius* is open and next to it, ... *e libre* (Wine Tasting, Feel Free to ... eatly on a piece of wood.

... vine will be just the thing for your ... gn has invited, you walk through the ... enclosed courtyard. To the right a ... dwelling is up the stairs over what ... ne cellar on the ground floor. Closed ... ther two sides of the enclosure.

... a steaming pile of composting manure ... es high would have filled (in more ways ... nter of this courtyard. Now a tractor ... f the barns is the symbol of the change ... machines and manure to chemical ... d German shepherd, chained, lies on ... ade under the stairs with one eye open ... Wisteria, past its bloom, is espaliered ... e.

"Allô!" you call out.

No response.

"Allô!" again. A rattle of chain; the dog rises but still does not bark.

You expect someone older in this setting, but it is a surprisingly young woman who appears in the doorway of the house above. Removing her apron, she apologizes—for what?—as she clatters down the stairs, keys in hand. You in turn mumble apologies for having interrupted her meal preparations.

"Non, non!" she laughs. But she is, nevertheless, all business as she unlocks and then enters the wine cellar. When the light is switched on you are surprised by the large size of two looming tanks, one wooden and the other stainless steel. They dominate the room. Separate rows of empty and full bottles are carefully stacked six feet high and three deep against the walls. The only "furniture" is a board set on two barrels, where she places two glasses and, with a flourish, pours the 1997 red for each of you. Sadly, she explains, the 1996 is sold out, just last week. "It was *so* good. But, even so, the '97 is not bad." When you agree, she adds with a blush that her husband has raised and vinified the grapes, made the wine. *Maison Marius* is just a small family operation, she says with pride. You sip carefully, trying not to gulp. The air is damp and cool in the cellar, and the smell of spilled wine mixed with evaporating alcohol fills the space. The heady odor is intoxicating by itself.

Politeness aside, the wine is truly good, certainly better than all but the most expensive wines likely to be available in the town's grocery store. You look quizzically at your companion who nods a yes, so for 18 FF you buy a bottle.

"Bonne route," she says as she relocks the cellar door. She smiles openly at your packs and hurries back up the stairs to her kitchen.

Happily, on the village's small central plaza there are not one but *two* cafés. An *épicerie* (grocery store) is on one corner, and visible up a small side street are a *boulangerie* (bakery) and a *charcuterie* (meat shop). The picnic is assured.

But first you choose the more active of the two cafés and, sitting outside under the welcome shade of an umbrella advertising Kronenbourg beer, order and quickly drink first a one-liter bottle of cold, sparkling Badoit water and then, more leisurely, a second bottle. Ahhhh.

On the square lone women, each with a straw or plastic basket over an arm, hurry from shop to shop, all business, little talk. In the center of the square on a bench next to the community bulletin board, two older men dressed in black, each with a cane, one wearing a beret, sit facing the sun without speaking. One of the men holds a smoldering cigarettes between thumb and middle finger.

High on the plastered wall of the building opposite is painted a large mural of some idealized vineyard, and, incongruously, one of the building's windows with bright red curtains sits right between two rows of vines. The painting's perspective is slightly skewed and its colors are faded. Below, the name of the village is in script along with the slogan, *Ses Vins Reputés* (Its Well-Known Wines).

Beer-stained air flows out the open door of the café where, inside, there is laughter and animated conversation. Men wearing blue overalls and black rubber boots are in from the fields for a quick glass of wine

In the cafés the walker will have a good opportunity to meet and interact with French people.

before going home for lunch. A knot of four stands at the end of the bar near the door, and their small glasses of wine tossed off at a gulp seem secondary to the kidding, the laughter and the talk; this is an informal club and it probably meets daily.

It is nearly noon when all the stores will close for two hours, so you pay your bill and reluctantly reshoulder your packs. It's time to buy the picnic. You go up the side street to buy a baguette at the bakery and a slice of country paté at the butcher shop while your companion enters the grocery store to buy a soft, just-made round of goat cheese, two ripe tomatoes "from Sicily" and a bar of chocolate. As you walk south out of the square the church bell is sounding twelve and a young boy is lowering the shutters that completely cover the front of the small hardware store—a rush of noise that echoes in the narrow street. Two men in suits hurry down the sidewalk toward the square, and you nod.

"Messieurs," you say in greeting.

"M'sieur-dame," they reply in unison and they too nod as they pass. *"Bonne route!"* one of them adds.

Ahead, just outside town, is a shallow, wooded valley and running through it is a sluggish, meandering stream whose source lies up in the hills to your left, the same hills you were walking that morning. The GR trail keeps to the paved road and with it crosses the stream on a stone bridge. On the far side, off to the right near the water, are two wooden picnic tables under the shade of large cottonwood trees. You look at each other and nod. It's hot in the direct sun; it will be cooler here. And, after all, you don't often come upon a picnic table just when you need one. Packs off.

Like a magician producing a silk cloth from his closed fist, you pull a brightly colored sarong from the side pocket of your pack and then lay it with a flourish on the table closest to the water. You bring out your pocket knife, open the wine and spread the picnic.

During the lunch hour there is only sporadic traffic on the narrow secondary road that leads out from the village to the main highway a few kilometers ahead, and it is peaceful here under the trees. The smells, basic and deep, are of grass and mossy water. Boots come off. You start to eat, slowly. The bread could be better, but the small, fragrant tomatoes are delicious for this early in the season, full of sweet-acid juice, which at first bite runs down your chin. As usual, you remark that you've certainly bought too much paté

Photography

For the French photography is still an expensive hobby. A roll of film in France costs almost half again as much as in the States, and a one-hour photo lab, when you can find one, will charge as much as a one dollar for each print. The quality of the work, it must be said, is superb, but anyone used to the very low prices elsewhere will be shocked by what is charged in France to develop and print a casual roll of snaps. If you enjoy taking pictures, my advice is to buy your film at home and to bring the exposed film back with you for processing after your walk.

France on Foot

and too much cheese, but, as usual again, the two of you seem to be nibbling your way steadily through both.

A kingfisher flies by, swooping and rising, going downstream fast. The bird blinkers iridescent blue as it passes through the dapple, sun to shade to sun. You exclaim in surprise at the display, then take another slug from the bottle. The wine tastes especially good with the last of the goat cheese.

Out on the road a young man in a battered *deux-chevaux* truck rattles past. He waves out his open window and calls out something unintelligible. You smile and wave back. He disappears over the crest of the hill into the village and it is quiet again. The bittersweet chocolate is very good.

According to your map the town you plan to stay in that night is still about twelve kilometers or seven and a half miles away. At your average pace of four kilometers an hour, that's three hours more of walking, so just after one o'clock, you reluctantly pack away the empty bottle, the paper wrappings and your sarong and set off again.

The GR trail follows the paved road up through the trees out of the valley and continues on the road through wheat fields and pastures for another kilometer. The sun is hot, and you start to perspire immediately. Walking on a hot and smelly tarred pavement is less than enjoyable, so when you do finally spot the GR turn sign painted on a telephone pole, you are happy to veer left onto a dirt track. Though you are still in the full sun, it's cooler here.

The growth on both sides between the track and the hedgerows that border the fields has not been cut, and here bloom wildflowers, clumps of red American Legion poppies, bluebells and smears of buttercups. They are so pretty that you just have to stop and stare.

For an hour and a half you zigzag your way through the fields on this gentle slope, all the while slowly reapproaching the hills. Overall, your direction is to the south and slightly east, but the confusing geometry of dirt paths, tracks and narrow one-lane pavements separating the fields requires that you pay close attention to the trail signs signaling the twists and turns of the GR. Map in hand, at each junction point you look

Traditional agriculture mixes a variety of crops—wheat with vines and truck gardens with pastureland.

carefully to spot the white and red stripe of the trail marker; here in the open fields they are painted on whatever is handy, fences, posts and even rocks in the ground. New spring growth hides some of the marks, causing you to miss a few turns, but with the help of the detailed map, you are easily able to pick up the trail again further on.

A meadowlark hovers in a fixed position overhead and, to proclaim his territory, burbles a cascade of notes. Crows protest your passage and croak resentfully when your closeness threatens them into the air. In the shade of a rock wall you find two kinds of orchid, the one a tall spike with spiraling rows of flowers, each of which resembles a miniature elephant head, the other a single more traditional orchid that, though muddy brown, still looks like a doll's corsage. A cooling breeze stirs the winter wheat in the fields, and puffy clouds offer occasional shade, but still you perspire.

A bit later, closer to the hills, the soil becomes rocky, and wheat gives way to grapevines. In one of the vineyards a couple—the man in blue overalls, the woman with a blue apron, both in rubber boots—remove by hand the energy-sapping secondary shoots that surface from the ground and emerge from the base of the vines themselves when spring growth begins. The labor is obviously hard, but they move quickly, stooping to cut the shoots. Your greeting interrupts their concentration. *"M'sieur-dame,"* you say, the mantra of polite social discourse. (How many times each day?) They look up, surprised by your presence. *"M'sieur-dame,"* they reply as they come fully upright, blank-faced. They stare after you as you continue down the dirt track past their white two-door Renault 4.

As you reach the base of the hills, the trail approaches but then skirts a very small village, an ancient huddle of eight or ten farmhouses. You walk through the *back*yards, three of which have large kitchen gardens laid out in careful geometric rows. Chickens run loose ranging indiscriminately through the vegetables and flowers. Up ahead an isolated gang of tall, purple iris lounges along a fence and partially obscures a pen confining a small flock of white ducks. Heads under wings, they are hunkered down in a mass in the small shade of their shelter. Pink peonies bloom by the back wall of the largest farm. Somewhere in the center of the buildings a motor wheezes to life and then dies. Otherwise all is very still. The sharp smell of farm, decomposing manure, hangs in the air.

Beyond the village the trail turns left abruptly, quits the vineyards and takes off up the wooded slope. The trees here are deciduous, mostly young oaks with a scattering of chestnuts and maples. The climb is short but steep, and you rest in the shade at the top of the first rise. As you bend to sit you feel a tightness, a protest from your legs. Your shirt is plastered to your back by perspiration; with the pack off, the evaporative coolness feels delicious. You pull the half-liter plastic bottle of Evian water from the sidepocket of your pack, take a long swig and pass it to your partner. In the woods a

Herbicides are used less often in France so a bewlidering variety of wild flowers grow along the lanes and trails. This is one of the many kinds of wild orchid you will be able to find if you look carefully.

hundred yards up the slope, a cuckoo starts his repetitive, monotonous call. Cuckoo, cuckoo, cuckoo... for at least a minute before, abruptly, the soft afternoon quiet folds in again. Already on this trip you have heard at least a dozen cuckoos but have not seen even one. The birds are very secretive.

After four hours of walking you are tired. The two of you amble along the GR, which follows what is apparently an overgrown fire trail. Every fifty meters or so small, hand-lettered signs announce that the collection of mushrooms is strictly regulated. Higher on the trunks of the trees larger signs proclaim *chasse gardée* (private hunting).

There is a confusion of paths, trails and roads here in these woods, and you find the red and white blazes useful. The shade is dappled under the canopy of leaves, and the undergrowth, given sunlight, is thick with the green of bushes and the blue haze of forget-me-nots. As you walk the breeze rustles the tops of the trees but doesn't penetrate the canopy to reach the ground below, and the still air is close and warm. Like this morning, you are following a ridge line, but here the terrain is more broken, filled with ups and downs; it may be your imagination, but the ups seem to predominate.

Suddenly, two hikers, a young couple, appear from around a bend in the trail ahead. Startled, you stop. As they approach you step to the side off the path and greet them, *"Bonjour,"* you say, and after a mumbled reply they also stop.

The four of you stand facing each other on the narrow trail, and there is a short though not awkward silence (everyone is smiling broadly) before the other couple speaks tentatively, first in what sounds like German and then after a pause, in English. You respond in kind. Your conversation has found a home.

They are Dutch, they explain, and they are spending a two-week vacation walking through this part of France. Attractive and athletic, they seem to be in their late twenties. They inquire where you are from and express surprise that you are there.

"Imagine! Americans walking!"

You exchange information about the trail ahead and behind, and they inquire specifically about the village two and one-half hours back where you bought your picnic. It is their destination for the night, they say. Before you can blurt out the information that there is no hotel, you notice that their packs are much larger than yours and surmise they must be camping out. Then, abruptly, they smile, nod and bid you a polite, almost formal goodbye before striding away. They move purposefully and disappear down the trail as quickly as they appeared.

You stare after them and then look down to examine your map. The brief rest is welcome. The map shows that the GR continues through these woods, crossing a height of land about four kilometers ahead before descending onto the plain of a major river. But almost all of that will be part of tomorrow's walk, for just a few hundred meters up the track the Dutch couple has said, the GR crosses a major highway. There you will leave the official trail to follow the road down off the ridge into a town where you will stay this evening. You start off.

Five minutes later you climb an obviously manmade bank and emerge from the woods onto the anticipated highway. Looking both ways, you cross the cement and then begin your descent facing the cars. The traffic and noise of laboring trucks is jarring after such a bucolic day. There is litter—glass, bits of plastic and even a dead paper diaper in the gravel verge where you walk.

Farther down the hill, right at the highway's first switchback, your map shows a trace that cuts straight down the hill away from the highway, avoiding the road and the hairpin turns altogether. Grateful to get away from the pavement and vehicle exhaust, you take this obscure trail. Down below you spot a storage yard full of brightly colored, new farm machinery. Just beyond, across another highway, is a three-steeple town, not a city but, nevertheless, the largest place you've visited over the past four days of walking. You can hear the hum of it already.

In town there are at least three hotels and a *Michelin* "good food at moderate prices" restaurant, but your mind is focused on a more immediate concern—a glass of cold beer. Here, on this west-facing slope, you

---

How strenuous is a walk in France?

A reasonably fit walker might wish to cover ten to fifteen miles over the course of a day, and by "easily" I mean at a pace of two and one-half miles an hour, which translates into four to six hours of walking between sun up and sun down. This pace leaves plenty of time for leisurely breakfasts, for picnics, for visits to wineries or châteaux and for, perhaps, a restorative beverage at any café you might come across.

But *you* will set your own pace. *You* will determine how far you go each day. There are no minimum or maximum requirements. One of my daughters and her husband recently walked for ten days in Provence and averaged more than fifteen miles a day, a figure that included a full day of rest. Some particularly fit and from my point of view masochistic British walkers think the day hasn't even begun unless at least twenty miles have been covered before lunch. I prefer a slower pace, something, as I've said, between ten to fifteen miles per day, but others, preferring to walk five or eight miles one day and then rest the next, might consider *that* pace masochistic.

The important fact to remember is that the strenuousness of your day is *up to you*. It is *your* vacation, and with a bit of planning, almost any pace, any distance you find comfortable is possible.

After walking for days without seeing even one other party, you may wonder why the French have bothered to establish and then so carefully maintain the elaborate trail system if they themselves don't walk it more than they seem to. It's a perplexing question and one for which I don't have a good answer.

The scarcity of walkers may be partially explained by the fact that the French are more rigid than we when it comes to vacation time. They *all* take vacations in the summer, and it's only at this time that they have the leisure to take to the trails. But even in July and August it's possible to walk all day without encountering, outside the villages, anyone else on foot.

The explanation may also lie in the mindset of at least some French walkers. You will occasionally encounter a large group of men and women walking in festive togetherness. This organized mass of perhaps thirty or even fifty hikers from the same walking club, all participating in a one-day group outing, seems typical of the way the French prefer to walk. Rather than walk alone or with one or two friends, they plan excursions that can be experienced with many other people.

But no matter the reason for the unexpected emptiness of the French trails, the happy consequence for you is the tranquility you will experience as you wander through this densely populated country.

perspire freely in the heat of the late afternoon sun.

The steep, weedy trail, slippery in places, disappears at one point, but you are able to pick it up again farther down. At last the trace levels but at the same time fades out again as it skirts the chain link next to the equipment yard. Plowing through the weeds, you reach the highway just before a traffic circle. The brightness, the hazy late-afternoon heat and the confusion of zipping cars is annoying as you dart your way across an arm of the circle, but then a narrow sidewalk paralleling the *centre ville* (town center) road brings you through a gate onto the relative calm of a shaded boulevard.

This broad street descends gently under big trees past the solid fronts of houses and apartments toward the commercial heart of the town. Tired, thirsty, your legs stiffening by the minute, you walk slowly. The stone carvings on the façade of an apartment building—nouveau? moderne?—catch your eye. Rafts of young children, all with book bags or outsized leather briefcases that flap against their legs, sweep by in noisy groups on their way home from school. After five short blocks you arrive at a large, tree-shaded *place* (square). Surrounding it are a beautifully proportioned church, the *Hôtel de Ville* (town hall), two of the three hotels you'll be looking at later, as well as a bank, stores and, thankfully, a large café with three rows of tables under the shade of a long, faded yellow awning.

You head straight for the café, shed your pack and settle out of the sun at a table in the second row. Your muscles ache in a pleasurable way. You wish you could take off your boots.

"Une grande bouteille de Badoit et deux demis, s'il vous plait," you say to the waiter. A liter bottle of Badoit water to soften the thirst followed by a draft beer for each of you. After twenty-two kilometers, well, twenty at least—twelve and a half miles—you've earned it. The water goes down first, quick glass after glass, but then you savor the beer. How can something so simple taste so good?

The center of the square under the shade of sculpted plane trees is paved with bricks and is three-quarters full of parked cars. There is commerce here. People pass on the sidewalk intent on errands and the pace is quick, almost urgent. But the square, with the façades of the three-story buildings softened by the trees, still feels comfortable.

Three of the nearby tables fill with a group of high-school-age students. Self-absorbed, they pull the tables together, settle and order draft beers or coffee. Most of them smoke, and their cigarettes are not Gîtanes but Marlboros or English Players. A haze gathers above them in the still air. Leaning in toward each other they speak animatedly and laugh often, these boy-men and girl-women. What you can hear of their French is unintelligible, full of shortcuts and slang, a private code.

Back in the corner in the deepest shade, three grey-haired women in coats and prim hats are chatting amiably over tea. At a table near the front a lone man in suit and tie sips a beer and stares into the square.

After a while, relaxed and happy following a good day's walk, you order two more beers from the friendly waiter. Pausing at your table, he asks where you have come from and expresses approval of your mode of transport. *"Courageux,"* he calls you. He too is surprised that you are American and walking.

Ahead, no hurry at all, are a hotel room, a long shower, a change of clothes and a leisurely exploration of town including, perhaps, a look into that pretty church across the square, which the Michelin green guide for the area describes as being "worth a detour." Your appetite is stirring and you're looking forward, at around eight o'clock, to sitting down to a good dinner.

At this point you're not at all sure which is best—walking or having walked?

The typical day

You might have a day in France like the one I have described. Of course, it could have included a visit to a

---

château or some other historical monument, a lunch in a country restaurant rather than a picnic, a showery wet day instead of unbroken fine weather or a route through a more inhabited area and, consequently, more frequent interactions with the local inhabitants, but the essential elements of any successful walk are there. Ultimately, it is the leisurely pace, the rhythm, the sensual stimulation, the pleasure of discovery and the feeling of peace and accomplishment that are central to any day on the trail. They are, after all, among the best reasons to walk in the first place.

Rural life

As you travel on foot through the French countryside it is easy to feel that what you are seeing and experiencing—the villages, the unhurried pace of life, the specialized businesses that are passed from generation to generation, the small churches smelling of damp stone, the closeness and camaraderie in the cafés—is timeless and immutable. It's natural for a visitor to assume that the buildings and the way of life that have been there for hundreds and hundreds of years will continue to be there virtually unchanged for more hundreds of years.

It's not only the tourist who senses that French country life embodies permanence and stability; the French population itself feels a deep kinship and attachment to the rural lifestyle that transcends sentimentality and goes to the heart of French national character.

Ruggedly individualistic, yet tied to everyone else in the village by proximity and mutual need, the paysan *(literally "peasant," but the meaning is broad enough to encompass rural occupations other than farming) as depicted in song, literature, movies and on* TV *is for the French the guardian of an important part of the nation's identity. In the past it is to the values, sensibilities and beliefs of this segment of the population that France has turned in time of stress and change.* Paysans *and an idealized vision of the life they lead are a sort of national anchor. In sometimes contradictory terms, they are perceived to be honest but not foolish, stolid, hardworking, parsimonious yet generous to those in need, conservative, crafty, stubborn and loyal.*

Change

The problem today is that the real-life version of the rural farmer working his own small plot of land is (and has been since the last *turn of the century) disappearing at an accelerating rate. Even as recently as 1968 fifteen percent of the French population still worked* the *land to produce agricultural products—timber, grains, vegetables, meat, wine—while twenty-five years later in 1993 less than six percent did so.*

*Some types of modern agriculture require machinery not horses, chemical fertilizers not manure and most important large plots of land that can be farmed efficiently, not small scattered plots—*one hectare *(two and one half acres) here,* three hectares *there. In some areas a few large-scale farmers have bought up and combined the small individual fields and have brought in modern, mechanized agricultural equipment—air-conditioned tractors, combines and threshers—to work their enlarged holdings.*

Only a few people work these large plots, which, when still fragmented, supported, marginally, many more. The process has accelerated unchecked as the efficient larger farms undercut the prices of the inefficient small, family-based operations. In the end, many rural French people have, like those in other industrialized nations, become unemployed and have moved to the cities seeking work. Thus over the past fifty years the infrastructure and cohesiveness of rural life has undergone a profound and, to the French, disturbing alteration in the affected areas, all but obliterating a once vibrant if insular culture.

This wholesale transformation of parts of the French countryside affects the walker in many ways. First, of course, larger fields have simply absorbed many of the ancient rights-of-way, but, in the less touristed areas, the complete abandonment of some rural villages is the most disturbing. It can be downright eerie to walk into an uninhabited agglomeration of houses that still retains the semblance of a lived-in place. The death of a village is so unnatural, so disturbing, that sometimes to provoke a response you want to yell as loud as you can, "Allô!"

Most properties in small villages are surrounded by

high walls, so your only clue other than silence that such a place is truly abandoned may be a glimpse high up of a broken attic window or lower down an entry gate long

St-Saturnin-d'Apt, a small town in the Luberon region of Provence, is in two parts: the upper village and the lower village. As is sometimes the case today in rural France, the less-accessible upper village has been abandoned while the lower village continues to thrive.

shut with a rusty chain and padlock. In some regions the abandoned houses have been bought by outsiders who have converted the properties into summer homes. But there are still many less popular areas where the walker's puzzled "Allô!" will go unanswered.

The death of a village

A community whose economic raison d'être has disappeared wastes slowly away.

In a very small village surrounded by fields of sugar beets—farmed today on large plots of land worked with modern machinery—the elderly café owner who runs the only commercial enterprise in town buries his wife. Bereft and alone, he loses his will to run the business, which, even though there is no mortgage, makes very little money. But he cannot pass the café to another generation because his only son is settled comfortably near Paris where he works as an engineer for Renault, and his only daughter (a great help when she was younger) is happily married and raising four sons far away in Clermont-Ferrand. He lists the business and the property with a realtor but realistically he knows that no one will buy. He simply shutters the doors.

The café is missed most of all by three men, old friends who spent their mornings there talking and smoking. The bread man, who, every day but Monday, used the café as a drop for the village's daily ration of twenty-five baguettes, *takes the town off his route. For years the village has been served by a traveling butcher who, as he drove into town, blew his truck's distinctive horn loudly and then parked on the small square in front of the church. He arrived at four o'clock every Tuesday and Friday to sell chops, roasts and pâtés. But because business is bad, he stops coming on Tuesdays. Then, a year later, he stops coming altogether.*

The people left in the village now drive two or three times a week instead of just once a week to a nearby town, where a supermarket, the French equivalent of

Village cemeteries in France are not restful green glades but fenced patches of unshaded ground in the middle of fields. The walker who peeks over the wall will see plastic flowers and a crowded jumble of ornate stone and iron monuments, often embellished with photographs of the deceased.

Safeway, has opened. Elderly, pensioned, they find one-stop shopping both convenient and economical. They buy bread and freeze it. They stop raising a few chickens for the table because the chickens from the United States that they can buy in the market are so cheap.

The curé *of the village's small Catholic church is transferred to a more lively parish and he is not replaced. Where once many years ago there were three masses on Sundays and morning services every day, a young (too young, the parishioners mumble) traveling priest now celebrates one mass on Sunday for the four women and one man who still bother to attend.*

With no central meeting place or commerce to bring them together, indeed with nothing to do except attend the occasional funeral, the inhabitants who remain in the village are increasingly isolated one from the other. When their televisions are turned off for the last time there is no one to take their place. The village is abandoned.

This is, of course, a worst-case scenario. If all French villages were like the one I just described, there would be little point in recommending that anyone walk through the French countryside. The person on foot will undoubtedly see shuttered cafés, empty houses and lifeless small communities, but in many areas small-scale agriculture not only survives but thrives.

Vibrant villages

Tiny, scattered plots of land, if they are planted in vines that produce good wine, can still support a hard-working family willing to adopt modern marketing methods. Fine wine is one of France's principal agricultural products supporting whole economies from the Loire to Provence and from Alsace to Bordeaux. Other products—foie gras, cheese, olive oil, Bresse chickens, to name just a few—can also support a family that owns relatively little land. Happily, in areas where such family farming survives there will be viable, often vibrant villages.

In a very different way, tourist economies also contribute to the survival and prosperity of some villages that would otherwise have declined. Obvious areas like the Côte d'Azur—an impoverished backwater before the British "found" it in the 1870s—come to mind. But the tourist influence in the form of second homes for both the French and other Common Market Europeans is widespread elsewhere in the south of France as well as along the north and west coasts. While tourist economies do not preserve rural life as it was, they do offer the unemployed farmer an alternative to moving to the city. Tourists must be housed and fed. Summer residents buy crafts and art, drink in the cafés and eat bread from the bakery every day. Second homes need repairs and re-modeling. If there's work where friends and family live and where the house has been in the family for hundreds of years, then there's reason to stay.

Another less obvious aspect of the support tourism can give the rural way of life are the large number of cham-bres d'hôtes *(bed-and-breakfasts) and* gîtes ruraux *(farms that accept guests) scattered throughout rural France. (See chapter 7 for a full discussion.) Established with the help and encouragement of the French gov-ernment, they provide extra income to rural people who otherwise might have to move away or become wards of the state. They also permit city people to come into contact with their country roots and thereby relearn the value of* paysan *culture.*

As the chambres d'hôtes–gîtes ruraux *system illus-trates, the French are strikingly active in their support of their nation's social fabric; unlike the United States, that help amounts to much more than just ineffectual hand-wringing. They legislate tax incentives and extremely restrictive zoning laws. Generous government subsidies protect traditional farming and industry and prevent inappropriate development in some thirty areas called* parcs naturels régionaux *or regional natural parks. The French are willing to spend a great deal of public money in support of their conviction that the* quality *of life and not just the accumulation of material goods is a large part of what makes life worth living.*

So despite the fact that the French countryside is home to far fewer people today than at the end of the Second World War, the walker will still find there the pace and spirit of simpler, less complex times. In the face of an evolving economy and social structure, rural France remains a fascinating and often lively area in which to walk.

Calais
Dunkerque
Boulogne
Lille
Arras
Abbeville
Amiens
Dieppe
St. Quentin
Charleville-Mézières
Cherbourg
Fécamp
Le Havre
Rouen
Reims
Caen
Seine
Metz
Paris
Marne
St-Malo
Granville
Argentan
Châlon-sur-Marne
Meuse
Nancy
Strasbourg
Brest
St-Brieuc
Fontainebleau
Dinan
Nemours
Seine
Troyes
Moselle
Colmar
Pontivy
Quimper
Rennes
Le Mans
Orléans
Sens
Mulhouse
Loir
Auxerre
Saône
Belfort
Auray
Loriem
Vannes
Angers
Tours
Blois
Avallon
Dijon
Besançon
St Nazaire
Saumur
Vierzon
Doubs
Nantes
Loire
Cher
Châteauroux
Bourges
Nevers
Chalon-sur-Saône
La Roche-sur-Yon
Poitiers
Moulins
Saône
Les Sables-d'Olonne
Niort
Montluçon
Mâcon
Bourg-en-Bresse
La Rochelle
Limoges
Clermont-Ferrand
Chamonix
Cognac
Loire
Lyon
Angoulême
Le Mont-Dore
St-Etienne
Isère
Royan
Val d'Isère
Périgueux
Brive-la-Gaillarde
Isère
Grenoble
Libourne
Dordogne
Cère
Drac
Bordeaux
Bergerac
Figeac
Le Puy
Valence
Gap
Arcachon
Lot
Montélimar
Durance
Agen
Cahors
Lot
Aveyron
Carpentras
Mont-de-Marsan
Montauban
Tarn
Alès
Avignon
Apt
Monte Carlo
Biarritz
Bayonne
Toulouse
Montpellier
Nîmes
Durance
Nice
St. Jean-de-Luz
Garonne
Ariège
Sète
Aix-en-Provence
Cannes
Tarbes
Carcassonne
Béziers
Marseille
St.Tropez
Lourdes
Aude
Narbonne
Toulon
Foix
Perpignan
Rhône

Where to Go
Contemplating your trip

Down on the floor with IGN map 903 spread out in front of you, it quickly becomes obvious as you study the tangle of GRs that each of the regions in France has at least one long marked and maintained trail running through it and that most have many more. The large number of paths, their length and their ubiquity means that choosing a route for your walking trip is not a matter of selecting an area where there are trails but a matter of choosing a region that intrigues you in some particular way. The trails are everywhere in France, but your interests may not be.

This book is not meant to be a guide that will lead you to specific restaurants, hotels or towns. But if you don't know France well, this chapter should help you become more familiar with the country by outlining briefly what each region offers the walker and indicating the best time of year to walk there. To pique your imagination I will also suggest several routes in each area.

Geography

Though it is western Europe's largest country, France is small by American standards. At 211,000 square miles, it is smaller than Texas or, from another perspective, just a little more than three times as big as New England. Yet within its borders there are differences in terrain that range from 15,771 feet at the top of Mont

The world is a country which nobody ever yet knew by description; one must travel through it one's self to be acquainted with it.

– Lord Chesterfield

Blanc, the highest point in western Europe, to below-sea-level polders near Mont-St-Michel. Scattered over the landscape are such diverse features as the geologically young Pyrénées and Alps, the volcanic Massif Central, the older, worn-down Vosges, and the folded Jura. And in between is even more diversity: the flat farmlands near Paris, the sparse forests on the swampy soil south of Orleans, the rolling, vine-covered hills of Burgundy and Beaujolais, the rocky coast of Brittany and the sandy plain south of Bordeaux.

Dividing the country are four major river systems: the Seine, which flows north into the La Manche (the sleeve, the French name for the English Channel); the long Loire, which ends in the Atlantic; the Rhône, which transports snow melt from the Alps and the Jura into the Mediterranean; and the Garonne, which carries water from the Pyrénées and the rest of southwestern France to, again, the Atlantic.

To better understand France's topography, it's useful to envision the country divided by a straight line that starts at the Spanish-French border on the Atlantic coast and extends northeast, passing near the cities of Limoges and Bourges, to end where the borders of France, Belgium and Luxembourg come together. The terrain to the west of this line is for the most part rolling or flat, suited to modern agriculture and heavily populated. Land to the east of the line, on the other hand, is broken, mountainous and consequently less suited to agriculture. Population in this part of the country is unevenly concentrated in the river valleys and in the industrial cities along the Rhine, the Rhône and the shore of the Mediterranean, where deep water and topography have allowed a port.

Walking vacations to the west of the line are less demanding. These areas are also tamer; the countryside along, say, the Loire, the Seine or around Bordeaux is quite populated and will, even in its remotest parts, seldom resemble an area you might call wild. In contrast, there are many areas to the east of the line that are rugged, isolated and quite far, at least on foot, from any significant human activity.

Population

With only fifty-eight million people France is one-half to one-third as densely populated as the other western European industrial nations. This relatively small population is due to two factors. The first is that republican France, though it is in name a Catholic country, has traditionally had birthrates lower than the rest of Europe. (The town of Condom, which gave birth to that utilitarian device, is located in southwest France.) The second is the lingering effect of a pause in growth caused by the death of a significant part of a whole generation of young French men during the insanity of the trench warfare during World War I.

Three-quarters of the French population, forty-four million people, live in cities and larger towns, and ten million of those are in and around Paris, the most populous city in western Europe. The typical Frenchman is often pictured in movies as a taciturn peasant who wears a beret, downs endless glasses of bad red wine and smokes roll-your-own, vile-smelling cigarettes. But as I pointed out in the last chapter, the truth is that Marius has moved to the city, where he wears an Armani suit, drinks Perrier and smokes Marlboros. France, like most developed countries, is predominately an urban nation.

Climate

There are three major climate zones in France—four, if you count the alpine climate that prevails in the mountains above an altitude of four to six thousand feet.

All along France's west and north coasts a climate called maritime predominates, the result of the moist west winds off the Atlantic Ocean and the English

Centigrade to Fahrenheit

$$9/5 \times C° + 32 = F°$$

One aspect of the metric system is the centigrade scale used in France and the rest of Europe to measure temperature. The freezing point of water, 32° Fahrenheit, is equal to 0° centigrade, and the boiling point of water, 212° Fahrenheit, is equal to 100° centigrade. 0° to 100°, logical and easy to use for those who grow up with the system, but walkers from the United States must translate those degrees centigrade into degrees Fahrenheit to get information that is at all meaningful. The formula is somewhat complex, but once you have memorized the drill it's easy enough to use if you have any facility for doing math in your head.

Nine-fifths of the centigrade temperature plus thirty-two equals the Fahrenheit temperature; 10° centigrade, then, is 18 plus 32 or 50° Fahrenheit, 20° centigrade equals 68° Fahrenheit, etc.

Channel. This climate is characterized by mild winters, cool summers and considerable rain throughout the year, particularly during the winter when the jet stream and, with it, the storm track shift to the south over Europe. As you travel inland, the effect of the ocean air lessens until the climate becomes what is called continental, a weather pattern characterized by more extreme temperatures in winter and summer than those experienced nearer the coast and by occasional but ample precipitation. This climate prevails over most of France and, indeed, over most of Europe. The last climate zone in France is the aptly named Mediterranean, which holds sway along a relatively narrow strip of land in the south bordering the sea with the same name. As in other Mediterranean climate zones like coastal California and South Africa, wet winters followed by dry, hot summers are characteristic.

Sometimes a persistent, strong north wind, the *mistral,* will blow for days down the Rhône Valley corridor through western Provence. The same type of wind also blows from the northwest across Langedoc, where it is called the *tramontane.* The weather is always sparkling clear and cool, even cold when a *mistral* or a *tramontane* blows down toward the Mediterranean at forty, fifty or even seventy miles per hour. The wind is so unrelenting that it becomes an irritant for the population, so much so, it is said, that living day after day with the accompanying dust and noise has been used, sometimes successfully, as an excuse for murder and other crimes of passion.

When the person on foot is caught by these winds, dust can be a problem. Faith and I once made the mistake of walking through the ocher quarries outside Roussillon in the Luberon area of Provence during a particularly fierce *mistral*; we emerged painted red from head to foot with a layer of extremely fine pigment.

If I had to characterize French weather briefly, I would use the word *fickle.* Though walkers from New England or the Rocky Mountains won't be surprised by cold snaps that may occur anywhere in France all through the springtime, visitors from California or Florida could be caught unprepared. The weather *can* be warm and sunny as early as late March or April (particularly in the south), but as I can attest from experience, it's also possible for snow to fall in the flatlands of northern and central France as late as mid-May. The weather is changeable in France, and the person on foot will in all probability encounter storms and rain sometime during a walk. Happily, the mutability of the weather *usually* means that the sun will follow the clouds.

Culture

Equally impressive and surprising are the varieties of culture in this small country. Though the various separate and ancient languages such as Alsatian, Breton and Provençal are fast disappearing in this age of high-speed trains and television, there remain subtle and not-so-subtle differences from region to region in architecture, cuisine and attitude. Even the walker who travels for only a week will likely encounter changes in rooflines and building materials as well as in the list of traditional dishes that appear and reappear like a refrain on menus in each particular region. You will walk over some physical barrier, perhaps only a low ridge, and gray slate instead of orange tiles will roof the houses and *confit* will replace *cassoulet* on the menu. When this happens you will know that you have crossed some invisible but venerable cultural border.

To the outsider, France seems monolithic and unified, but in truth it is made up of many separate regions, each of which has its own insular and distinct manner of dealing with the outside world. As Gillian Tindall points out in her illuminating book on rural France, *Celestine, Voices from a French Village,* even as late as 1900, in some isolated rural towns the word *étranger* (foreigner) applied, not as it does today, just to groups of people like the Peruvians or the Chinese, but also to "those people" from the neighboring village only miles away. They were unknown. They were not to be trusted. They were strangers. More than just a hint of that attitude persists today.

The regions:

My division of France into thirteen areas is arbitrary. With the walker in mind, I have sometimes lumped together contiguous but traditionally separate regions that are similar in climate or terrain. In some cases I have ignored historic borders by amalgamating or carving up regions, but willy-nilly, all of France is covered. First, I'll discuss those areas to the west of that line that divides France into two parts—the flatter, more urban north and west from the higher, more mountainous east and south.

Please note that I myself have not (yet) had the time to walk anywhere near a majority of the trails that I mention in connection with each of the regions, but I am quite familiar in a general way with all of the areas. Many are trails I hope to walk in the future. For some of the recommendations, I am indebted to a variety of FFRP guidebooks and to two British books, *Long Walks in France*, by Adam Nicholson, and *Walking in France*, by Rob Hunter. (For more about these two informative but out-of-print books see the reading list at the end of this book.) Keep in mind that these suggestions are meant to fire your interest, not narrow your choices. Use map 903 to choose any trail that interests you.

Normandy and Brittany

Terrain: In both Normandy and Brittany, the terrain is for the most part flat to gently hilly, with some short but steep ups and downs when a trail descends to a beach from the seaside heights or when a path crosses a river valley. But each area also has one older, worn-down mountain chain. Brittany was formed by the uplift of the Amorican massif almost six hundred million years ago. The ancient peaks are now rounded, but some hills near the western tip of the peninsula in the Arrée still manage to rise to bald, wind-blown

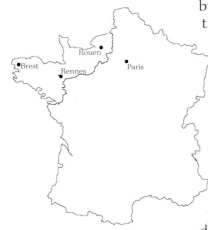

knobs that top twelve hundred feet. In Normandy the eastern extension of that same uplift has left a small chain of granitic hills. The two highest rise exactly to exactly 1368 feet and are at the center of the Normandie-Maine Regional Park. The Brittany coast, where exposed to large waves from the Atlantic Ocean, is rocky, broken and very beautiful.

Weather: These coastal areas are the wettest in France. The westernmost reaches of the Brittany peninsula at Brest receive at least some rain on half the days of each year, and though it's damper in winter, precipitation can come at any time. If you walk from east to west, you will often face a strong, even fierce, wind off the Atlantic or the English Channel. During winter storms these winds can reach hurricane force, strong enough to blow heavy slate tiles off roofs and send them scaling dangerously down the length of cobbled streets. The bath of air from the Atlantic moderates the temperature year-round.

Some walks:

5 days:	Dieppe to Etretat; GR 21; about 60 miles; a seaside walk
7–10 days:	Bagnoles-de-l'Orne to Mont-St-Michel; GR 22; 90 miles; hilly country
10–14 days:	Paris to Rouen; GRs 2 and 25; about 120 miles; an easy river walk
10–14 days:	Lannion to Paimpol; GR 34; 115 miles; a coastal walk in northern Brittany

Comments: When I think of Brittany and Normandy, I think of the ocean, but two of the four walks I list are inland. The first, on the GRs 2 and 25, would actually start in or near Paris, enter Normandy near Vernon, follow the wide meanders of the Seine past Monet's beautifully restored home and gardens at Giverny and end in old Rouen, with its fine cathedral and impressive collection of medieval buildings and gates. The second inland walk is also in Normandy. It follows the GR 22 along the granite spine that divides the Normandie-Maine Regional Park, which is east of Mont-St-Michel. These rambles are quite different; the walk up the Seine is urban and peopled, while the one in western Normandy is rural, full of cows and apple trees, butter and cider.

The walks inland are fascinating, but the walks along the coast, almost anywhere in Normandy or Brittany, are among the most spectacular and varied in France. I have singled out two particular seaside strolls, one in Normandy on the GR 21 along the cliffs—often painted by various Impressionists—between Dieppe and Etretat, the other on the GR 34 along the rocky Brittany coast, but there are many others—the invasion beaches in Normandy, the Cotentin Peninsula—that would be just as enjoyable. This entire coast, and in particular the rocky north coast of Brittany, has huge tides that fill whole bays and then empty them to the horizon. Walks by the sea bring the sharp smell of iodine and seaweed, the screech of greedy gulls and the hiss of the waves retreating over pebble beaches.

The walker has a variety of good choices in Brittany. Because hoards of tourists jam Mont-St-Michel and because the town itself is devoted almost exclusively to them, this jewel is perhaps best viewed from afar. But no crowds will spoil your appreciation of the many Celtic menhirs that dot the fields inland. You might

Mont-St-Michel seen across the bay from a point of land north of Avranches. Notice the blaze for the GR 223 on the bench.

even wish that more attention were paid here as you wade through the trash and new-age messages from the faithful that surround Merlin's grave in the forest of Brocéliande. Reflecting the history of the regions, there's a definite English flavor to these areas with their hedgerows, thatched-roof houses, herds of dairy cows in green fields and always the sea.

Normandy produces no wine, but this being apple country, hard cider with a spritz, about as alcoholic as beer, is often available in the cafés. A small part of the vineyards that produce the dry Muscadet white wine are in the southernmost part of Brittany and that wine, which accompanies shellfish so well, is served in many seaside restaurants. Oysters said to be the best in the world, fish of all kinds, small Breton lobsters and a bewildering variety of other shellfish await the hungry walker at the end of a day on the trail. And there is more: delicious lamb raised on the salt flats near the ocean and, from all those cows, dairy products that include thick cream, superb butter and a large variety of cheeses—Pont-l'Evêque, stinky Livarot and the famous Camembert among them.

Huitres, *or oysters, are a specialty of Brittany.* Belons *and* Marennes *are two of the better known from the over one hundred varieties of oyster available in France.*

Normans—originally descended from Viking pirates—have a reputation (undeserved, as far as I am concerned) for being taciturn. The weather is often wet in Brittany and Normandy, but this shouldn't keep the walker from these two very beautiful regions. Given good weather (never guaranteed), the coast could be walked at any time of the year, but warmer if not necessarily drier conditions would prevail from April into November.

The north and Champagne

Terrain: The terrain is flat to undulating throughout this region. Even the hills of the Ardennes reach only 1500 feet in altitude at their highest point. The seashore, like that across the Channel in England in Dover, is in large part made up of chalk cliffs. Major rivers—the Somme, the Aisne, the Marne and the Meuse—divide and define this countryside.

Weather: Near the English Channel the climate is maritime. The Ardennes hills and Champagne are far enough inland to escape much of the precipitation that keeps the shore so green. As you move away from the coast, temperatures become more variable. During storms, particularly in the winter, hurricane-force winds can blow off the Channel from the west and north.

Some walks:

Day walks:	From Epernay in Champagne; walks on the Montagne de Reims
and	From Charleville-Mézières on the Meuse; walks in the Ardennes forest
2–3 days:	Calais to Boulogne-sur-Mer; GR *littoral;* a seaside walk; about 25 miles

Comments: Dunkirk, the Somme, the Marne—these names immediately call to mind the two World Wars. But this is country that has been fought over for centuries as towns with names like Crécy and Agincourt (Azincourt to the French) remind us. The flat terrain—a highway for cavalry and tanks—and its proximity to Belgium and England make this area naturally desirable to generals and the like, but there were and are other reasons to covet this region. It is rich and heavily populated, full of forests, good agricultural land, manufacturing centers like Lille and, until recently, coal mines and steel mills.

If this sounds interesting but not necessarily like a countryside you might want to walk through, I would have to agree. Frankly, despite its beauty spots, this is the least attractive of all the walking areas in France.

People here in the north, though they greatly enjoy their beer, are for the most part hard-working and serious, and the food, once you leave the mussels and Dover sole on the coast, echoes that hard-working and serious theme. Pig's feet. *Andouillettes* (tripe sausages). Ham. And all of it cooked using not butter or olive oil but the traditional lard. Taken one at a time, the region's specialties are delicious, but day after day they may prove too heavy for even the most active of walkers. You'll find trout in the Ardennes and of course champagne in Champagne, but food is not this region's strong point.

There are some beautiful timbered buildings scattered through this area, and Louis XV's castle at Compiègne as well as the cathedrals at Reims, Beauvais and Amiens are certainly worth a visit. But for the most part, this is a countryside that has been repeatedly ravaged by war and in places disfigured by mines and industry. To top it all off, modern agriculture has emptied many villages in the countryside.

Charleville-Mézières or one of the smaller towns along the Meuse River—Revin for one—would be a convenient base for day walks in the Ardennes. This beautiful and surprisingly wild area is heavily forested. Walking paths are everywhere here, even extending into Belgium. Epernay, south of Reims, is the other day-walk center I would recommend. It sits on the edge of the Montagne de Reims Regional Park. Walks through forests and vineyards followed by picnics with Champagne. What could be better?

The coast walk I cite is a short but spectacular stroll along the chalk cliffs between Calais and Boulogne-sur-Mer. The French call this area the Opal Coast. If you are staying in England and wish to get away for a long French weekend, a quick trip to Dieppe or Boulogne by ferry would put you on the trail.

The coast could be walked at any time of the year, though storms in winter frequently bring unpleasant conditions. Inland, the walker should wait at least until late March or April before attempting a cross-country walk.

Paris and the Ile-de-France

Terrain: Level in Paris. In the Ile-de-France outside Paris, generally level except for some short, sometimes steep drops or climbs when crossing or walking along the Seine and its tributaries, which include the well-known Oise and Marne.

Weather: Continental. Cold and often foggy in winter; warm, sometimes hot in summer. Evenly but not excessively moist the year round.

Some walks:

Day walks: From Fontainebleau on the GR 1 as well as regional and local trails in the forests surrounding the town; also in Paris anywhere your interest lies

Comments: Two official trails cross Paris, one running north to south, the other east to west. The east to west trail can lead the walker at either end through the suburbs out of Paris on marked paths to the GR 1, which encircles the city within an area called the Ile-de-France. Including all its variants and detours, the GR 1 is over 375 miles long. For anyone living in or staying in Paris, the GR 1 is an excellent and convenient trail to use for day or weekend walks. Almost every branch of the RER (Paris' newer urban subway, which supplements the venerable Metro) crosses the GR 1 or one of its side shoots. It is easy to use this efficient system to "get out of town" for walks of a day, a weekend or longer.

Paris? Who would want to trail-walk in Paris? Though the staff in the FFRP office seemed quite enthusiastic and proud of the two trails through Paris established in 1996, I, having walked the east-west trail one cool, cloudy November day, cannot recommend them. The FFRP, it seems, applied the usual criteria when they established and marked these itineraries: avoid bustle, people and heavy traffic. As a result the sights you see are, well, not sights at all.

Instead, you are shunted onto minor streets that seem to have been chosen not for their beauty, charm or interest but solely because they are quiet and obscure. Following the marked trail, you will walk monotonous roads lined with apartments while only one parallel street away from the marked route a bustling market takes place. You will stroll down long cavernous alleys lined with hospitals or, more accurately, the walls around hospitals. Yes, there are parks, the lovely Jardin du Luxembourg among them, but they are not enough. My advice would be to ignore the established paths and make your own way through Paris with a home-made itinerary, which can include whatever interests you—markets, museums, the parks, the Seine. Walking in Paris is a delight but walking there on the marked trail is less so. Dull was the word that came to mind that November day, and Paris should never be dull.

It's almost equally hard to imagine walking in the outskirts of Paris, but the GR 1 has a great deal more to recommend it than the trails inside Paris. Though on average only twenty-five miles from the city, much of this trail passes through the forests that form the Paris greenbelt. This green band is in part made up of the numerous woods and preserves that were, before the French Revolution, hunting grounds for the French aristocracy. Happily, many of these relatively unspoiled areas have been preserved—Napoleon, a great admirer of the English system of parks and gardens, was instrumental in saving much of this land for the State and the public—and they are now crossed not only by the circular GR 1 but also by many other trails that radiate out from that trail like spokes on a wheel toward Champagne, Burgundy, the Loire and Normandy.

You would need a great deal of time to walk even half of the 375 miles that make up this circuit. Because many of the forests just outside Paris were hunting

grounds for the nobility, there is much of historic interest to see. Fontainbleau and Versailles are but two of the better-known playhouses that lie along or just off the route, but there are many other châteaux, chapels, churches and museums as well. This is an urban walk, and equally interesting are the houses, gardens and backyards of the locals.

Because a regional trail that connects with the GR 1 passes very close to the Charles deGaulle airport northeast of Paris, it would even be possible, after your flight has landed and you have cleared customs, to shoulder your pack and walk out of the airport. With time you could end up, always on foot, anywhere in France.

Once the walker leaves the forests, the Ile-de-France is quite populated and, since this is after all suburban Paris, sophisticated. Hotels and fine restaurants should be easy to find at the end of the day. Because the area is not wildly popular with visitors as a place to stay the night, it might even be possible to walk the Ile-de-France during the months of July and August—bus-loads of tourists out from Paris for a guided tour crowd the better-known monuments during the day but, because they are herded back into the city late each afternoon, not the hotels and restaurants in the evening. There's only one problem: during the summer some of the small hotels catering to business people or the restaurants serving the local residents take a cue from their regular clientele who during August have fled to a beach somewhere. As a result they too close up while the owners and the staff take their own vacations. Some of the suburbs of Paris can be, in August, just as bereft of local businesses as Paris itself.

How 'ya gonna keep 'em down on the farm, after they've seen Paree?
– Sam M. Lewis & Joe Young
World War I song

As a practical matter, the GR 1, given a sunny day, could be walked at any time of the year, though the ground is likely to be muddy during November, December, January and February. More pleasant conditions can (never say will) prevail from March through October.

The Loire

Terrain: In its lower reaches the Loire crosses land with few changes in elevation. But upstream past Orléans the river enters hillier country that becomes progressively more rugged though, never quite mountainous, as it approaches its source only thirty miles west of Valence. The Loire, at 634 miles, is France's longest river. The principal tributaries are the Loir, the Indre, the Cher and, closer to the source, the Allier.

Weather: The lower reaches of the river are strongly influenced by storm systems streaming westward off the Atlantic Ocean, and the weather there is changeable and frequently wet, though less so in summer. Further upriver past Tours, the climate becomes more and more continental until once east of Orléans the weather is entirely typical of that zone—hot with sporadic showers in summer, cold with frequent rain or snow in winter. Temperatures are moderate near the coast, more extreme—colder *and* hotter—inland.

Some walks:

5–7 days	Tours to Chambord; GR 41 and various GRPs; about 70 miles; flat
7–10 days	Tours to Vierzon; GR 41; about 90 miles; gentle terrain
8–10 days	Châteaudun to Angers; GR 35; about 115 miles; gentle terrain
14 days:	Saumur to Orléans; GR 3; 160 miles; flat terrain

Comments: The GR 3, which follows the Loire, the GR 41, which parallels the Cher, and a few interconnecting regional trails between the two manage to pass near to or by most of the well-known châteaux between Saumur and Orléans. This area would be a wonderful choice for walkers who enjoy level paths and interesting cultural monuments during the day and the creature comforts at night. At all times of the year, many tourists, French and foreigner alike, visit the popular and picturesque small towns and cities west of Orléans, so the hotels and restaurants are well developed. Luxury, if you want it, is never very far away in the Loire. But, even if luxe is not one your priorities, the Loire château country with its abundance of facilities of all types, its flat terrain and easy-to-follow routes would be a good choice for a first long walk in France.

The list of attractions seems endless: the châteaux at Chenonceaux, Chambord, Azay-le-Rideau and (my favorite) Cheverny; the abbey at Fontevraud, where

Richard the Lionheart and Eleanor of Aquitaine are buried; the vineyards and wineries that produce the wonderful Loire wines—Vouvray, Saumur, Chinon and Bourgueil. All this is available to the walker. In places, the river banks are honeycombed with limestone caves where the locals not only store wine but also make homes and even restaurants—the wonderfully evocative word *troglodyte* is everywhere on signs and advertisements. It's never boring in the Loire. If you tire of the sights, you have only to fix your attention on the day-to-day life of the local population, friendly, prosperous, maybe even a little smug. Though not overcrowded, the Loire between Angers and Orleans is highly civilized, tame not wild, and the walker there is never far from people or activity.

The exterior of the château at Azay-le-Rideau is, like many of the Loire châteaux, a delightful mix of towers, moats and gardens. But the interior is less impressive. Many of the châteaux were looted during the revolution. Some of the rest have been given or sold to the government by owners who find the expense of maintaining such a luxurious home prohibitive.

The foot traveler already familiar with the château country or those simply unwilling to deal with that area's inevitable shortcomings—a relatively expensive tourist economy and at times crowds of bus-borne visitors—might consider instead a walk in a different area. The GR 35 follows the masculine *le* Loir (no "e" on the end) valley, a picturesque and much less touristed tributary of the feminine *la* Loire (with the "e"). The Loir runs down from the north near Chartres for 150 miles to Angers. This valley is beautiful and quiet in a way that the busier Loire could never be. As in the Loire, there are châteaux, abbeys and churches to visit as well as vineyards and wineries, but everything, starting with the river and its valley, is on a much smaller and more intimate scale.

Again, I would recommend that the walker plan a trip in this area anytime from April through June or from September through October.

The center and the Atlantic Coast

Terrain: The terrain in these areas is quite flat, though seldom monotonously so. Along the Atlantic, the cliffs and rocks of Brittany give way, south of the Loire, to a more subdued coast and, below the mouth of the Gironde, long sandy beaches.

Weather: The easternmost part of this area is the geographic heart of France, and as you would expect, the climate is continental in nature. The weather along the Atlantic Coast—that part of it south of the mouth of the Loire—is of course maritime, but being further south, it is warmer and drier than similar areas to the north, so much so that during the summer the southern part of this coast can be quite dry if the storm track has shifted to the north into Scotland and Scandinavia.

Some walks:

Day walks:	From Mézières-en-Brenne near Châteauroux in the Berry; on regional and local trails; flat
3–5 days:	Arcachon (west of Bordeaux) to Mimizan; GR 8; a 40-mile stroll in the Landes; flat
7–10 days	Vierzon to Sancerre; GRs 41-31; about 80 miles; some hills

Comments: This is a huge section of France, and by naming only three walks, I have obviously left out many other fine candidates. The pastoral country in the center encompasses what the French call *la France profonde,* literally "deep France," but the meaning includes concepts like "ancient" and "traditional." Because this area has neither spectacular natural features nor a plethora of well-known monuments, it will, in all probability, not be your choice for a first-time walk in France. But you should remember when you plan your second or fourth walk that it has a great deal to offer.

Mézières, the day-walk center I recommend, is in A flat region called the Brenne; the land here is half-covered with ponds and small lakes. This quiet, rural area, another in the series of French regional parks, is a paradise for those interested in birds. The lakes and ponds supply a great variety of freshwater fish—pike, perch and the delicious *sandre* (defined as pike-perch)—to French commercial markets and, of course, to the local restaurants. At the end of a stay in Mézières the person on foot could easily walk for two days across the park into the nearby town of Le Blanc.

The second walk I recommend is through the pastoral Collines du Sancerrois (Sancerre Hills), which lie between the Cher River and the upper reaches of the Loire around the wine town of Sancerre. This walk passes through a beautiful, little-visited region. The grapes for Sancerre wine are grown here; you will drink and eat well. If you have the time, a walk all the way from Sancerre to Tours along the GRs 31 and 41 combines the peaceful, rural countryside you would find during the first part of the walk with the modicum of sophistication you would find on the periphery of the château country during the second half.

The short walk on the GR 8 south and west of Bordeaux is, like some walks in the north, an ocean walk, but here the terrain and the weather are different. Fortunately, there is quite a bit less rain along this coast, particularly during the summer. The biggest difference, however, is that the land south of the mouth of the river Gironde is sandy and flat. A beach 140 miles long (Europe's longest) begins at the mouth of the river and extends south to Biaritz near the Spanish border.

The prevailing west wind blowing inland off the Atlantic has formed large dunes behind this beach, and it is in this area you will walk, using a path that passes through pine forests and along the shore of ponds and lakes trapped behind the piles of sand. The restaurants serve local seafood, which you can wash down with the less well-known but delicious dry white wines of Bordeaux.

South of Mimizan the GR 8 quits the dunes for the edge of the beach; accommodations are sparse along this section of the trail, but anyone willing to put in a long day or two, would be rewarded with a spectacular stroll along the Atlantic.

These areas can be visited anytime between late March and November though the beach towns are certain to be crowded in summer.

Alsace–Lorraine and the Jura

Terrain: The Vosges mountains rise above the flat alluvial plain of the Rhine to the east and the slightly hilly to flat terrain of Lorraine to the west. The Vosges, like the mountain-hills of Britanny and Normandy, are old, worn-down mountains, but the highest point, the Grand Ballon, still manages to rise to 4671 feet above sea level. Lorraine is drained by the Meuse and Moselle rivers, which flow north toward Luxembourg, Germany and eventually the Rhine. The Jura are a series of folded mountains with heights from 3000 to 4500 feet. The ridges that characterize these mountains run from the northeast to the southwest and parallel the Swiss border. There are numerous lakes and rivers in the heavily wooded Jura.

Weather: The weather here is continental except at high altitudes where, specially in winter, it can be characterized as alpine. Many trails in the Vosges and Jura mountains are closed by snow from November through April.

Some walks:

Day walks:	From Les Rousses in the southern Jura; hilly
7–10 days:	Wissembourg through the northern Vosges to Schirmack; GR 53 and variants; 100 miles; a hill walk in the Vosges
10–14 days:	Fesches through the Jura to Nyon; GR 5; 160 miles through hills and along ridges; for the in-shape walker

Comments: In the ninth century Charlemagne divided his kingdom into three parts for his three heirs. Ever since that time, the middle part, Alsace and Lorraine— left to the weakest son—has been fought over by the descendants of the other two sons and by their subjects, the French and the Germans.

Alsace, in particular, is a mix of the two cultures, and the resulting blend borrows some of the best features from both. You will see timbered buildings, drink excellent beer and eat delicious food that emphasizes the German love of pork and cabbage, yet the respect for privacy and independence is French, as is the preparation of all that pork and cabbage. Alsatian wines are made from grapes we think of as German—

riesling and gewürztraminer—but are more delicate and refined, more French, than those made further down the Rhine. The Alsatian people are fun loving, *gemültlich* without that hint of underlying smugness sometimes found further east.

Walking trails in Alsace are in the Vosges mountains above and to the west of two of my favorite French cities, Colmar and Strasbourg. The walk on the GR 53 that I recommend begins in the Vosges du Nord Regional Park in France's northeastern corner right up against the German border and ends in the mountains west of Strasbourg. The northern Vosges is an untouristed area full of picturesque villages and ruined castles. If you have more time, continue south into the beautiful Ballon d'Alsace Regional Park where you will walk through high treeless meadows called *chaumes*.

Lorraine is less German than Alsace. The region is dominated by two large rivers, the Meuse and the Moselle, and in the north active and defunct industries crowd the banks of both. But south of Metz and Verdun, the gently rolling terrain is wooded and pastoral and offers many fine walking opportunities. Nancy, with its graceful Place Stanislas and fine garden called la Pépinière, is worth a visit.

The Jura is sparsely populated and heavily forested. At first encounter it seems to be a dark and somewhat mysterious region, but once you become accustomed to the dense woods and the deep valleys and after you've met the friendly inhabitants, your impression will soften. But to enjoy the Jura, you must enjoy that somber mood, which involves the primitive, the wild and the beautiful all wound up in a vague, not displeasing feeling of self-sufficiency tinged with loneliness. This is country that brings to mind the fairy tales of Grimm, not Disney.

Les Rousses, the day-walk center I recommend, is a winter and summer resort nestled right up against the Swiss border in the southern Jura. This walking center par excellence offers a huge variety of paths that wind their way past lakes in the valleys and into the forests up in the hills. You could end your stay here with a delightful two-day walk on the GR 5 across the border to the Swiss town of Nyon on the north shore of Lake Geneva.

The long walk on the GR 5 that I have mentioned begins in southern Alsace and ends in Nyon. This trail doesn't traverse extremely difficult terrain but it does demand that the visitor sometimes walk long distances between accommodations. This is a ridge walk through a wild and beautiful country full of lakes, dark valleys and deep forests. The restaurants here serve *civets* made with wild boar and succulent trout simmered in an acidic broth until their skin turns blue.

The highest areas of the Jura and Vosges do not clear of snow until late April or May, and snow could become a problem again as early as October. Lower areas can be visited anytime, but winter is likely to be cold, dark and unpleasant.

Burgundy and the Beaujolais

Terrain: The Burgundy and Beaujolais regions are hilly and for the most part forested except where vineyards have been planted. Both regions have been blessed or cursed, depending on your point of view, by relatively poor soil of a type that, in some areas, is excellent for growing grapes but not well suited for other crops.

Weather: Continental.

Some walks:

3–5 days	Dijon to Beaune; GRs 7 and 76; about 40 miles; some hills
8–10 days	Vézelay to Luzy, GR 13; 80 miles; gentle at first, hilly at the end
10–14 days	Beaune to Villefranche; GRs 76 and 76A; about 135 miles; rolling

Comments: The famous part of Burgundy between Dijon and Chagny encompasses the Côte d'Or wine region, where the grapes for many of the region's well-known red and white wines—Chambertin, Clos de Vougeot, Montrachet and Meursault—are grown. At first glance, this part of Burgundy seems to be rural and uncomplicated, but reflecting the high prices that its wines command, it is in truth wealthy and sophisticated. The locals are not ostentatious, so it's only when the person on foot visits the luxe shops in Beaune or Dijon, eats in one of the many fine restaurants or takes a room in one of the region's fancy and expensive hotels that the underlying wealth becomes apparent.

The walk in this area between Dijon and Beaune climbs from Chambertin up through the famous vineyards to the top of the slope, but near Nuits St-George it descends back into the vines. This is a superb short stroll, a leisurely wander that will reward your efforts with good food and even better wine.

Walking the Côte d'Or is like visiting a rich and somewhat stuffy uncle. You enjoy the creature comforts and the luxury, but the formality can be inhibiting. Walking through the three less well-known wine regions to the south, the Mâconnais, the Chalonnais and the Beaujolais, is like visiting good friends; the amenities may not be so grand, but the atmosphere is relaxed and casual. The second walk I recommend, along the GRs 76 and 76A, is through this welcoming comfort zone. Here you will eat delicious but simple food, drink good, inexpensive wine and be greeted warmly and sincerely by the locals, who seem to find many excuses to smile.

The other Burgundy, that larger part to the north and west of the wine regions, is forested and relatively poor. It encompasses the Morvan Regional Park, a large and beautiful area of dense forests, lakes and hills, and it is here that another fine but less civilized walk is located. The GR 13 from Vézelay to Luzy traverses the full length of the park and near the end rises to the summit of the 2,693-foot Mont Beauvray. This was the site of an immense barbarian fortress where, at a convocation of all the Gauls in 52 BC, Vercingetorix was elected chief just before his battle with Caesar at Alésia. Traces of the camp with its five kilometers of ramparts are still visible.

Burgundy is said to have the best food of any region in France; five out of twenty-one of France's finest restaurants (according to the 1998 *Michelin Hotels-Restaurants* guide) are there. Two of these are in the Morvan Park, and you could start or, better, end your trip on the GR 13 at the one in St-Père, only three kilometers from Vézelay. The walk down the Côte d'Or ends in Beaune, but another day on the GR 76 would bring you to Chagny, the site of another of these famous restaurants.

This area is best visited from April through June and from September through early November. In September during the *vendange* (grape harvest), hotels in the wine regions can be crowded with visitors, particularly the Swiss.

Many of the best restaurants in the Beaujolais north of Lyon and in Lyon itself are unpretentious establishments where the walker will feel comfortable and welcome.

Périgord and the Dordogne

Terrain: Rolling country interrupted on occasion by deep canyons where rivers cut across the plateau. Hilly in the south.

Weather: Maritime, but typically less wet than similar regions farther to the north. Some summers are quite dry.

Some walks:

7-10 days:	From les Eyzies to Cahors in the Dordogne; GR 36; 86 miles; hills, some steep climbs
8-11 days:	Périgeux to Rocamadour; GRs 36 and 6; about 100 miles; hills, some steep

Comments: In many ways the Périgord–Dordogne region embodies what foreigners picture the French countryside to be. Full of romantic castles and spectacular fortified towns, this area has a rich history, and the extraordinary fact is that much of this history is visible, available in concrete form to anyone interested enough to look. There are prehistoric paintings in a myriad of limestone caves like Pech Merle, traces of the Romans in the town of Périgueux and an amazing collection of medieval castles and buildings not only in well-known places like Sarlat-la-Canéda and Rocamadour but scattered everywhere in the region. This is a quiet, thickly forested area with little heavy industry,

and when traveling there, it is easy to feel that time has forgotten this corner of France.

Both the walks I mention will take the person on foot through the heart of this beautiful area. The first is from les Eyzies, the so-called capital of prehistory, to Cahors, a busy town that, with its plane trees lining the broad Boulevard Gambetta, has an unabashedly south-of-France feel. The museums of les Eyzies will give the visitor a full dose of interesting information about the prehistory of the region, but along the trail you will see the real thing: the dark interior of limestone caves with horse outlines and handprints as well as immense solitary menhirs standing in the fields. There are *bas-tides*, the fortified towns built by both the English and French during the Hundred Years War. Even the farms of the Quercy region surrounding Cahors look like miniature castles.

The second walk from Périgeux to the fortified town of Rocamador is similar to the Cahors walk but has the added advantage of passing through the restored medieval town of Sarlat-la-Canéda. The old section of Sarlat is lit by gas lamps, a touch that sounds hokey. But the lights along with the restoration of the Gothic and Renaissance buildings have been so well done that the overall effect works. Because the buildings are still in use the visitor has the feeling of being in an active small town, not a museum. The Saturday market in Sarlat is famous all over France.

Truffles, foie gras and confit are but a few of this area's specialties. No one pretends that any of this is diet food, but the walker who hesitates to try the fat-laced local cuisine should remember that in this region the "French paradox" was first noticed. The puzzle was that, though the inhabitants here ate the richest diet of any in France, the heart-attack rate was much lower than that in the United States and even slightly lower than that in the rest of France. So far at least, research has pointed to the consumption of wine as the miti-gating factor. So eat hearty, but wash everything down with plenty of the local Bergerac or Cahors wine!

Late March through October is the best time to visit Périgord and the Dordogne, though the more popular towns like les Eyzies, Sarlat-la-Canada and Rocama-dour are crowded in summer.

The Auvergne and Languedoc

Terrain: Though there are no spectacular peaks as in the Alps, this is mountainous country. The highest point in the Auvergne rises to over 6000 feet. The Languedoc is, except along the coast of the Mediterranean, also mountainous, though here the hills are lower and characterized by long ridges and not the jumbled mass of peaks and valleys found to the north in the Auvergne and, farther to the east, in the Cévennes.

Weather: Mediterranean on the coast and continental inland. Drier than areas in the north. The weather in the highest country is alpine; in winter considerable snow tops the peaks and passes, which can linger in the Auvergne until late May.

Some walks:

5–7 days:	From Florac to Millau in the Gorges du Tarn; a variety of local and GR trails; 55 miles; some short steep parts when the trail leaves or returns to the river
10–14 days:	Volvic to Murat in the Auvergne; GRs 4 and 400; 100 miles; a difficult but beautiful walk full of steep climbs
10 –14 days:	From Mazamet to Lodève in the Langedoc; GR 71; 100+ miles; hilly

Comments: Thirty-five million years ago two volcanoes, each eventually thirty miles across at the base, erupted in what is today the Auvergne. These volcanoes are now extinct, but their eroded though still formidable remnants, Mont Dore and Mont du Cantal, dominate and define the region. As recently as eight thousand years ago another flurry of smaller eruptions near Mont Dore in the north further disrupted the landscape there leaving fresh lava flows, small cinder cones and a series of stark volcanic necks.

The soil throughout this region is ill suited for agriculture, and the almost treeless plains, hills and valleys support only summer grazing. The herds of cattle and sheep are driven up to the pastures in the high country in the spring and back to lower country in the fall. (This practice, called *la transhumance*, has been carried on for at least three thousand years in the Auvergne. It is common everywhere in southern France.)

Excepting the industrial city of Clermont-Ferrand, the Auvergne is the most sparsely populated area in the country. The people here are poor and have a reputation among the French for being as harsh and as hard as the country they live in.

The walk on the GRs 4 and 400 from Volvic to Murat is difficult because of many steep climbs and descents and because the sparseness of the population means that lodging options are few and sometimes quite distant one from the other. But the fit walker will experience an area almost empty of people, primitive and spectacularly wild. This is a walk through a country thoroughly dominated by its violent geologic history. The food is simple, good and, as you might expect in this poor region, inexpensive. Cheeses are a specialty; among the best are the blue from Ambert, firmCantal and St-Nectaire, delicious when carefully ripened.

Languedoc is a less intense version of Provence, less touristed, less fancy yet still picturesque and comfortable as only the south of France can be. The walk I cite on the GR 71 is in the hills above the vineyards, fishing ports, industry and city of Montpellier on the Mediterranean. Like the high country away from the coast in Provence, there are surprisingly few people, but accommodations for the person on foot are close enough together to make walking pleasant. The walker here will experience a beautiful untouristed area of heavily wooded hills, open plains and friendly, easy-going people.

Seafood is available at the coast, but inland the simple straightforward cooking features lamb and game. Again, as in Provence, olive oil and garlic are used liberally. Many of the wines from Languedoc are excellent and, because they are not well known, good values. These wines have improved greatly since the 1960s, when almost all the grapes from the region were made into the cheap wine that was shipped in drums to cafés all over France where it was sold for as little as forty cents a liter. At the time the English called this wine *plonk,* which somehow described it perfectly.

The last walk I have singled out is through the spectacular Tarn gorge. This steep defile is a popular spot during the summer for French tourists but is less

visited in the spring and fall. Many restaurants and hotels dot the route of this relatively easy walk. Tour boats will even float you down the gorge if you become too tired to walk.

The hills of Languedoc are heavily wooded and sparsely populated. In this region there are sometimes long periods of good but cool weather in the fall when the tramontane *wind blows toward the Mediterranean. The yellow and red blazes mark a regional trail.*

Though the Auvergne and Languedoc are in the south, both receive enough snow in the winter to preclude walks before May.

Rhône Valley and the Alps

Terrain: Between Lyon and Avignon the Rhône is bordered on both sides by hilly terrain, which to the east culminates in the extremely rugged Alps. Mont Blanc is higher than any mountain in the lower forty-eight United States. The French Alps, particularly in the north near Chamonix, spawn many glaciers.

Weather: Continental and of course alpine in the mountains. Snow stays on the high trails until June or, after a heavy snow year, July.

Some walks:

Day walks: From Chamonix in the high Alps; local trails

and From Barcelonnette in the Ubaye region midway between Grenoble and Nice; on local trails and the GRs 6 and 56

10-14 days: Larche to the Mediterranean; GR 5; 95 miles; mountainous

14+ days: The tour around Mont Blanc; 125 miles; mountainous and rugged; a classic walk for the very fit

Comments: The Rhône river south of Lyon is an industrial artery, full of barges and lined in many places with factories and power plants. But just fifty miles to the east are the Alps, where many snow-covered peaks rise to between two and three miles above the sea. Here herds of cows graze in high pastures that resemble vast manicured lawns. Picturesque farms with overhanging roofs bring Switzerland to mind. And there is frequently a deep blue sky with air so limpid that what appears to be only a mile away turns out to be five.

In this region the walker will find a different country. Because the climate is harsh and agriculture border-line, the people who live here are used to tests of their ability to survive both physically and, until the recent advent of winter and summer tourism, economically. They are independent but, like many people who live relatively isolated lives, friendly. These mountains were part of the separate (and influential) Savoy state before it was joined to the French nation in the 1860s. Savoy included much of the northwestern part of Italy where, even today, French is spoken.

Chamonix is a ski resort that in summer doubles as a superb walking center. Not only can you walk the many trails in the valley near town, but the ski lifts, some of which run in summer, give the person on foot almost unlimited access to the trails in the mountains to the south and, particularly, to the north of town. To some it

may seem like cheating, but I like nothing better than to take a ski lift into the high country in the morning and then spend the rest of the day walking *downhill* back to town.

Chamonix would also be a good place to start the demanding tour of Mont Blanc. This classic two-week walk, which passes through France, Italy and Switzerland, brings the walker in stages completely around western Europe's highest peak. Though the country traversed is spectacularly alpine, accommodations and food are available throughout; despite the terrain, no camping or cooking gear is needed. But since cold storms can occur at any time in the Alps, the walker tackling this circuit should bring waterproof rain gear and carry warmer clothes than would be needed in the flatlands. The tour of Mont Blanc can be attempted anytime after the snows melt from the highest passes in mid-July; some writers say that the last week in August to mid-September is best because the weather is likely to be better and because accommodations are less crowded than at other times.

The walk on the GR 5 from Larche to the Mediterranean in the southern Alps is less demanding than the tour of Mont Blanc, but this ramble still rewards with views of mountains and glaciers. The GR ends in the northern suburbs of Nice, but two variants are available, both of which lead into the town of Menton right on the Mediterranean. The variant onto the GR 52 passes through the beautiful Parc du Mercantour on the Italian border. Because deep snow lingers on the passes, even this southern portion of the GR 5 should not be attempted before mid-June.

Walking the GR 5 from Lake Geneva all the way to the Mediterranean (or vice versa) is a goal for many Europeans. Some who cannot afford the eight to ten weeks needed to complete the walk in one season do it, instead, in stages, traveling parts of the walk for three or four weeks each summer over a two- or three-year period. The season is short and the route popular; the GR5 in summer is one of the few French trails that could be called crowded, though "crowded" is a relative term.

Barcelonnette is a small alpine village in the beautiful Ubaye valley. From the town and from the other small

Day walkers returning from a hike toward the Col du Larche on the GR 5 south of the town of the same name. Larche *means larch, a tree with needles like a pine. But unlike the evergreens the needles of the larch turn yellow and drop to the ground each autumn.*

villages up and down the valley many trails can lead the day walker up into the hills and low mountains, from the tops of which views into the higher Alps to the east are spectacular. Barcelonnette supports a small market on Sundays where many of the specialties of the region—delicious ham, flavorful *tomme* cheeses and a variety of dry sausages—are sold. Aside from the ubiquitous Côte du Rhône, which comes primarily from the south nearer the Mediterranean, the Rhône valley produces many excellent red and white wines like Condrieu, Côte-Rôtie, Hermitage, St-Joseph and Cornas. The white wines from the Savoie, particularly Seyssel, are refreshing and reasonably priced.

Alpine walks are more serious than walks on the flat. You must be fit and prepared for bad weather, even snow. For the long-distance walker accommodations serving food are scattered along almost all the routes, so no camping equipment is needed, but many stops will be in *refuges* (alpine huts) or *gîtes d'étape* (simple rural inns), not hotels.

The Pyrénées

Terrain: Mountainous and steep. To the north of the mountains, the foothills are cut by the many streams

and rivers that drain the mountains.

Weather: A mix of climates, depending on altitude. Snow stays on the high trails until June. Some summers are dry, though thunderstorms are always possible in the high mountains.

A walk:

6–10 days: From Aire-sur-l'Adour to St-Jean-Pied-de-Port; GR 65; 110 miles; a part of the Chemin de St-Jacques pilgrimage trail

Comments: When I think of the Pyrénées, I think of Andorra, Spain and the Basque people, not France. Like other regions far from Paris such as Brittany and Alsace, this area of France seems slightly foreign and divorced from the mainstream. Yet despite the unpronounceable Basque place names—full of Zs and Xs—that still stick to local landmarks and despite the proximity to Spain, the northern side of the Pyrénées is as stubbornly French as any area in France.

The medieval pilgrimage trail, the Chemin de St-Jacques, was in reality not one, but a series of different trails from all over Europe that led eventually to the shrine at Compostela in western Spain. From the twelfth century on, Compostela, along with Jerusalem and Rome, was one of the three holiest places in the Catholic world. Today, four major St-Jacques pilgrimage trails are recognized in France: the first runs from Tours on the Loire, the second from Vézelay in Burgundy, the third from le Puy west of Valence and the fourth from Arles in Provence. The walk on the GR 65 that I cite covers the last part (in France) of the most famous of these trails, the one from le Puy.

Though some parts of the original Chemin de St-Jacques are under highways and no longer part of today's trail, the GR 65 still follows whenever possible the ancient way and almost always passes through the towns and villages where the interesting ruins and landmarks that served the pilgrims—abbeys, châteaux, Romanesque churches and structures called *hôpiteaux* or shelters—are located. The *hôpital* at Ostabat on the trail near St-Jean-Pied-de-Port was able to accommodate five thousand pilgrims at one time. There were many more walkers on the trail seven hundred years ago than now!

On the French side the Pyrénées are abrupt, steep mountains, an almost continuous barrier between France and Spain that is difficult to travel over in an east-west direction. Nevertheless, the GR 10 does manage to traverse the mountains from the Mediterranean to the Atlantic, but the person on foot using this trail must be in excellent physical condition. By staying in the many refuges and other more or less primitive shelters, it might be possible to walk the GR 10 without camping out, but most hikers on this trail carry full back-packing equipment.

While the food of the Pyrénées region is no reason to make a special trip there, the lamb and the sheep's milk cheeses are very good as are the dry sausages and hams. Wine from the nearby Bordeaux region as well as some less well-known wines from the foothills are excellent.

St-Jean-Pied-de-Port, only ten miles from the 4409-foot Bentarte pass on the Spanish border, is itself only about 500 feet in altitude so the GR 65 can be walked at any time of the year, though conditions will be more pleasant from March into June and again from September into November. The summer months will be very hot except high in the mountains where snow remains on the passes until late May or June.

Provence and the Côte d'Azur

Terrain: The terrain in Provence is flat only at its western border near the Rhône river. It becomes increasingly rugged as you move east until, near Sisteron, it becomes truly mountainous. Similarly, the northern areas of Provence are more mountainous than the southern areas; Mont Ventoux, just east of Orange on the Rhône, rises to 6263 feet. The Côte d'Azur is broken country, full of ravines and cliffs. The land there rises from the Mediterranean abruptly, often to 3000 feet just three miles from the coast. Near the Italian border the spine of the Alps is, a mere fifteen miles inland, already 6500 feet above the sea and still rising. Because of the dry climate the vegetation in the lower areas, a mix of pine and deciduous bushes called the *maquis*, can be very dense where the tangle has not been burned away by one of the summer forest fires that periodically ravage—and eventually renew—the low-lying parts of this region.

Weather: Extremes of weather are common. The climate is Mediterranean—dry in summer and wet in winter—but the altitude differences and the distance from the sea cause great variations; in March one person could be basking in the sun along the shore near Cannes while, only a few miles inland, another could be skiing. The Rhône Valley is often swept by a cold dry *mistral.* This entire area can be very hot and tinder dry during the summer months.

Some walks:

Day walks:	From Vauvenargues near Aix; GR 9 and local trails
and	From Sospel in the hills above the Côte d'Azur; GR 52, regional and local trails
7–10 days:	Castellane through the Gorges du Verdon to Manosque; GR 4; 50 to 60 miles; very demanding in the gorge, hilly otherwise
10–14 days:	Gordes through the Lubéron Regional Park to Sisteron; GR 6; 120 miles; rolling at first, mountainous at the end

Comments: It's a truism that the people in the southern part of any country are more friendly, generous and open than the citizens of that same country who live in the north. Provence proves the rule. It is, I must admit, my favorite area for walking in all of France. Not only are the people more welcoming, but the weather is generally sunny, the countryside varied and the hill towns stunning. The land vibrates with light and warmth; it's little wonder that Van Gogh was overwhelmed here.

Day walks from Vauvenargues near Aix-en-Provence involve some steep hills, particularly if you are ambitious enough to climb to the top of the nearby Mont Ste-Victoire. Tiny Vauvenargues is a fascinating town, full of art left by visitors who came to pay homage to Picasso when he lived (and died) there in his rather dark and formidable château. In contrast, day walks from the active walking center of Sospel twelve kilometers inland from Menton on the Côte d'Azur take the walker directly into the Alps, where those mountains begin their final disordered descent into the Mediterranean.

The walk on the GR 4 along the Verdon River involves

one very difficult day *if* the walker decides to take the seven-hour route through the roughest yet most spectacular part of the gorge. Walking this part of the canyon involves climbing ladders fixed to the sides of cliffs, traversing kilometer-long tunnels and experiencing some daunting exposure to steep drops on narrow trails. However, a short three-hour cross-country off-GR walk can be substituted for this day in the gorge. Regardless of your decision, the other days on the GR 4 involve nothing more than spectacular views, Roman roads, less dangerous walking in and around the canyon and, at the end, pastoral countryside. If you do decide to take the seven-hour trail, inquire carefully before you venture into the area. Special rules apply. You must carry a flashlight and have certain equipment before you will be allowed to start. In this, the narrowest part of the canyon, the possibility of a sudden flash flood from a thunderstorm or heavy rain is another factor to consider. Watch the weather.

The walk on the GR 6 through the Lubéron is one of the great French walks. If you start at the western end (as I would suggest), the first days are spent in the heavily touristed but beautiful area around Gordes but, once you are past the ocher quarries in Roussillon, tourism fades and the relaxed pace of Provençal life reasserts itself. Forcalquier is worth a day's stop before tackling the two-day climb to the top of the Lure where, on a clear day, the view of the snow-capped Alps makes all the effort worthwhile. This walk, like the western end of the walk on the GR 4, takes the visitor into the heart of a Provence that is far from glitzy, into a land of quiet narrow streets, hill towns, *pétanque* and friendly, independent people.

In the south of France you will eat simple but delicious food—*socca* (a pancake made with chickpea flour), lamb flavored with rosemary, *bouillabaisse* and a bewildering variety of goat cheeses. Garlic is used liberally, and this is the land of the olive, not only of the oil but also the fruit itself, which is preserved in a myriad of forms displayed colorfully in the open-air markets. The local wines with unfamiliar names like Palette, Lirac, Bandol, Gigondas, Cassis and Côtes du Lubéron taste of the earth and herbs. They, like the familiar Côtes du Rhône, can be consumed young and are particularly attractive when drunk with food outdoors on a warm Provençal evening.

Facing page:
Hill towns in Provence, like Roussillon pictured here, are specially beautiful in the spring when poppies and other wild flowers are in bloom.

The higher areas of Provence and the Côte d'Azur do get snow in the winter, but the lower areas can be walked at any time of the year during a period of good weather. However, Provence is at its best in spring when the land is still green from the winter rains and the wildflowers are in bloom. The relentless sun makes walking in summer difficult, and at this time, hordes of tourists crowd every available hotel room making long-distance walking next to impossible anyway.

The island of Corsica

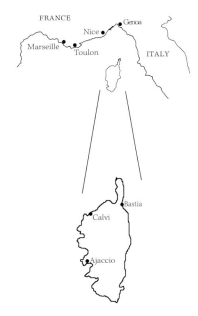

Terrain: Rough and steep except for a section of the northwest coast that slopes gently up from the sea and a narrow swampy strip along the central part of the east coast. The island's spine is very mountainous. Corsica is only 110 miles long and fifty miles wide, yet Monte Cintu, the highest point, rises to 8884 feet. The word *maquis* is Corsican in origin, and as in Provence, it describes the maze of dense, tangled bushes and herbs along the coast.

Weather: Mediterranean climate. Wet and, at the highest elevations, cold in winter. Hot and dry from April–May through September–October, with scant precipitation. What does fall during this time comes in the form of thundershowers. The tops of Monte Cintu and other high peaks are above the tree line. They and many of the highest trails and roads are covered with snow in winter.

A walk:

10 days:	Regional trails along the northwest coast from Calenzana to Cargèse, rough terrain

Comments: There is only one national trail on Corsica, the GR 20. It starts near the town of Calvi in the northwest and traces a tortured course across the highest terrain of the interior to end in the mountains above Porto Vecchio in the southeast. Three regional trails, starting and ending on the coasts, cross both the mountains and the GR 20 on east-west tracks. Another regional trail, the one I recommend, runs not through the mountains but through the *maquis* along the island's spectacular west and northwest coast.

Though I have visited the island twice, I have yet to

walk in Corsica. However, having driven most of the roads in the interior, I imagine that a walk on the GR 20 would be very difficult for all but the most in-shape walker. The terrain, to understate, is steep, and the trail climbs or descends constantly in great 1000 and 2000 foot swoops—there is virtually no level ground in mountainous central Corsica. Also, because the interior is sparsely populated, there are few hotels or restaurants to shelter and feed the weary walker. On some long stretches of the GR, it's even impossible to obtain supplies.

Walks in Corsica's high country must await late May or, after a severe winter, even late June, when the trails are finally clear of snow. By that time the weather is hot and dry everywhere. But just to make things a bit more difficult, as in the Alps, snow or hail can fall on the highest peaks and passes during every month of the year. Frankly, walking the GR 20 would mean that you would be backpacking in the true sense. Camping equipment would have to be carried.

Nonetheless, the island's rugged terrain does shelter some of the most spectacular landscapes in Europe, an astounding mélange of picturesque fishing villages, mountain hamlets, beaches, peaks, flowers, snow and cliffs. The high villages, often perched on the side of some deep ravine, are few and small, with the houses huddled protectively. They, like the people who inhabit them, belong to some ancient and simpler age that was made of stone and gnarled wood, secretiveness and dogged perseverance. In April and May, when the *maquis* bordering the sea is covered with flowering bushes—fragrant thyme, savory , rosemary and caper among them—the whole area is so thoroughly permeated by the smell of herbs that, though you are outdoors in the open air, you feel physically assaulted, stunned by the heavy scent. Even the food absorbs the perfume as if by osmosis; the sheep's milk cheeses, the lamb, the wine, the bread and, yes, the vegetables taste the way the landscape smells even when herbs are not used in the actual preparation. Corsica, a land of strong tastes, strong smells and strong contrasts, assaults the senses.

I would recognize Corsica blindfolded, by her scent alone.
 – Napoléon Bonaparte

Because of the ruggedness of the terrain, a walk on the regional trail along the northwest coast would be a somewhat strenuous but beautiful undertaking. Here there are towns with restaurants and accomodations so no camping gear would be required. If you plan to walk in Corsica, I urge you to consider this coastal trail in late March or April. At this time of year tourists are rare, the weather is cooler and the *maquis* is in bloom. (Anyone considering this walk should buy FFRP guide 065, *Corse entre mer et montagne*—see page 92.)

Corsica can be reached by air from Marseille or Nice and by boat from Nice, Toulon, Marseille or Genoa.

Other factors

Having read the descriptions of the various regions above, you may have already decided that one or another of the areas is a likely candidate for your first walk. But before you make specific plans, there are three factors to consider. They apply to all regions and could affect, if not the area chosen, at least the timing of your walking vacation.

July and August vacations: I have hinted above that walking cross-country during the summer is difficult, and the reason is the vacation habits of the French and the rest of the European population. Many businesses in France, Italy, Germany, Belgium, Holland and the Scandinavian countries shut down during the month of August to allow the workforce to take a month off at the beach, in the mountains or in a pretty village somewhere in Europe. Since the beaches in France are attractive, the mountains beautiful and the villages picturesque, many of those people end up there.

Baldly put, in any area that might appeal to tourists, the hotels and restaurants are fully booked during the months of August and—since it seems that everyone who doesn't vacation in August does so the month before—July as well. Even in areas not popular with tourists, walking in summer is never as easy or as carefree as walking in the spring or fall when most of the rest of Europe is working.

Certainly there are some mountainous areas that, for long-distance walks, can only be visited in the summer. The southern end of the GR 5 in the Alps between Lake Geneva and Nice is one such trail. The fact that deep snow lingers on the passes until late June or even mid-July and returns in September restricts the walker

to a short period during the summer. It would, I suppose, be possible to rigidly plan the daily details for a long walk during the summer in a popular area like the Loire Valley, but all accommodations would have to be reserved well ahead of time and then—weather and whim be damned—an inviolate schedule adhered to. I much prefer a less scripted vacation.

On the other hand, establishing a base in a hotel or bed-and-breakfast where you have reserved a room in advance and then venturing out for day walks is certainly a possible and enjoyable summer option. Any walker who *must* take his or her vacation during the two high-season months of July and August should, as I have already discussed on pages 18 to 20, seriously consider day walks rather than long-distance walks. This is exactly the way most French people who enjoy walking but also face the it's-overcrowded-and-how-do-I-get-a-reservation problem spend *their* holidays.

Hunters: The second factor is the autumn hunting season, which announces its arrival with tentative small-gauge pop-pops—quail—from the open fields in late September and erupts in a crescendo of eight-gauge booms—wild boar and stag—from the woods in November. The late season hunts in particular attract French trophy hunters, many of them wealthy city people out for a bit of country living on the weekend. They sometimes fire at anything that moves.

With some planning, though, the hunters can be avoided. Luckily, the best autumn months for walking are September and October, when the shooting season is just getting under way. At this time it is largely confined to hunting for quail, partridge and pheasant in the open fields where both the hunters and you yourself would be quite visible. Hunting in the woods for bigger game like stag and boar most often takes place later in the year when the shorter days and colder weather make it unlikely that you would be roaming the forests. Too, the majority of the hunts in France are on Saturday and, in particular, Sunday when groups of hunters, their cars parked in the woods and on the shoulders of rural roads, chase game cooperatively, often with dogs.

When the French hunt big game in this way, hired men accompany baying hounds, beat on tin cans and

In the autumn the person on foot should be aware that hunters may be about, particularly on the weekends. Here a hunter waits quietly at his station for a drive to start; when it and with it the shooting begins the noise makes the affair easy to avoid.

crash through the woods to drive game to the hunters stationed in a cordon around a specific area. Preparations for the drive are carried out as quietly as possible, but once the drive (and with it the shooting) starts, the ruckus will be evident to any but the comatose.

If you should encounter hunters *make sure they see you. Stay visible. Shout if necessary.* When you are sure that *all* the hunters in the party know that you are about, leave the area quickly.

Light: The third factor that affects the walker in all regions is the fact that France compared to most areas in the United States lies quite far to the north. Paris, at 49° latitude, is as far north as Newfoundland on our continent, and even Nice on the Mediterranean, at 44° latitude, is no closer to the equator than Portland, Maine, or Boise, Idaho.

Because Europe is bathed by the warmth of the Gulf Stream, the climate is much milder than you might expect, given the high latitude, but being so far north does affect the light in summer and winter. Days are delightfully long in June but equally short and dreary in December. For the walker this means that during the spring and early summer months it's possible to take a stroll after a late dinner to enjoy the sunset. By early September, however, the sun is already setting at seven-thirty, and by late October it's dark at five.

I find myself gravitating toward the spring and early fall as my favorite times to walk simply because I enjoy the surfeit of light, the lack of heavy-duty hunters and the ease with which I can, on the spur of the moment, get a bed and a meal. It's possible to walk somewhere in France at any time of the year, but to do so from late March through June or from September into October will usually prove most pleasant.

Maps

Planning your trip

Aɴʏᴏɴᴇ ᴡʜᴏ ᴄᴏɴᴛᴇᴍᴘʟᴀᴛᴇs, then plans and finally takes a walking trip in France will need at each of the three progressive steps new, ever-more-detailed maps.

A map for dreaming

In chapter 2 I discussed briefly the first map you will need, *France grande randonnée,* ɪɢɴ map 903. Showing all the ɢʀs and some of the major regional trails on a map drawn to a large scale (1/1,000,000—see "scale", page 88), it illustrates the broad sweep of the French national path system and it is the one tool you will need when you are first considering where to take a walking vacation. General in nature, it presents a thorough overview of the choices, showing clearly where the major trails run. Map 903 is the dreamer's map, full of possibilities and what-ifs. But once you have actually decided in which area and on what trail you will walk, you must then turn to a more detailed map to actually plan the specifics, the reality of your trip.

The planning map

The map or maps you will use for this next step come from Michelin, not the ɪɢɴ and they are called *Michelin cartes routières et touristiques* (Michelin road and tourist maps). Quite understandably the target market for these maps, given that Michelin makes automobile

Journey over all the universe in a map, without the expense and fatigue of traveling, without suffering the inconvenience of heat, cold, hunger, and thirst.
  – Cervantes,
    Don Quixote de la Mancha

---

tires, is the motor tourist. But happily these maps, unlike IGN maps of similar scale, do also show the GR trails. They are not prominent but they are there when you look for them.

Locating your GR as well as the hotels and restaurants along that GR and then highlighting everything with a Magic Marker is part of the planning process. The Michelin maps are five times as detailed as the IGN 903, and this means that many more towns and villages can be represented. In fact, the maps are so carefully done and complete that virtually all of the villages and towns mentioned in the *Michelin Hôtels-Restaurants* guide, the *Logis de France* guide and the *Chambres & Tables d'hôtes* guide—guidebooks you will need to consult—can be located on them. By marking your trail and then the hotels and restaurants along that trail you will turn the Michelin map into a tool that you can use to make a light-weight guide of your own to carry in place of the heavy and bulky guidebooks themselves. The details of how to assemble your own guidebook are explained in chapter 9.

You can buy these Michelin maps in two forms. The easiest to find in the United States is a series of sixteen large, conventional fold-up maps. (See the appendix for a map showing the general area covered by each.) The *Atlas Routier France* (French road atlas), a 180-page compilation in book form of the information on all the separate fold-up maps, is the other incarnation of these maps. This book, superficially similar to our Rand McNally road atlas, can sometimes be found here in travel bookstores. It covers the whole of France; if you want that much information, this atlas is the most economical way to get it.

The working maps

The blazes used to mark the GR and regional trails— the white/red and yellow/red painted slashes—though almost always frequent and prominent, are not in themselves enough to guide the person on foot from one town to the next. A moment of inattention on a wide trail results in a missed turn onto a smaller path. New growth covers a turn marker leaving you confused once you walk past that point. Two GR trails cross, and since the trails are not signposted—GR 7 this way, GR 76 that way—you don't know which of the three other paths to take. In all sorts of ways relying solely on the trail markers can lead to confusion and even a bit of aimless wandering, but luckily there are good maps— the third level of detail—that the walker can buy, carry and consult to supplement the information from trail blazes.

In fact, the *cartes IGN, série bleue* (IGN maps, blue series) are not just good, they are fabulous, and fabulous is not a word I use indiscriminately. GR trails are marked in red on these maps, and, because they are eight times as detailed as the Michelin road and tourist maps, it's a simple matter to find your exact location on that wandering red line.

For example, let's say that you are standing at the corner of a field on a GR path that has just emerged from the woods. From the IGN blue map in your hand you would be able to see that the path will stay on the edge of the rectangular field until the next corner, turn to the left there and continue, again hugging the edge of the field, until, down about two hundred and fifty yards, right before a small building, the trail will again turn, this time sharply away from the field onto a dirt track, and enter the surrounding woods. Everything— the trail, the field, the woods, the building and the dirt track—is clearly marked and, because of the map's small scale, easy to discern. You can walk two hundred and fifty yards in three to four minutes, and that distance translates to three-eighths of an inch on the map. You will not need a magnifying glass.

The scale of these maps is such that, even though the average *carte bleue* is over twenty-two inches wide, the distance those inches represent is only fourteen kilometers as the crow flies; in flat country it's entirely possible to walk the twists and turns of an east-west GR all the way across one of these maps in a single day.

To cover the whole country the IGN has published two thousand blue maps. If you could afford the fourteen thousand dollars needed to buy them all and then had the space to lay them out side by side, each attached to the other, the result would be a map of France 130 feet across and 125 feet high. The detail is amazing. Calvaries, caves, springs, golf courses, high-tension electric lines, water towers, ruins, cemeteries, earthen levees, hedgerows, aqueducts, not to mention contours (one

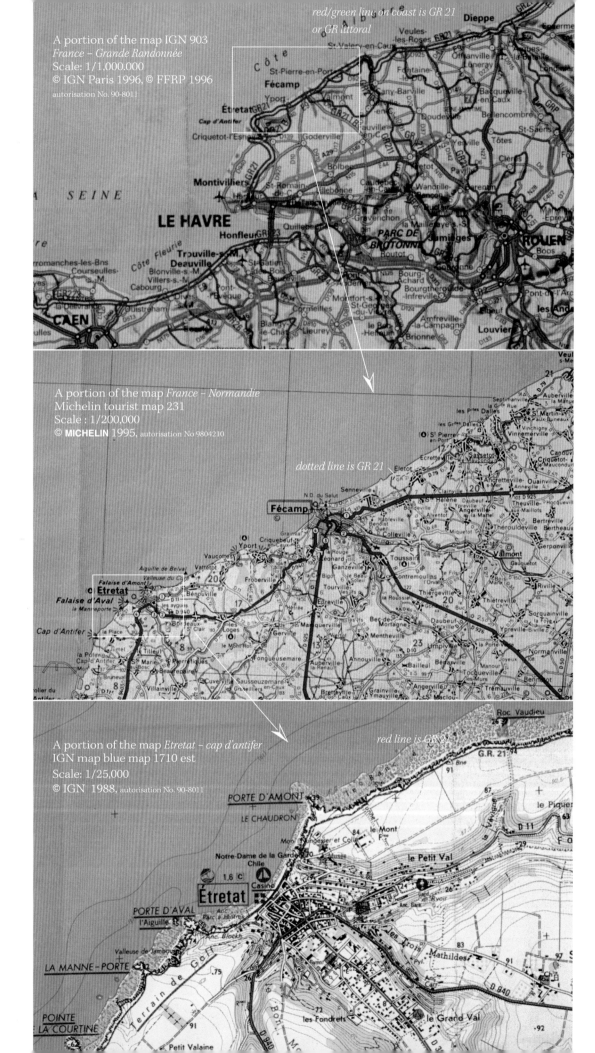

A portion of the map IGN 903
France – Grande Randonnée
Scale: 1/1,000,000
© IGN Paris 1996, © FFRP 1996
autorisation No. 90-8011

*red/green line on coast is GR 21
or GR littoral*

A portion of the map *France – Normandie*
Michelin tourist map 231
Scale : 1/200,000
© **MICHELIN** 1995, autorisation No 9804210

dotted line is GR 21

A portion of the map *Etretat – cap d'antifer*
IGN map blue map 1710 est
Scale: 1/25,000
© IGN 1988, autorisation No. 90-8011

red line is GR 21

for every ten meters or thirty-two feet in height), all buildings outside urban centers no matter how insignificant, every kind of road or trail as well as any imaginable water course and administrative border are just some of the features illustrated.

When you carry maps with this level of detail, a landmark that is shown on the map is always within sight, and along with the trail markers, it can be used with confidence to navigate your way through the countryside. Truthfully, I consider the blazes as supplements to the information I get from the maps, not the other way around. When walking in France I navigate first by using the maps. I *then* look for the trail markers to confirm what the maps have shown me.

Can I walk off-GR?

In fact these maps are so reliable that it's entirely possible to use them to quit a GR and strike off cross-country. Actually, on your first walking trip you will be required to navigate off-GR to a limited extent anytime you leave the trail at the end of the day to walk the few hundred meters or the few kilometers into the town or village where you will be spending the night. Sometimes a road or even a highway will be the only practicable way from the GR to your lodging, but often by carefully examining your *carte bleue* you can find a local, non-GR trail on the map that will turn out to be a more enjoyable, traffic-free and perhaps shorter alternative.

After you've become accustomed to the trail system in France it's also perfectly possible to walk for days through an area that interests you but has no official trail running through it. The French prefer to locate their trails as far from civilization as possible, but sometimes it is the civilized places that call to you—for example, the actual vineyards of Bordeaux, which have no GR trail. The service roads between the fields, the tow paths beside the canals, the fire roads through the forests are all shown on the *cartes bleues* and more than ninety-five percent of the time they are public and open to anyone careful to respect the property and crops on either side. I would not recommend that the first-time walker plan a trip off-GR, but anyone who feels entirely comfortable readings maps and who has also completed a couple of long walks using the GR

What does the "scale" of a map mean?

Look at the maps on the opposite page. The scale of the map at the top of the page, IGN 903, is 1/1,000,000 and that fraction means that 1 inch on map 903 is equal to 1,000,000 inches (83,000 feet or just short of 16 miles) on the ground in the real world. On the other hand, the IGN blue map on the bottom is scaled at 1/25,000, which means that 1 inch on this map equals in the real world only 25,000 inches (2083 feet or less than ½ a mile). If 1 inch equals almost 16 miles on 903 and 1 inch equals less than ½ a mile on a blue map, then it's obvious that you can draw a great deal more detail—houses, fences, obscure paths—on a blue map than it would be possible to draw on map 903.

This is what scale is meant to convey: the detail or its lack available on a particular map. On a large-scale map more real country and therefore less detail will be pictured in a given area. On a small-scale map less real country will be pictured on the same piece of paper, and therefore the map will contain more detail. The juxtaposition of the three maps opposite illustrates the principle clearly.

Facing page:
Examples of the three principal maps discussed in this chapter. They are, from top to bottom, IGN map 903, a Michelin touring map and an IGN blue map. Each small section of the maps (reproduced here to actual size) focuses in ever increasing detail on the town of Etretat on the English Channel in Normandy.

system should be able to do so.

All those maps

The territory covered by each of the two thousand *cartes bleues* is superimposed over a map of France on the reverse side of IGN map 903, and when you look there you will see that the detailed maps, colored light blue, are numbered sequentially from left to right and from top to bottom. You will also notice that most of the maps are oddly numbered, with 2042O right next to 2042E. The first is not 2042 zero but 2042 letter O, with the O being the abbreviation for the French word *ouest* (west). The 2042E means 2042 *est* (east). In other words, the number 2042 is used for two separate maps, 2042 west and 2042 east, and you must be careful when buying your maps to know not just the number but whether you want the eastern or western part.

When you examine even more closely the layout of all the maps on the back of map 903, you will see that some are colored white, not light blue, and that these are often larger or odd sized. These are the newer *Top 25* maps that have been published to cover the most popular areas and they are, if it's possible, even more carefully done than the regular blue maps they have superseded. They illustrate topography with shaded colors as well as contour lines, and the territory each covers is determined more by the logic of the terrain and not, as the regular maps are, by arbitrary lines of latitude and longitude. *Top 25* maps are issued with an E or O version followed by the letter T, 1016ET for example. *Top 25* signifies *topographie 25,000* and not, as I thought for a while, the franglais "top 25."

Another convenient feature of the map on the back of 903 is the fact that the various GR trails are drawn in dark blue. This allows the walker to see exactly which blue maps any particular trail will cross and make a list, before departure, of all the maps that will be required while walking that trail.

Older editions of the blue maps

Years ago when these *cartes bleues* were first published, they did, of course, show all the trails and paths, but no one at the IGN office had thought to single out and highlight in red the specific GR trails. The various ways that made up the GR trails were, like all the paths, illustrated only in black. You may occasionally have to purchase one of these older maps, a few of which are still in circulation, and when you do you will be deprived of immediate access to the information—a clear representation of where exactly the GR goes—you need when walking.

But if you have brought to France the Michelin tourist map you used to plan your trip, it is a relatively easy task—performed perhaps over breakfast before you start your day—to find and then highlight with a pen or pencil your specific route on the blue map. Each of the Michelin maps is so detailed that you can translate the information from it to the blue map. *We go down some path when we leave town—it must be this access road here—turn into the woods and continue on a small path until we reach a road—ah, there, I see it.* All you have to do is locate your route on the blue map in this way and then mark with a pen or pencil the major intersections. By doing so, you will have highlighted the trail yourself, and, with the blazes to back you up, you'll be ready to walk.

Where do I get blue maps?

Cartes bleues are purchased as you travel, not before you leave. Unless you visit the superb two-story IGN map store just off the Champs-Elysées in Paris, you are unlikely to find a place outside the area you will visit that carries any of the maps you will need. However, when you arrive in your area you will find that bookstores in the larger towns and cities carry most of the *cartes bleues* for the region, and that even in the tiniest villages along your route many of the small shops that sell postcards, newspapers or tobacco also stock the IGN blue maps for the immediate area.

Because I prefer to walk with as detailed a map as possible, I try, when on the trail, to keep ahead of the game by buying the maps for the next area and even the area after that before I walk there. I'm constantly scanning the racks for the maps I will need.

These maps at 42 FF to 55 FF apiece are expensive, and because each one covers only a small area, on a long trip you will quickly accumulate a pile of them, a small fortune's worth if you are on a tight budget. But despite

the expense, I still urge you to buy all you will need. They will serve as your personal guide as you walk, helping you on your way, all but whispering in your ear: *turn here by the cemetery... the trail crosses the stream up ahead... there's a village just over that ridge.* If your collection of blue maps becomes too bulky and heavy, put those you have already used in an envelope and mail them home.

Other maps

Two private companies working closely with the IGN have published 1/50,000 scale maps covering two areas in France, the southeast and the Pyrénées. These maps, produced with the walker specifically in mind, highlight not only the GR and regional trails, but also many of the non-official trails and routes open to anyone walking cross-country.

Didier Richard, a publishing company in Grenoble, concentrates on the southeast. There are at this writing twenty-eight *éditions didier richard* maps, each of which is named for a prominent geographic feature, and because of the various versions these maps have gone through over the years, numbered somewhat randomly. Didier Richard has issued maps for the Alps from Geneva to the Mediterranean, the island of Corsica, the Jura from Montbéliard south to Geneva and the rugged terrain on the western side of the Rhône from St-Etienne south to just north and east of the Cévennes.

Though only half as detailed as the IGN *cartes bleues*, these maps are still full of information. Some but not all buildings, springs, water towers, ruins, châteaux, cemeteries and other prominent landmarks are represented on them as are forested and cultivated areas. One unique feature is that they give the location of the *gîtes d'étape* (simple rural inns for hikers) located near the trails.

But the real reason to buy these maps is not to find *gîtes* but to find, instead, all the many non official long-distance paths highlighted in the same way that GRs are highlighted on the IGN blue maps. A day walker in any of the areas covered by these maps should buy that map just to learn the possibilities, and any experienced walker who contemplates walking off-GR will find a a great deal of important information about alternate trails detailed here. If you lack the appropriate *cartes bleues*, these maps could be used as your primary navigation tool, but I prefer to walk using the more detailed information on the blue maps.

Rando éditions does the same thing for the Pyrénées mountain chain that Didier Richard does for the French Alps. Numbered from west to east and named for the regions covered, their twelve 1/50,000-scale maps, called *cartes de randonées Pyrénées*, detail the features, contours and, again most important, the

Detailed IGN blue maps for the local area are usually available in village tobacco and newspaper shops. Though the rack pictured here is from Michelin, most of the maps in it are from the IGN.

significant unofficial trails of this rugged region. Like Didier Richard, Rando also details the location of *gîtes d'étape*. All the information given for France, including the location of unofficial trails and *gîtes*, is also given for the tiny country of Andorra and for the areas of

Spain immediately adjacent to the French border. Again, these maps could, in a pinch, be used to navigate your way along a GR.

The French seem to be map crazed, more than mildly obsessed with picturing their country at all possible scales and in all possible formats. Both the IGN and Michelin publish many, many maps other than those I have already described.

Both print, of course, a plethora of specialty one-sheet maps of France similar in format to IGN 903 but different in subject matter. Super highways, camping areas, waterways, cheeses, historic churches, relief, wine and geology—these subjects and others are mapped in mind-boggling detail. Beyond that, the IGN publishes sixteen 1/250,000 maps covering all of France, while Michelin, as explained above, covers France with 1/200,000 maps in two formats. But it doesn't end there. The IGN has recently started to publish a series of 1/100,000 maps called *Top 100* that illustrate tourist attractions. Both Michelin and the IGN go on to publish a series of conventional 1/100,000 maps for the entire country, and then, for good measure, IGN adds a complete series of orange-covered 1/50,000 maps just to fill the gap, so to speak, between the green-covered 1/100,000 and the extremely detailed 1/25,000 blue-covered maps.

There certainly are other maps I know nothing about, but I think you get the idea. For anyone seeking information about France the variety is wonderful if bewildering. For a walking vacation, however, you will need only the three I have described: first, IGN map 903; second, one or more of the Michelin road and tourist maps covering your region; and third, once you're in France, the IGN blue maps for the specific areas where you will walk.

Are there trail guides?

FFRP Guides: The national headquarters of the FFRP, the organization responsible for all the official trails, also publishes a series of guidebooks that cover in great detail some (but far from all) of their trails in France. There are about one hundred and fifty (they go in and out of print as they are revised and updated) of these small five-by-eight books, called *Topo-guides,* and each contains a carefully written description in French of one specific trail or group of trails. My translation of just a small part of the text describing the GR 71 trail, printed on page thirty-nine of guide 716, *Traversée du Haut-Languedoc* (Crossing the High Languedoc), will give you a good idea of the minutiae these guides contain.

...take the red dirt path on the right that leads to a wide road: follow it to the right; just a bit later take route D 8E, again to the right. Walk through Valquières (medieval houses) *and, on the road, cross a stream called the Brayou; 400 meters further on, take a path on your right and then follow the dirt road on your left. Go to the right of the Calvary and stay on the trail that passes above the church at Dio* (390 meters in elevation)*, a picturesque village situated below a château. Be sure to see the two water mills dating from the 1600s...*

The layout of this written description follows a pattern used in all the *Topo-guides*: the text is on the right-hand page, and on the left-hand page it is embellished with a 1/50,000 scale topographic map (sometimes in full color) where the route is clearly marked.

These publications describe the route at a level of detail meant to be usable on the trail as a book-in-hand, real-time guide. As if this were not enough, they then go on, as in the example above, to call attention to historical sights.

Topo-guides would seem to be a godsend, combining as they do in one volume a good enough map with a written description of the trail, but if you don't read French, they will be of little use.

However I have an objection that goes beyond the language difficulties: I find it close to impossible to use the written word as a trail guide.

When carrying and using a map, I must glance down frequently to consult that map and sometimes must actually stop stock still in the trail to locate on it the landmarks I can see—annoying but necessary inter-ruptions that involve only visual information. But when carrying and using a *Topo-guide* I find that *every* time I consult this bulky object I have to stop, find my place and then actually read some text that must *then* be translated in my head into usable, visual informa-tion. This becomes doubly difficult if the guide des-cribes the trail from, say, east to west while you are walking from west to east. The order of the text must then be turned around in your head—it must in effect be read backwards—before it can be translated into the physical objects you see around you. Left becomes right, uphill becomes downhill. Try that process out in your imagination using my translation up above. Confusing, isn't it?

Some people who are not visually oriented have a difficult time interpreting and using the information on a map. I find reading maps easy and am comfortable with the process but I imagine that it *might* be more informative for some other walkers to use the written word as a guide, and there is a solution—partial and far from ideal—for them. An English company, McCarta (until recently known as Robertson McCarta), has translated into English the information from some of these *Topo-guides*. The area covered in one of these English-language guides does not correspond directly to the area covered by one FFRP *Topo-guide* but is, rather, a regional compendium of information. For instance, the cover of the *Walks in Provence* book states that it contains descriptions of GRs 4, 99, 98, 9, 6 and 92 (nowhere to be found), condensing five *Topo-guides* into one book.

Unfortunately the translators have omitted many of the subtleties contained in the original French guide-books and, much worse, have allowed omissions to creep in that make it hard to maintain complete confidence in the text. And given that some of these guide-books were translated in the 1980s, the information concerning what lies along the trails and even the physical description of the trails themselves may now be out of date. Use these translations, if you must, with caution.

It would seem, then, that the English-only speaker would have no reason to buy one of the FFRP *Topo-guides*, but one aspect of these books could be useful to English-only walkers—particularly to those venturing off into the more remote and less populated regions.

At the front of all but very oldest editions, the FFRP prints a comprehensive table listing for each town and village along the route the availability there of a *gîte d'étape, refuge,* hotel, camping ground, food market, restaurant, bus stop or train station. It also gives the distance or, alternately, the time between the towns on the trail. This table may supply you with information about hotels or restaurants not mentioned in any of the other guides you will be consulting. The newest editions of the FFRP books contain other interesting but nonessential information in visual form—graphs showing the elevations along a route as well as an overall highlighted color map of the GRs and regional trails discussed. All this might prove interesting, but for most non-French-speaking walkers, an FFRP guidebook is an option, not a necessity.

If you do buy a *Topo-guide* for hotel information, buy the French-language edition. Unlike the version in English, it will contain relatively up-to-date information.

Other trail guides: In a country with such an extensive trail system, it should not be surprising that there are numerous privately published trail guides for sale in book and newspaper stores everywhere in France. Chamina publishes carefully produced books on the Massif Central region that describe in a complete and detailed way both long distance point-to-point-to-point walks and shorter day walks. Solar publishes guides that emphasize day walks in areas like the Cévennes and the Vosges. Edisud publishes similar guidebooks for Provence, and there are other firms that cover other regions. None of these French language guidebooks is readily available outside of France, but French-speaking walkers will be able to purchase those they need either at the IGN store in Paris or in the area covered by the book.

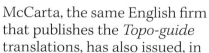

McCarta, the same English firm that publishes the *Topo-guide* translations, has also issued, in

---

conjunction with the IGN, five English-language *Touring and Leisure Guides*, one each for Brittany, the Loire, the Pyrénées, Provence and the Riviera. These are attractive, compact books, full of color photographs. They present the general tourist as well as the walker with an summary of the history, geography, culture and attractive places to visit in those areas. And, for the person on foot, an interesting variety of about a dozen short walks, scattered over the whole of each region, are mapped and described. The guides, available in bookstores in the United States for $19.95, could prove useful to the day walker planning to visit any one of the five regions they cover. In the future McCarta may publish guides for other areas.

Where can I buy all these maps?

Since Michelin publications are more widely distributed on this side of the Atlantic than those produced by the IGN, at least some of the Michelin touring maps can usually be found in large bookstores and travel stores, where they will likely cost around eight dollars each. Map 903 and the McCarta guidebooks are harder to find in the United States, and the rest of the material—Didier Richard and Rando éditions maps along with the French-language FFRP guides—are available (at this writing) *only* from England or France.

You will find in the appendix the phone and FAX numbers for mail-order sources and in chapter 9 a full explanation of how to order maps and guidebooks from companies here and abroad. The detailed blue IGN maps you will, as I have explained, buy in France while you walk.

The excellence of French maps—their detail and their reliability—is one of the main factors that make an independent walking trip possible. Map 903 will familiarize you with the scope of the trails while the Michelin maps will take the mystery out of the planning phase. And once you're actually in France, the IGN blue maps will eliminate confusion on the trail. By doing so they will allow you, the traveler on foot, to concentrate on important matters: the beauty of the countryside, the people and the intriguing montage of history and culture unfolding at just the right speed, before your eyes.

A few rules

In the United States and to a lesser extent in England, landowners jealously guard the borders of the land they own, careful to exclude outsiders who have leisure rather than business on their minds. Two factors mitigate against any impulse toward openness that the individual landowner might feel: first, the Anglo-Saxon tradition that says a man's home (and by extension the land around that home) is his castle and, second, a legal system that holds the landowner liable for injury to anyone, authorized or otherwise, on the property. Sadly, load up the shotgun with rock salt and keep 'em out *sums up the usual attitude all too well.*

The success of the French walking system—the relative lack of acrimony between those who walk and those who own the private land the trails cross—depends to a great extent on a less-litigious legal system, which operates on the assumption that the individual is responsible for his or her own actions. It is the person on foot and not the landowner who is primarily responsible for accidental injury on the trail.

Equally important is the less selfish attitude of the owners of the land, a point of view that is based not just on the fact that the landowner in France is less likely to be sued but also, at its root, on the French appreciation for the importance of community as well as individual rights. Unlike their Anglo-Saxon counterparts, most French landowners believe that the rest of the population—so long as they do no harm to property, crops or livestock—should have access to the land.

French walkers return the respect given them by observing the customs and safeguarding the property of the landowners. If while you are walking you practice the ten common-sense rules below, you will contribute your part to the continuation of this happy state of affairs.

1 – No open fires in the French woods. No fire of any kind, and this includes smoking, during the summer in the south and in Corsica. During times of high fire danger, it may be illegal to even carry matches or lighters, and in times of extreme fire danger, the trails anywhere in France may be closed completely.

2 – Leave all gates as you find them. This means that you should reclose any gate you open and leave gates you find open just as they are, open.

3 – If you encounter a shepherd with a flock be extremely careful not to disturb and thereby panic the animals. Indicate to the shepherd on which side you wish to pass. Don't plunge through a flock. Equally important, never harass animals that have been left unattended in fenced fields.

4 – Never walk through a cultivated field. Remember, grass is a crop too (hay) and it is impossible to harvest when trampled flat.

5 – Never pick fruit or nuts from trees on private land. In wine country do NOT sample the grapes unless you are specifically invited by the vineyard owner to do so.

6 – Everything you carry onto the trail should continue with you until you reach your lodging in the evening. Do not litter.

7 – Avoid loud noises that might disturb others. Radios do not belong on the trail.

8 – Don't take shortcuts, particularly those that plunge straight downhill. Doing so contributes to erosion.

9 – Admire and photograph the wildflowers, but leave all but the most common where they are. It is actually illegal to pick flowers in National Parks and illegal to pick certain rare flowers like orchids anywhere.

10 - Remember, almost everywhere in France the land on which you are standing belongs to a person, a family or a group. Treat it with respect. Treat it as if you *owned* it.

Equipment

The essentials

Discussing the details of equipment—zippers, water-proof jackets, sturdy straps—can be a yawner for many people, yet a successful walking trip is predicated on gear that is chosen with care. First, of course, equipment must serve a useful purpose, but to make your experience in France as enjoyable as possible, it should also be comfortable and light in weight.

Utility, comfort and weight. With these criteria in mind, then, I will discuss here in some detail all the can't-do-without-'em items you'll be bringing—your equipment—with special emphasis on the three I consider the most important: your boots, your pack and your rain gear. I will wait until chapter 10 to address the clothes question—what to bring and, equally important, what to leave at home.

What should I wear on my feet?

There are diverse opinions on what is and what is not proper footwear for a long walk. The following, though it's based on my experience walking over both flat and rugged terrain, is still just one opinion among many. In the end, the boots you wear will depend on your own needs and preferences.

It is said that a person who puts the mugwort plant in his shoes each morning, can walk forty miles before noon without tiring. Don't you believe it.

– Rob Hunter & David Wickers
Classic Walks in France

Support: I urge anyone taking a long walk to wear boots instead of the now popular low walking shoes for one reason: boots offer ankle support. Some flat dirt paths such as those in the Limousin or the Loire certainly *could* be walked without boots and the support they give, but since a twist of the ankle can occur anywhere, even as you exit your hotel in the morning, I *always* walk in boots. Boots are travel insurance; by wearing them, you greatly reduce the risk of vacation-ending sprain. Boots with sturdy uppers that fully envelop the ankle can be laced tightly or loosely to give more or less support.

Weight: During the sixties when I lived in Colorado I shouldered my trusty Kelty framepack and, as often as I could, hiked up to high mountain lakes where I fly fished for big but finicky trout. At that time the conventional wisdom among backpackers had it that *a pound on your feet is the same as five pounds on your back.* I'm not sure now whether this is literally true or not, but I *am* certain that weight on your feet—lifted at least a few inches off the ground with every step—does tax your body more than weight carried smoothly on your back. The weight of your footwear becomes, then, doubly important. You must have enough shoe for the terrain, but not so much that you waste energy lifting them. My boots, size eleven, weigh two and three-quarters pounds—not exactly light, but not overly heavy either.

Traction and steadiness: Your boots should have a sole that offers good traction on both smooth and broken surfaces. This usually means Vibram soles or something similar. Walking in boots with poor traction is frustrating and sometimes dangerous. Even in flat terrain, rain can make clay soil, rock or cement extremely slippery. The sole should also be broad enough to support your weight without rolling over on uneven ground. A proper boot should *feel* stable.

Most brands of boots come only in one width, and Faith is someone who finds it difficult to deal with that one-size-fits-all approach. Unable to find a comfortable pair of leather boots, she walks instead in a pair of what I would call light leather sneakers. These come with a corrugated sole, have uppers that extend above the ankle and weigh a full pound less than my boots. Envious of the light weight, I tried to walk in a similar pair, but to me they felt too narrow and unstable. Faith insists that, for her, the sneakers are just fine. If you feel comfortable and steady wearing these light-weight boots, they could be a satisfactory choice, particularly if your trip will be over flat terrain.

Cushioning: Boots should offer enough cushion in the sole to allow you to walk day after day for as many miles as you plan to cover without bruising the bottom of your feet. If you plan to walk twenty miles a day you will need a sturdier, more cushioned sole than if you expect to walk only five miles each day. Remember that your feet will be bearing not only your own weight but also the weight of your pack. Terrain is also a factor. The flat paths in Normandy don't require the same padding as the rock-strewn trails in the Alps. If you have not traveled on foot over long distances you may not believe that bruising could be a problem, but the poorly equipped walker—someone, say, in street-shoes—who travels any distance over rocky, broken ground can quickly bruise the soles of his or her feet sufficiently to make walking extremely painful, if not impossible.

My boots come with a set of removable leather and foam rubber innersoles and lugged outer soles that (though I seldom slam-dunk) have built-in air cushions. To increase the cushioning even more, I wear two sets of socks, one thin woolen pair under a thicker outer pair. Pay attention to what you wear under your boots. Socks have gone high-tech, and some of the newer designs offer a great deal of extra cushioning.

Shopping for boots: If you don't already own a pair of comfortable walking boots, I advise you to buy your new ones as soon as possible after you decide that, yes, you are going to walk in France. The reason for an early purchase is to make absolutely sure that you have the right—and that means, primarily, comfortable—boots for the trip. This admonition may seem unnecessary, but I have known people who have compromised their trip because they were "too busy" to buy their boots a month or so before their departure. As a result, they waited until the last minute and ended up with foot-wear that was not just uncomfortable, but painful.

Take enough time and use great care when making this purchase.

When trying on boots in the store wear the same type of socks you plan to wear when you're on the trail. Be

---

deliberate. Be skeptical. Once you've found a pair that you think might work, put both the right and left on and walk around the store in them for at least ten or fifteen minutes. Don't judge too quickly—you should give your feet a chance to settle in—but do, in the end, be extremely critical. Make absolutely sure that the boots are not too tight or, equally bad, too loose. Close enough is not acceptable when the result may be blisters, bone spurs or jammed toes.

Once you have made the purchase you should walk as much as possible in your new shoes. Wear them for a whole weekend. Put them on when you come home from work and wear them until bedtime. Wear them every time you walk to get in shape for your trip. Unlike the bad old days, when the acquisition of new hiking boots meant almost a whole summer of discomfort during which you (or, at least, I) struggled painfully to break in unnecessarily stiff and stubborn leather, most modern walking boots need little or no break-in time. Today's boots have no hardened toe and are quite pliable, but even pliable boots can be wrong for your feet—they can rub, chafe and irritate because they were made with wider, narrower or just differently shaped feet in mind—so you do need to assure yourself that your choice will remain comfortable when worn, as they will be on your walking vacation, for days on end. The only way to do that is to wear your new boots for long periods of time *before* you land in France.

Your pack

Equally important for comfort on the trail is the pack you will use to carry your clothes, toiletries, reading material and other items like a camera—that is, everything you will need over the whole of the time you will be walking. Readers who have never walked with anything heavier than a light day pack may view this prospect with some misgiving, but modern packs are so well designed and so comfortable that eighteen to twenty pounds—probably very close to the final weight of your pack—can be carried with ease day after day by even the smallest person. In fact, twenty pounds in a good quality large pack can be much more comfortable to carry than five pounds in a sloppily designed day pack. Though you're the one who must in the end be happy with your pack, I do have more definite ideas for its specifications than I had for boots. My criteria for a proper pack inevitably lead the shopper to a narrow range of choices.

Interior and exterior frames: While exterior-frame packs, that is, packs with a rigid, exposed support system like the classic Kelty, are cooler to carry because air can circulate freely between the pack and the back of the person carrying it, the newer interior-frame packs, which hug the back, are the kind I strongly recommend. Interior-frame packs gain their rigidity from a series of flexible metal wands that are bent and shaped to fit exactly the contours of your back when they are inserted into special pockets inside the pack. If time and care are taken during the process, a very comfortable fit can be made.

Modern packs are designed to carry weight not on the shoulders but the hips, and both exterior-frame and interior-frame packs do a good job of transferring weight to a wide, padded strap cinched just below the waist. This arrangement allows the person on foot with a properly adjusted pack to walk in a natural, upright position. But the interior-frame packs have two advantages over the exterior-frame models. First, they are considerably lighter; an exterior-frame pack weighs approximately half again as much as an interior-frame model of the same capacity. Second, an interior-frame pack is much more compact and thus far easier to carry onto airplanes or into hotels than the exterior-frame model with its protruding maze of metal tubes and webbing.

Pack size: Packs are sized by their interior capacity in cubic inches. I strongly recommend that you obtain one with a volume of between 2400 and 3200 cubic inches, a size range that is commonly labeled for use as an "overnight," not "multiple night" pack. Dedicated backpackers who read this may be lifting an eyebrow, for they, when heading out for even just a weekend in the high country, often shoulder a pack with a capacity of 4000 or even (obsessive) 5800 cubic inches, but I would remind them that to walk in France is not to backpack in France. You will not carry a sleeping bag. You will not be lugging a stove, cooking pots and enough food for three days.

Though you won't find it in the physics texts, it is a well-known law of nature that any pack will inevitably

Compression straps

Panel-loading back

My own 2900-cubic-inch internal-frame Kelty Redwing pack, large enough for weeks of travel

fill to its capacity. A too-large pack is sure to invite a too-large burden; if you have room to include an item you may reason *what the hell, I may need it so I might as well bring it along,* and this attitude will quickly lead to a very heavy and very bulky load. Instead I urge you to limit yourself to, say, a 2800 cubic inch pack, a size so small and compact that it will absolutely guarantee, even if you load yourself down with camera equipment, that you will be carrying a reasonably light pack. You may imagine that you couldn't possibly live for two weeks out of something as small as a pack of the size that I recommend, but be assured that you can and, more important, that you will enjoy the freedom and flexibility doing so will bring.

Compression straps and panel load: Two other features that I consider necessary are compression straps and a "panel-load" design.

Compression straps do exactly what their name indicates, compress. Packs with compression straps usually have four, two on each side; these straps are like belts that can be cinched tight to compress the pack's contents inward toward your back and thereby prevent a loose load—your carefully folded clothes—from shifting to the bottom in a heap while you're walking.

Similarly, a pack with a panel-load opening will maintain your clothes in much neater condition than a pack with the conventional top-load opening. Panel-load packs have a zippered back that allows the whole outside of the pack to fold open, revealing all the contents from top to bottom. Top-load packs allow entry only at the top; you can imagine the mess if, on the trail in the middle of the day, you needed to dig out an item at the bottom of a top-load pack. Panel-loads are also much more convenient at the hotel in the evening since, with the easy access to all your belongings they allow, you will not have to unload every item in order to change your clothes.

Shopping for a pack: As I indicated at the beginning of this discussion, my recommendations—interior frame, small size and panel load—narrow the choices considerably. At a web site, www.gearfinder.com, which maintains a list of the specifications for all available outdoor equipment, there are between twenty and thirty packs that seem to meet my criteria. A major retailer of outdoor gear, Recreational Equipment, stocks over ninety models of packs large enough for overnight loads, yet when I checked their large store in Berkeley, California, and, later, their web site, I was able to find only three that met all my requirements. You may have to search more than one store to find a proper pack in your local area.

If you are taller or shorter than average, I advise you to shop in person at a store that specializes in outdoor equipment. The salespeople are usually knowledgeable about the merchandise and can help you choose and fit the proper size pack. Taking the time to find the right pack and then fitting it to the contours of your back will pay you dividends in comfort later.

Rain gear

Given the climate in France, it's safe to say that it *will* rain sometime during your walking trip. If you are a city person who spends the day in an office and the night in an apartment, the weather is at best a peripheral concern, never more than an inconvenience. But once you start walking—outdoors, exposed for hours on end to cold wind, showers, heat or whatever else comes your way—the weather assumes half of its primordial importance. ("Half," because you will, happily, retreat into modern, heated shelter at night.) Rain is potentially the most disruptive element you will face. Past the shower stage, it can make a day's walk less than pleasant or, in extreme cases, impossible. In the mountains it can even be dangerous.

What you carry to protect against rain depends primarily on your determination to complete the whole of the route you have set for yourself. When it comes to reaching a stated goal, I am quite casual when I walk. I may have set out to cover, say, one hundred and fifty miles of coastline in Normandy, but if rainy weather makes walking unpleasant, I am more likely to stop, find a hotel room and then retreat with a book to some warm café than to brave it out. Too many days like this can quickly cut the number of miles covered overall making it unlikely that you will reach the destination you may have set for yourself at the beginning of your walk. A "failure" like this can make the goal-oriented person uncomfortable. Though it was hard for me at first, when slowed by the weather I am now able to convince myself with Faith's help that I'm on vacation and that it's the experience that's important, not the destination. As a result of the decision not to walk during downpours, in all but mountainous areas I carry nothing more than a collapsible umbrella.

Umbrellas: *You carry an umbrella?* Yes, though the picture of a hiker with an open umbrella over his head might seem ludicrous, I use an umbrella when I walk. Despite the arrival of Gore-Tex and other breathable waterproof fabrics on the scene, I don't believe that any of the hooded rain jackets actually work as intended

I carry nothing more than an umbrella to protect myself from the rain. In really bad weather I retreat to a café, but many walkers prefer to use waterproof rain gear, which allows them to continue on the trail in bad weather.

because perspiration is still trapped inside under the not-breathable-enough-for-me cloth when I am buttoned up against the rain. Though no rain may be penetrating the jacket, perspiration is condensing in my clothes and soaking me from the inside out. An umbrella, on the other hand, doesn't trap moisture at all. Also, while a jacket can't protect your pack from the rain, an umbrella does a fair job of sheltering at least the top in all but a wind-driven tempest, a time when I would be safely sheltered in a café anyway.

I carry the lightest possible fold-up umbrella with a curved handle. The handle's crooked shape fits the hand comfortably and makes it much easier to hold the umbrella at the desired angle when the wind is blowing. Also, my pack has two open passages behind the side pockets (originally intended for skis), and in good weather I slide the folded umbrella down one of them. The bent handle, hooked over the edge of the pocket, prevents the umbrella from slipping through.

Ponchos: Some walkers insist on walking in any weather. They are bored by too much time off in cafés and consider the feeling of accomplishment at reaching a goal to be an important part of their trip. Some of these ambitious people report that they have successfully used a modern hooded poncho in persistent rain. Because these coverings are open on the bottom the air circulates up freely, and this feature, at least in theory, prevents evaporated perspiration from condensing in your clothes. Also, the poncho covers and protects the pack from the rain.

Weather can change quickly in the Alps. This picture taken in the morning shows high cirrus clouds moving in. They presaged a cold rain by mid-afternoon.

Old-style ponchos were heavy and bulky, but the newer models are light and compact. The decision to carry one or not should be based on your intentions, not mine. Remember, though, anyone walking in a light rain will be as comfortable as is possible under the circumstances using nothing more than an umbrella. It's only a real storm that requires more, and then only if you insist on walking through it.

Rain gear in the mountains: Of course, the exception to all this advice about needing nothing more than an umbrella is when you are walking in the Alps, the Pyrénées or indeed in any isolated area at high altitude where a sudden cold storm might catch you far from shelter. In the mountains you may not plan to walk in bad weather, but circumstances—the sudden arrival of a cold front on a warm muggy day or a thunderstorm with hail—may dictate otherwise. Mountain walking is

a more serious affair than walking on the plains, where the worst a sudden downpour can do is to wet you and your gear.

Water, when it replaces air in your clothing, destroys the insulating qualities of that clothing. So even if what falls is not snow (and snow is always possible in the European high country), a mountain storm is still cold as well as wet, and, if you yourself become cold and wet, you can develop hypothermia, a cooling of the body's core temperature that is potentially life threatening. To avoid getting wet in the first place, anyone walking in the mountains should carry and use rainpants and a waterproof jacket with a hood . Though an umbrella might be useful as a sunshade at high altitudes, it is not sufficient protection from precipitation in the mountains.

There are a number of other items that are so basic that I would classify them as equipment.

First-aid kit

One person in every walking party should carry a rudimentary first-aid kit containing a piece of moleskin for blisters, bandages of different sizes, a disinfectant like Polysporin, tweezers for splinters and bee stings, a few packaged medical wipes and an elastic bandage for strains or mild sprains. Unless you have special medical problems, anything more is unnecessary because you're always close to help in France.

The first line of defense—post first-aid kit—is the local pharmacist. This well-educated person is very likely to speak English and has a great deal more authority to diagnose and prescribe medicine for illnesses than does his or her counterpart in the United States. A pharmacist is all you need when you are suffering from a sore throat, the flu or a cough.

The second line of defense is, of course, the French medical establishment—the doctors and the hospitals. It is unlikely that you will ever need a doctor in France but if you do, it's reassuring to know that they are well trained and competent. The French government has stressed the importance of having medical help in as many villages as possible. Should you need to see a

---

Travelers' insurance

Anyone requiring a helicopter lift from the trail to a hospital—for, say, a broken leg—will be required to pay the costs of that evacuation unless he or she has some form of travelers' insurance. Your travel agent should be able to obtain such insurance for you if you desire it. Some policies also cover lost or stolen luggage.

France on Foot

doctor immediately, you will probably be sent down the street to an office rather than to an emergency room in a large city hospital miles away. In some cases the doctor may even come to you in your hotel. Happily, I have had little contact with the French medical establishment, but on the few occasions I or a friend have needed attention, it has been provided promptly, efficiently and, because medicine is socialized, inexpensively.

Your hat

With holes in the ozone opening wider and wider, most people know that it's prudent to wear sunblock. But doctors also recommend that anyone out in the open over an extended period of time should, even if they aren't as balding as I am, wear a hat to protect the skin of the face and neck from the sun's ultraviolet rays. Even if you dismiss these warnings, you will find it necessary to wear a hat when walking because without one, sunblock or not, you will likely get a painful sunburn.

If you lose the hat you brought with you or arrive in France without one, you can easily acquire a cheap, broad-brimmed straw hat from one of the open-air stalls that appear on market day in most villages. Hats are also available in *quincailleries* (hardware stores) or *drogueries* (general stores) in any country town that serves the agricultural sector. I like to wear straws when walking because they are cheap, easy to replace and, because of the open weave, cooler on the head. Also, with their wide brim they shade the back of my neck and ears as well as my face—not to mention my bald pate.

I also pack a light cotton billed hat as a backup and as a warmer alternative for cool or cold days. If I'm planning to walk in the late fall when I am sure to encounter colder weather, or anytime in the mountains, I substitute a light wool watch cap for this cotton cap.

Knife

When you picnic on the trail you need a knife with a blade, a bottle opener and a corkscrew. Well-known Swiss Army produces an excellent, lightweight knife that has two blades and a wine opener, but my favorite

Hat shops

Fast disappearing from France is the dedicated hat shop with its stock of bonnets, fancy-dress hats—seemingly right out of the 1890s—as well as an extraordinary selection of straw and felt hats for men. If you are lucky enough to run across one of these anachronisms while you are walking, you should not miss the chance to meet the proprietresses (usually charming, fastidiously-dressed elderly women with bright smiles) and look over the inventory.

My bet is that you will come out with a new hat. I did.

picnic knife is still the sleek, wood-cased knife I bought in France. The French make many brands of knives with wooden cases—they range from the reasonably priced Opinel to the very expensive but superbly crafted Laguiole—that are available throughout the country in hardware stores, cutlery shops and at special knife stalls in open-air markets. Bring a pocket knife from home when you go because you may not find the right French model before your first picnic, but then buy one of these practical and aesthetically pleasing knives when the opportunity presents itself.

You should not bring a hunting knife. Your pack will be small and light enough to qualify as carry-on luggage when you fly, but a long-bladed knife inside that pack will not be allowed through the security checkpoint when you board. Pocket knives are permitted, but anything larger will raise alarms. And if this is not reason enough to avoid a pigsticker, you should know that carrying a knife with a long blade is, under some circumstances, illegal in France.

Also, resist the temptation to bring a Swiss Army knife with a multitude of blades and an array of gadgets. A few extras—toothpick, awl, scissors—might prove useful, but the *very* elaborate knives weigh a great deal and are too bulky and heavy to carry in your pocket. All you really need is a blade, a bottle opener and a cork screw.

Walking stick

I had never used a stick until halfway through a walking trip in the Loire valley where, in an orchard early one foggy morning, I picked up a handsome branch that had been pruned from an apple tree and placed in a burn pile by the resident farmer. Once I had trimmed away the side limbs and rounded the narrower end with my pocket knife, the stick proved to be nicely balanced in the hand and comfortable to carry. Later, when it had been burnished by a combination of oils from my skin and friction with my hands, I became so attached to that stick that I have since carried it back and forth across the Atlantic many times. Leaning against the wall in my office at home, it has become a sort of talisman, a prod and reminder that it is time to go walking again.

Why bother to carry a stick? There's the conventional reason: as a third leg it helps with balance on a steep stretch of rocky trail or when crossing a small stream. Balance is always less sure with the top-heavy weight of a pack. A stick is also useful for knocking some of the moisture off dew-laden branches overhanging the trail in the morning. But the main reason I carry a stick

Dogs are almost always fenced or chained in France, but I still carry a stick to warn the occasional escapee.

is that I have found it indispensable when dealing with the rare but startling appearance of a loose dog.

The French are careful to fence or chain their dogs, and the walker will seldom encounter one that is not restrained. Many people, particularly those living in isolated homes in the French countryside, will keep a dog to guard their property and they fully expect that dog to bark when strangers approach. The intention is that the noise will frighten a potential intruder and warn the proprietor, particularly at night, that someone is about. While almost none of these dogs are trained to bite, many of the larger ones seem quite intimidating.

The rare loose dog is a confused dog because the accustomed limits—the end of a chain or the edge of a fence—are gone, but these dogs are easily frightened away or at least kept at bay by the tapping of a walking stick on the ground or pavement. French dogs are stick savvy and wary of anyone who carries one; even the most aggressive dog, once it has heard your tapping and seen your stick, stays well out of range of any potential swipe while allowing you—as you carefully maintain eye contact with the dog—to continue along the trail until it stops barking and turns toward home after you have left what the dog considers to be its territory. For this reason alone—to frighten the rare loose dog—I believe that at least one person in every group should carry a stick.

It's not necessary to forage for and then shape your own stick as I did, though doing so can be quite satisfying. Sports stores now sell telescoping walking poles that, when collapsed, are much easier to carry back and forth across the ocean inside or strapped to the outside of a pack. These manmade sticks are of course considerably more expensive than a free branch, but the folding pole is perhaps worth the money for its ability to disappear into your pack when not in use. If you do purchase a high-tech stick, be sure to choose one with a rounded tip; airport security may not allow you to carry anything as sharply pointed as a ski pole onto an airplane.

Compass

Because French trails are so well marked and the maps so detailed, I have found that a compass is of little use on the trail. Hanging from one of the zippers of my pack is a plastic-encased thermometer that also holds a small compass, and I can remember using this rather imperfect instrument only once. In a heavy, disorienting fog, four of us came to a junction point in heavily wooded hills where three paths, two GRs and one regional trail, crossed. It was easy to dismiss the regional path as our route because of its yellow and red markings, but we were confused as to which GR path to take because for once the marking system was not explicit enough and we had not bought the IGN blue map that covered this portion of the trail. Only after we had lined up our Michelin regional map using the little compass on my pack, were we able to choose what appeared to be (and was) the right path. Caution dictates that one person in your party should carry a compass, though the odds are that you'll never have to use it.

But if you are walking in the mountains you *should* carry a good compass. A mistake on the plains is inconvenient, but getting lost and taking the wrong route in the mountains can be dangerous because of the relative scarcity of shelter and the extremes of weather. Anyone walking up or down a specific drainage confined between valley walls will find it difficult to get lost even in heavy fog, but that same person, high on an open pass in fog, can easily become disoriented. When planning a walk in the Alps or Pyrénées, learn to use your compass before you leave, that is, before you need it.

Getting in shape

It may seem odd that I include getting in shape in the equipment chapter, but your ability to maintain your pace day after day depends to a great extent on the shape you are in before you leave. The ability to walk without becoming overly tired and out of breath is an essential part of the equipment you will bring with you to France.

I find repetitive exercise—walking the same four-mile route in the morning, skiing in place for twenty minutes every day on a NordicTrack—boring and when I am at home I find every excuse to avoid these sensible activities. However, four to six weeks before I leave on a walking trip I panic a bit and do, reluctantly, start a program of regular long walks through my neighborhood.

Walking is the best exercise. Habituate yourself to walk very far.
–Thomas Jefferson

How you get in shape depends on your regular exercise program (if you have one), on which trail in which region you have chosen and on the pace you plan to maintain on that trail.

Even an area like the Beaujolais pictured here, which is considered to be relatively easy to walk, can harbor long uphill sections. It's wise to be in the best possible shape for any walk, no matter how benign the reputation of the terrain.

If you will be walking on flat terrain and if you are in reasonable shape to begin with, then a minimum of preparation—a regular series of long walks to test and break in your boots, for example—would probably suffice. If you're planning to walk in an area that requires a great deal of climbing and descending—the Alps, the Cévennes and Corsica come to mind—then, unless you work out daily, a more serious conditioning program would be called for.

The best preparation for a walk is to walk, and the best preparation for climbing and descending hills is to climb and descend hills. But if you live in a city where walking is difficult and hills nonexistent, then, aside from walking up and down stairs whenever possible, you should join a health club and use the machines there to habituate your legs and strengthen your heart muscles for the work they will be doing. You're not preparing for an assault on Everest, but it's still logical that the stronger you are, the more enjoyable your walk will be.

People with health problems and indeed those who have the slightest doubts as to their ability to meet the challenge of the moderate to strenuous daily exercise needed to complete a long walk should consult their physician before they leave. Remember, though, walking in France is not a competition. You need do only what you and your companions are comfortable doing.

When good equipment is not good enough

Sometimes, no matter how well you think you have planned and equipped yourself, events intervene and remind you rather rudely that mistakes and the unexpected are part of life.

Four of us had just arrived late on a mild but rainy mid-May afternoon in the small Burgundian village of Mercurey, exhausted but elated after a marathon run from the western edge of the United States on a series of planes, the TGV, a shuttle train and, finally, a bus. We ignored the weather as we downed a bottle of Rully, a bottle of Mercurey and an expensive but only passable Michelin *one-star meal at the starchy Hotel Lion d'Or before falling into our beds. We all looked forward to our planned two-week walk down through the Beaujolais which would start the next day. It was good to be back in France.*

But as I peered out of the bedroom window the next morning, I saw that the rain had not stopped and the mild temperature of the day before had now been replaced by cold. A blustery wind was blowing straight out of the north, and, even though the calendar said May, the rain, wispy white streaks against the green of the leaves in the garden, was turning to sleet.

Over croissants *and* café au lait *good judgment was overwhelmed.*

In truth all four of us were inclined to start our walk, but because our friends lived in Colorado and were used to cold, they were more anxious to set out whatever the weather than we Californians. As the wind increased and the sleet turned to rain and back to sleet, we sat in the warm dining room talking of alternatives before we

Snow and cold can sometimes surprise the person on foot. Here in southern Burgundy on the 13th of May umbrellas were not proper equipment for our walk from Mercurey to Givry.

finally all agreed that, what the hell, we could do it; none of us wanted the first day of the walk to be the first day of rest. The ignominy! Also, another night at the Lion d'Or was not the brightest of prospects. The next hotel, a much more modest affair, was only fifteen kilometers away in Givry, and the route to it on the GRs 76 and 7—up over a low ridge, down into a valley and then up and over another ridge—shouldn't, we reasoned, offer any difficulty even in bad weather.

Faith and I should have known better, but it seems that good sense was off on its own vacation. We packed up and left.

Since everyone had followed my advice and brought nothing more waterproof than an umbrella, our first stop was a hardware store just down the street where we bought from the amused owner large black garbage bags to line our packs. Passing cars sent up waves of water that washed over the curb as we paraded single file down the narrow sidewalk, presenting, we were sure, quite a spectacle to those few startled inhabitants foolish enough to be out and about.

After we had walked only a few hundred yards up the first ridge, the snow, big wet flakes, began to pelt down with audible swonks onto our umbrellas and the arms of our far-from-waterproof windbreakers. Back at the hotel we had donned every conceivable piece of clothing, but slowly, layer by layer, the moisture penetrated to the skin of our arms and legs. Luckily, the wind was at our backs, but still, as we climbed, the gale mounted until at the top of the first ridge it pummeled and buffeted us so forcefully that we had to hold our umbrellas out horizontally to fend off the snow. Faith's was the first to go, caught and torn upward, splaying out suddenly in a cartoon tangle of bent ribs and shredded fabric.

To make a long story short, we had an uncomfortable, laughable and thoroughly memorable first day on the trail. Though we had brought a picnic from Mercurey, it was too cold and too miserable to stop for long, so lunch was a shared candy bar and some cheese gobbled quickly as the four of us stood under a tree in a huddle. We had jettisoned the bread, a soggy, disintegrating mass, an hour before. Of course the café in the small village located in the valley between the two ridges was closed, so we were forced to walk all the way to Givry without a fortifying hot drink in a warm bar. But by keeping our pace brisk, we stayed relatively warm even though the snow continued until we had walked and slid off the treeless second ridge.

Up there on that ridge the snow had actually stuck to the leaves, grass and gorse in a two-inch layer, sometimes covering the trail markers that were, for the most part, painted on rocks in the ground. The scene, heavy snow blowing horizontal and blurring away the landmarks only one hundred yards out, reminded me of some overdone black and white English movie shot on the moors during the 1930s. Poor Tess. But the flakes, which got drier as it got colder, were actually less wetting and consequently more comfortable to walk in than sleet or wet snow. The snow tended to slide off, not soak in, but even so, our boots, our packs and, despite the garbage bags, much of our clothing inside those packs was wet.

When we finally reached and then checked into our hotel, we found—hallelujah!—that both of our rooms had large, old-fashioned radiators that actually worked. If you had entered either room late that afternoon, you would have seen clothes and equipment draped and hung from every conceivable spot and smelled the unmistakable scent of a commercial laundry, a mix of moisture and scorched cotton. Anyone could have been forgiven for assuming that we were working our way through France by taking in washing on the side.

The lesson from all this? Well, first, the equipment I recommend is probably not adequate if you're determined to walk in a snow storm, but few readers will want to walk in snow storms. More important is the admonition that you should prepare for the minimum but be ready for anything because not every day of your walk is guaranteed to be uneventful. Perhaps that's even reassuring. After all, what's a vacation if there's not at least the possibility of adventure? It's experiences like these that are remembered, repeated and exaggerated as good tales long after the pleasurable but unremarkable everyday events have been forgotten.

Lodging

Comfort & charm

ONCE THE FOOT TRAVELER has absorbed the fact that marked and maintained paths crisscross France in a tight web, allowing anyone to walk anywhere, the next fact to accept is that, when you walk, a bed will be there at the end of the day. *Where will I stay?* is a question I hear frequently.

Here in the United States we are accustomed to having hotels and motels clustered near some Interstate exits and in large cities but virtually nonexistent in rural towns far from industry or tourist attractions.

But French villages *do* have lodging, and the surprising fact is that the next village over and the one after that, each only five, seven or ten miles from the other, also have lodging. In many of the more populated French regions such as the Loire, the Burgundy wine country, Alsace, the Côte d'Azur and the coastal areas of Brittany and Normandy, lodging is so ubiquitous that you will probably have a choice when you stop for the night—the lively inn on the square with all the young people in the café outside or the more dignified but perhaps stuffy hotel in the wooded park just outside of town? Like the villages, places to stay are rarer in the rugged areas like the Massif Central, the Alps, the Pyrénées and the higher areas of Languedoc and Provence. Nevertheless, they are, almost without fail, close enough to each other so that, with some planning and a willingness to walk more or fewer kilometers than

There is nothing which has yet been contrived by man by which so much happiness is produced as by a good tavern or inn.

– Samuel Johnson, 1776

normal, the person on foot will easily find a comfortable place to sleep each evening.

Reservations

When I am walking other than during the two summer vacation months, rooms in hotels are generally so available that I do not make reservations unless my research (done at home, see chapter 9) has told me that few rooms would be available in the town that I've chosen as my destination. And even then, to be sure that I will not be delayed by weather, I don't call more than twenty-four hours in advance. A walking vacation is truly a wander, scripted only insofar as the general route—*I want to walk from the Aix-en-Provence to St Tropez*—has been chosen and a time frame adopted. Of course, before you leave you should examine carefully the facilities along your proposed route to assure yourself that your trip is practicable, but in my experience advance plans are *always* modified when you are actually on the trail. Sometimes it's the weather, but most often it's circumstance and whim. An extra day of rest in a surprisingly pleasant spot is always hard to resist. Schedules are for home. This is your vacation!

As I pointed out in the sidebar on page 80, there's one exception to this don't-reserve-ahead rule. When any French holiday occurs during your walk it's wise to take more than the usual precautions concerning hotel and restaurant reservations, particularly if you're walking in a popular tourist area.

Telephoning for reservations

Picking up a telephone and attempting to make a reservation in any foreign country is a daunting prospect even if you do speak the local language. There's something about speaking into a receiver and, in particular, listening to a disembodied voice spout rapid-fire French that can discombobulate even the fluent. But there is an easy way around this problem. When you need an advance lodging reservation in France, ask the proprietor of the hotel you're staying in to call ahead for you. Everyone I have ever asked has been happy to help.

Using your personal guidebook (chapter 9) as a reference, note on a piece of paper the town along with the

name and the telephone number of the hotel or bed-and-breakfast that you plan to walk to the next day. Then, during the evening or when you come down for breakfast in the morning, give that information to the owner or to the person on the front desk and ask them to call for you.

This simple procedure benefits both of you. The hotel, by identifying itself when it makes the call, begins a relationship with a nearby establishment, and by making a reservation there, "does a favor" for them that might be reciprocated later. And you, of course, get your reservation.

Types of accommodation

Three types of accommodation are available to the long-distance walker. By far the most common are, of course, *les hôtels*, of which there are many, many thousands throughout France. The *Michelin* red guide lists over ten thousand and it is a very selective, far from all-inclusive resource. Next in popularity and numbers are the *chambres d'hôtes* (bed-and-breakfasts or B&Bs). Over seven thousand of these have been officially sanctioned. The last type of accommodation is the *gîte d'étape* (a simple rural inn for hikers and other *sportifs*) of which there were, in 1998, only about one thousand. These last are concentrated next to the national trails, often far from cities and towns.

In this chapter I will describe in a general way the different types of accommodation. In chapter 9 I will discuss the various guides that will allow you to find the hotels, bed-and-breakfasts and *gîtes* along your chosen route.

Readers who have traveled extensively in France are probably familiar with French hotels, but most of you will find the information about *gîtes* and bed-and-breakfasts new and, despite what some may think—*I'd never stay in a bed-and-breakfast much less something called a* gîte—informative and useful. I myself was quite prejudiced against all bed-and-breakfasts and I too thought *gîte* was just a fancy word for youth hostel. But the truth is that the French version of a bed-and-breakfast is different than most such establishments in the United States in several important ways. And the word *gîte* does *not* translate so easily. Read on.

Gîtes d'étape

Yes, the sleeping accommodations in *gîtes d'étape* are for the most part dormitory bunks, often double-decker, and the bathrooms are shared. But, before you conjure a vision of some marginal Asian "guest house" full of young "backpackers" and redolent with marijuana, you should realize that French *gîtes* are located far from the "action" which most often attracts peripatetic young people out to see the world for the first time. Instead, these facilities are patronized by active people of all ages who are there to enjoy the out-of-doors. *Gîtes* cater to people who arrive on a horse, by bicycle, on skis or on foot; in theory at least, *gîtes* are reserved exclusively for people who do not arrive by car. As you can see, they are certainly not *auberges de jeunesse* (youth hostels).

Gîtes d'étape *are the best lodging bargains in France. The walker on a tight budget should seek them out.* Gîtes *are usually simple establishments, but in my experience they are also clean and comfortable. While on the trail the walker can spot both* gîtes *and French bed-and-breakfasts by looking for the same Gîtes de France symbol.*

Nor are *gîtes d'étape* the same as *gîtes ruraux* (farm *gîtes*) or *gîtes de séjour* (holiday *gîtes*). Even the French often lump all the members of this *gîte* stew together, but both the farm and holiday *gîtes* require longer stays, a three-day weekend or a full week in most cases, and will decline to take anyone for only a night or two. These *gîtes de sejour* and *gîtes ruraux*, then, are of use only to the day walker—that person, group or family wishing to stay in one place that is used as a base for walks into the surrounding countryside.

Sometimes the only option for the long-distance walker in a remote area of France will be a *gîte d'étape*. No hotels, no bed-and-breakfasts, no choice. This is exactly the situation that Faith and I faced on the GR 9 late one May afternoon when we tentatively pushed open the rough wooden door of our very first *gîte d'étape*, located in Vitrolles, a small village high on a ridge in the Luberon region of Provence.

Just before noon that day we had walked into the town of Céreste down below on the valley floor, eager, since the weather was hot and clear, to continue walking. But queries in a café confirmed what we had already gleaned from guides: the only lodging on our route within walking distance during the half day remaining was the *gîte d'étape* up the hill in Vitrolles. Though unsure of what we would find, we had phoned to make a reservation. There was space, they said. so we set out. A short while later as we picnicked next to the GR, we concluded that we would not be disappointed because, frankly, our expectations were low.

Once through that door, though, we were greeted warmly in the commons room (a feature of many *gîtes*) by the friendly couple running the facility. After we had habituated ourselves to the routines and customs of unisex *gîtes* life—intuitive things like hurry in the shower because others are waiting and look anywhere but directly toward a person who might be changing clothes—we settled in comfortably and had a good night's sleep in our bunk beds.

But best of all, because we were thrown together with French people on more intimate terms than we would have been in a hotel, we enjoyed a much closer inter-action with them. Let's face it, the French like their privacy and, in general, go to great lengths to stay in their own cocoon and keep you—over there thank you—in yours. But in the openness of a *gîte,* reserve breaks down. Because everyone is in the same situ-ation *and* already shares a mutual interest in the outdoors, a camaraderie can develop that fosters openness and conversation. After all, it's much easier to talk to someone after you've inadvertently glimpsed them in their underwear. We were delighted by our experience in that first *gîte d'étape* where we made a friend with whom we still correspond many years later.

There may be shabby *gîtes* out there (my experience is not extensive), but all those that I have seen have been obsessively neat, clean and pleasant. Almost Swiss without the seriousness. Many provide only large, open *dortoirs* (dormitories) for sleeping, but some, like our first *gîte* in Vitrolles, are divided into alcoves and door-less areas that give a semblance of privacy. Some *gîtes* even have one or two private rooms with doors— available for a slight extra charge on a first-come-first-served basis—for two or four persons.

Your bunk in a *gîte* will have a blanket but sometimes no sheet or pillow. In that case, sheets and a pillow may be available for an extra 20 FF, but, if you are on a tight budget and plan to spend as many nights as possible in *gîtes d'étape*, I suggest you carry a sleeping-bag sheet, a mummylike liner made of cotton (weight: about one pound) or silk (only one-quarter pound but expensive), available in the United States in most places where sleeping bags are sold. Otherwise, if you'll only be staying in one or two *gîtes d'étape*, you might (again, only if sheets are not provided) have to sleep under the blanket in your clothes.

Aside from the chance to interact more closely with the French, one of the best things about staying in a *gîte* is the low price. Most charge between 50 FF and 75 FF per person per night, though some cost as little as 25 FF; still others, fancier and with more privacy, ask 100 FF. *Gîtes* are one of the best bargains in France.

Approximately half the *gîtes d'étape* in France either serve food (see chapter 8) or are within walking distance of a restaurant. The others provide kitchens where for a nominal extra charge guests can prepare their own meals. For me, cooking up some pasta or soup gets too close to backpacking. If faced with a situation like this (not so far) I would probably just eat a cold meal, another picnic.

Today almost all *gîtes* have a resident guardian, but some, particularly in the mountains, may not. These are run on the honor system. When you leave in the morning everything should be left as clean as you found it, and the posted fee should be dropped in the lockbox, which is usually screwed to the wall near the door. Most *gîtes* operate on a seasonal basis, but it is unlikely that you would want to walk in the area when they are closed.

Unlike hotels, reservations are a must when you plan to stay in a *gîte*. Most of these facilities are isolated and far from other forms of accommodation, so to avoid disappointment and the prospect of a night on a floor or bench, the walker should always phone ahead that morning or even the night before. Sometimes in the off-season, a *gîte* may be completely booked for four or five days by a group who gather to take some course or other—things like mushroom identification or technical climbing—so even though the region you are walking in may appear to be bereft of walkers, you

---

Franc–dollar conversion

$1 = 5 FF	then 100 FF = $20
$1 = 5.5 FF	then 100 FF = $18
$1 = 6 FF	then 100 FF = $16
$1 = 6.5 FF	then 100 FF = $15
$1 = 7 FF	then 100 FF = $14

should still phone ahead. If the *gîte* serves food be sure to mention when you reserve your bed that you would also like to eat.

Reservations at these facilities are normally held only until 7 PM. In theory, stays at *gîtes d'étape* are limited to three days so that others who may want to stay will have a chance to do so, but this rule seems to be enforced only during the busy summer months.

Cash is the usual method of payment since *gîtes* are not equipped to take credit cards.

Chambres d'hôtes

First, let me make one thing clear: I'm not a fan of American bed-and-breakfasts. There are undoubtedly pleasant ones out there somewhere—at least people keep telling me there are. But it has been *my* experience that B&Bs come in only two forms, two flavors so to speak, and neither of them is particularly tasty.

The majority, plain vanilla, are just a modest home where a lonely owner-host rents out the spare room with a fatigued mattress, a shag rug, a shared bath and access through the living room. "My daughter's in Des Moines now..." but her dolls are still propped in the bookcase, and the pictures of Kurt Cobain or, in a dusty worst-case scenario, Elvis, are still there on the wall. Bad enough.

But sometimes you're unfortunate enough to came across the second kind: a large, often Victorian house with five or so rooms for guests, each "done" in some bizarre theme, the expression of someone's elaborate and obsessive fantasy. Such places are arranged like stage sets, and your stay is scripted by a fussy, domineering innkeeper who is both playwright and director. "You'll want to join us at 5:30 for wine in the parlor and..." To continue the flavor analogy, places like this might be characterized as being mango peanut butter with sprinkles. Painful experience has taught me to avoid both types of American B&B, the first because I am annoyed by the overpriced discomfort, and the second because I refuse to play the assigned role.

But French *chambres d'hôtes* are different. You *will* stay in someone's home, but you will also either have a separate entrance, or the door to your room will be off a hall that itself has direct access to the outside. Your room will not be the abandoned bedroom of the son who just moved to Marseille or Lille, but rather will resemble more a room you might find in a nice residential hotel—large, spacious and sometimes suite-like. Newer French hotels like new hotels everywhere offer rooms that seem to have been made with a cookie cutter, each the same, each just as dull as the next, but your room in a *chambre d'hôtes* is sure to be distinctive and indicative of the proprietor's tastes. The decor, like that proprietor, may on occasion be eccentric, but it will seldom be boring.

And you will be left alone. No one will pester you to join some group activity, sherry at five, breakfast precisely at nine "so you can meet the rest of the guests." French reserve, which sometimes makes it difficult to interact with the people you meet, works to your advantage in this situation. The proprietor and his or her family—running the *chambre d'hôtes* is usually the project of either the husband *or* the wife, but seldom both—keep to themselves, sometimes so effectively that you actually might wish for a little *more* contact. You hear the giggles of the children upstairs but you don't see them. You hear the dog bark but you never get to pet it. The owners guard their privacy and, in the process, your privacy as well.

All *chambres d'hôtes* are limited in size by law to six rooms. Any lodging with more rooms than that must be classified as a hotel, which is subject to a much more complex and stringent set of government rules. But there is absolutely no limit to the amenities that can be offered. If your fantasy has been to spend the night in a French château, then a bed-and-breakfast might be the easiest and most affordable way to satisfy that dream. Most *chambres d'hôtes* are in houses, often attractive or unusual houses, but houses nonetheless. But some are in very grand country castles that have

Chambres d'hôtes *are usually in older homes or farms. Like* Gîtes d'étape, *they are always indicated— as above—by the official medallion of the* Gîtes de France *organization posted outside. Rooms are comfortable and often spacious. They and any communal areas (below) are similar to what might be found in a good residential hotel.*

either been converted by their aristocratic but impoverished owners to *chambres d'hôtes*—entities that might generate and not swallow money—or have been

bought and refurbished by new, necessarily wealthy owners.

While walking in the Mâconnais in the spring of 1996, two friends, my wife and I were fortunate enough to stay at one of these châteaux-*chambres d'hôtes* in the very small community of Sassagny. We walked into the town, nothing more than a crossroad, late in the afternoon on a cloudy day that threatened rain. You could smell the dampness in the still air, and the clouds were turning from gray to an ominous black. The approach to the château was up a long *allée,* and we admired the view during the five minutes it took us to hurry along its length.

The building that faced us had been built in one fell swoop during the 1700s and was a well-proportioned example of an unfortified country estate, not medieval, not squat and bristling with towers, but open and four stories tall on the downhill side with chimneys and windows everywhere. Nestled amongst ancient trees, it presented us on that dark afternoon with a grand and formidable façade. As we crunched through the fine gravel toward the front door, I found the grandeur of it

French bed-and-breakfasts are sometimes in grand homes like this château in the Burgundian hamlet of Sassagny. The owner, André Marceau, has worked hard to rejuvenate the buildings and grounds, which had fallen into disrepair.

all strange, even daunting. I fully expected to be greeted by a scowling old aristocrat as I knocked, but instead, the owner was a middle-aged gentleman, André Marceau, who greeted us warmly and put us immediately at ease.

Later, while rain fell outside, we sat in the library drinking wine made on the property. M. Marceau explained that he had grown up in Sassagny and had left at a young age for Paris where eventually he made his fortune "in computers." His wealth, he freely admitted, had allowed him to retire early and return to Sassagny where he was able to fulfill his childhood dream of buying the château.

The former owner, an elderly widow, had as she faded away closed off more and more of the building until, when she died at age ninety-five, she was living in only one room on the ground floor. In the abandoned and unheated parts of the château, winter cold had burst pipes, ruining plaster and buckling parquet floors, but now, after five years of hard work by M. Marceau and his wife, the bedrooms were comfortable suites, the library-common room was Louis XIV elaborate and the acres of grounds and forest were once again groomed and productive. M. Marceau was contagiously enthusiastic about the wine he made on the estate, the Limousin cows he raised and the improvements he had made to the outbuildings as well as to the château itself. He delighted in his castle and did everything in his power to make sure that his guests did too.

Prices in *chambres d'hôtes* vary as much as the amenities. A stay for two in the château at Sassagny, with an elaborate breakfast but without dinner, costs (in 1998) between 550 FF and 750 FF for two, depending on the view from your room, but the vast majority of places, less grand but nonetheless comfortable, range in price between 200 FF and 250 FF for two. A few are only 150 FF. Prices are less reasonable for a single room, usually only 50 FF less than the double price. Triple and quadruple rooms are often available for a slight supplement over the double price and these can be a money-saving option for the family walking with young children or for two couples on a tight budget.

One in eight *chambres d'hôtes* will serve an optional evening meal, a so-called *table d'hôtes,* if you request it when you make a room reservation. A few establishments also offer a *coin cuisine* (kitchen corner) where guests can cook their own meals, but most often you will eat in a (hopefully) nearby restaurant. Luckily for the person on foot, the more isolated establishments are the ones most likely to serve meals; those in villages with restaurants usually don't bother.

Since the number of rooms in any *chambre d'hôtes* is limited to a maximum of six and because most in reality have only two to four rooms, reservations are essential. Remember, these places are not hotels with an official front desk, so if you arrive unannounced, you may find no one at home or the place closed for a week while the family takes its own vacation. *Chambres d'hôtes*, best described as small inns, serve the traveler walking point to point very well, and the day walker will find a pleasant *chambre d'hôtes* in the countryside or in a small village an ideal base of operations.

Very few *chambres d'hôtes* take credit cards. You should be prepared to pay cash.

Hotels

Some Americans, those who haven't traveled abroad or stayed overnight in a big city, have never slept in a true hotel. Almost without exception, the motel has driven out of business the small-town hotels that did exist in the United States, so that now the hotel is the dominant form of lodging only in larger cities. And even there, the newer hotels are nothing more than multi-storied motels with each room the same as the next, the bathroom, the bed and the decor a carbon copy of what can be found in motels anywhere in the country. The only difference is that your car isn't right outside the door.

In France, however, real hotels, are everywhere, thriving in the cities and surviving in many of the small towns. Though motels are now appearing near the exits of France's expanding *autoroute* (superhighway) system, they are still relatively few in number.

While there are a scattering of new hotels, particularly in French cities, with sterile, you've-seen-one-you've-seen-'em-all rooms, the majority of the hotels in France are older places with rooms that are unique, each different from the other in size, decor and amenities. Many of these places were not built all of a piece but are the result, instead of accretions and changes to a small-town inn established as much as one hundred years ago and the property of one family since that time. One generation may have saved and scraped to buy and then incorporate into the business the building next door, another may have completely rebuilt or rearranged all the rooms to accommodate indoor plumbing, and certainly every generation will have redecorated. The result is a unique establishment about as far from a boring motel as you can get.

When checking into a hotel a French person expects to be shown the room he'll stay in that evening. The desk clerk or bellman will, if choice is an option, take two or three keys from a board in back of the desk and  walk the prospective client around to show a range of accommodations from which to choose. Americans are sometimes uncomfortable with this procedure, perhaps because we have been so conditioned by the uniformity of our motels. Once you've seen just one room in one particular Holiday Inn, there's really no need to inspect another room in that establishment or, for that matter, in any other Holiday Inn anywhere else in the world. They're all essentially the same—on purpose of course—but French hotel rooms are definitely not all the same, and I urge you to adopt the French habit and at least glance at the rooms that you may be shown.

And if the offer to see a variety of rooms isn't made, you should ask for a tour. By doing so you will, if there are other lodging options in town, be able to decide whether or not you want to stay in that particular hotel and, if you do decide to stay, which room suits you best. By that I mean that you will be able to choose the room that has the amenities most important to you, be it firm bed, balcony, good view or tub instead of shower. There is usually such a variety of rooms within one establishment that when my wife and I are walking with another couple, one couple gets first choice one night, the other first choice the next. That way each gets a fair share of the "good" rooms.

The French government tourist bureaucracy grades all

the hotels in France, from one ☆ up to five ☆☆☆☆☆, rating each against a limited and strictly-adhered-to list of criteria. These include television in the room, carpeting, average square footage and bath amenities, items that are, on purpose, easily quantifiable so the system can't be accused of being arbitrary and capricious.

These ratings do not measure charm but they do, in general, reflect luxuriousness or the lack thereof and, in a more general way, the price. A brand new ☆☆☆ hotel may have earned its rating by having been built with the ☆☆☆ criteria in mind but it may still remind you more of Best Western than the best that France has to offer. An older ☆☆☆, on the other hand, may have the same level of amenities *and* charm.

Out in the countryside you will find few ☆☆☆☆☆ hotels. These are the George Vs and Negrescos of the world, rare, very expensive establishments offering a level of service that pampers and flatters the guest. What you will find are many ☆☆☆, ☆☆, ☆ and no star— yes, such a thing exists—hotels.

The government rates all French hotels on a scale of ☆ to ☆☆☆☆☆ and most establishments—as here— post that rating outside. Hotel guides also indicate the number of government stars. The vast majority of rural hotels also maintain a café and restaurant.

Over the past fifty years France has upgraded the general level of its hotels. Gone are the days when a

majority had the "water closet" and, separately, the bath tub down the hall from the bedrooms themselves. Now I would guess that at least ninety percent and very likely one hundred percent of the rooms in any given ☆☆ hotel will have complete baths, while the rest of the rooms, if there are any such, will have at least a sink in the corner. Hotels with ☆ are almost certain to have some rooms with the bath down the hall, but it is just as certain that the best rooms, the most expensive rooms, will offer a full bath, though, in this more modest establishment, the decor may be less than new and the beds softer than you might like.

There are still a few relics without any in-room facilities whatsoever except, perhaps, a sink in the corner. These are the no-star hotels, and, while they may be short on amenities, a few of these, when they are located outside the train-station district of larger cities, can be long on charm. Personally, I like these older places when they are well maintained. Even that arbiter of quality, the *Michelin* red guide, sees fit to list a handful of these spartan but perhaps well-located or quaint establishments, and, when it does, you can be assured that the hotel will be squeaky clean as well. In general, no-star hotels in cities tend to be run-down and dirty while no-star establishments in isolated villages *can* be clean and delightful. Don't write no-star hotels off out of hand, but definitely ask to see the room before you agree to stay.

French hotel prices vary greatly, but as a general rule, you get the amenities if not necessarily the charm you pay for. The star rating system, it is said, carries with it some price constraints that, if they exist at all, I don't pretend to understand. But, in general, prices do rise as the number of government stars goes up. Obviously hotels in Paris and other large cities cost more than similar hotels out in the country, and prices in popular tourist areas like the Côte d'Azur are also higher, but whatever the area, a ☆ hotel will be less expensive than the ☆☆ down the street, which in turn will be less expensive than the nearby ☆☆☆ hotel.

Many travelers are surprised by the reasonable prices charged by nice if not luxurious hotels outside the big cities. A typical ☆☆ in a small town will charge between 225 FF and 300 FF for a double room, taxes and service but not breakfast included. A simpler but

The great advantage of a hotel is that it's a refuge from home life.
– George Bernard Shaw

France on Foot

comfortable ☆ in the same area will charge between 175 and 250 FF, while a ☆☆☆ down the street, complete with pool, might charge between 300 and 480 FF.

Because each room in older country hotels is different from the room next door and different again from the one down the hall, prices charged for rooms within any one hotel also vary. French *hôteliers* do not micromanage to the point that the price for each and every room is different, but certain features are often singled out, their lack or inclusion used as a point of departure for differences in price. A room with two twin beds costs marginally more than a room with one large bed. A room with a bathtub costs more than a room with a shower. A room with a better view—on the side facing not the town but the sea, for instance—will always cost more, sometimes considerably more.

The single traveler will usually pay almost as much as a couple. Some hotels do maintain a few small, more reasonably priced rooms for the lone traveler, but most rooms will accommodate two people, and the understandable attitude is that rooms are rented by the unit, not by the number of people staying in them. As a single traveler, you will pay considerably more for your hotel rooms on a per-person-per-night basis than will each of two people traveling together.

Many but not all hotel proprietors in France also operate a restaurant on the premises. Particularly when the hotel is located in a small village or when the restaurant and not the hotel is the principal business, you may, if you stay, be expected to take your evening meal there. To avoid this sticky situation when you have planned to eat in a special restaurant elsewhere in town, it is best to choose, if you can, to stay in a hotel without a restaurant. But if this isn't an option, almost every French hotel with a restaurant will tolerate (perhaps reluctantly) your eating elsewhere; you are only obligated to eat in house if you have agreed to do so when asked directly. Most often, of course, you *will* be eating where you are staying. Often that's the best option. Sometimes it's the only option.

All French hotels offer a continental breakfast for an additional charge of from 30 to 50 FF per person. You are not obligated to take this meal, but if you absolutely need your coffee first thing in the morning, you

> **The minuterie**
>
> To save on electricity, the hall lights in all but the most luxurious French hotels are activated by pushing a strategically placed button at the foot of the stairs or in the hall outside your room. Once the button is pushed the lights will stay on for thirty seconds, a minute or more allowing you, if you don't dawdle, to get where you are going.

may not have a choice.

As I said at the beginning of this chapter, during the months of April, May, June, September and October, in other words, outside the vacation months, there is no reason to reserve your room in advance other than on the weekends in popular tourist areas or perhaps during first week in May when schools are on holiday. Of course, if the only hotel in the village to which you're walking has only four rooms, then I would certainly advise calling ahead, but if the village has two hotels with a total of forty rooms, then I would wait until I arrived in town and had a chance to inspect the two hotels before I made a choice. In my experience, hotels in the countryside are seldom fully booked.

Visa and Mastercard are welcome in all but a few hotels, and in fancier establishments American Express and Diners Club might also be accepted. A number of years ago, French restaurants and hotels organized a somewhat loose but prominently publicized boycott of American Express to protest that firm's high fees and slow payment. Though this dispute has been resolved, you will still find that the American Express card is accepted in fewer places in France than you might expect.

No hotel

It could happen.

You walk into a tiny village on a Wednesday at five in the afternoon and find that the only hotel in town, thirty rooms housed in a large, attractive stone building, is closed. That morning you had perused your personal guidebook (chapter 9) and seen that this large hotel closed only for a week at Christmas and otherwise operated seven days out of seven. No need to call ahead, you had decided—on a weekday out here in the boonies during early June this big place should be almost empty. Now you peer in at the window next to the front door and see that the furniture is covered with sheets. You knock insistently at the door. Nothing. Well, you were right—the place is empty.

Happily, I have never been faced with such a situation, but it *is* possible. After all, the elderly owner of a hotel can die, businesses do go bankrupt and some buildings even burn down. The question is what to do if this should happen to you?

During the 1800s and early 1900s, when a traveler walked or rode into a village, he (itinerants were usually male) would as a matter of course ask the mayor where he could find lodging for the night. There were few formal inns during that era, but the mayor of a town with no inn would know which households were willing to take in a traveler for a fee. A vestige of this tradition still survives in France, and the person on foot who faces a proverbial night in the hayloft should ask to speak with the village's mayor who might know of a family willing to house and feed a stranger. If the mayor isn't available, then the owner of the café would be my next choice.

I have found, almost without exception, that the rural French are very willing to help anyone in need, and in an emergency such as I have just described, I believe that two people would have a good chance of finding a place to stay. Four people would have less of a chance and, even if successful, would probably end up in two different houses. More people than that, six or eight, and you should immediately call a taxi (or two) in the nearest fair-sized town to come to the village and transport you and the rest of the group to a hotel.

The traveler on foot has many options for lodging after a day on the trail, a fact that makes it possible to walk in France without camping. Burdened only with your personal effects, you are free to walk where you will, assured, if you do your research beforehand, that you'll find a place to rest your head at the end of the day.

<aside>
Time

Like the military in the United States, the French nation, military *and* civilian, operates on a day that starts at zero hours and ends at twenty-four hours, a system that by its very nature does away with any confusion that might arise between 8 AM and 8 PM. In France, 8 AM is 800 (spoken as eight hours) and 8 PM is 2000 (twenty hours) — they just keep adding hours once noon is reached instead of reverting, as of course the clock itself does, back to one as the afternoon begins. Plane, train and bus schedules are all written and referred to using this system. *"Le car part à quinze heures quarante."* (The bus leaves at fifteen hours forty.)

Restaurant and hotel reservations are also made using the twenty-four-hour system though you will certainly be understood, particularly if you are speaking English, when you tell your hotel that you will arrive at five o'clock instead of at seventeen hours.
</aside>

Our first French bed and breakfast

"We could always blame Balzac, or maybe even Calder,"
I said to Faith with a smile. "After all, we wouldn't be
here if it weren't for them."

"Honey, let's be serious about this," she replied. "We need
a room."

"Well, then, maybe Madame Calder could put us up. I

know he's gone but..."

"*Bruce,*" *she said, putting down her demi–tasse cup with a gesture that quite plainly said,* "Enough." *But then, in spite of herself, she too smiled, so to hide her softening, she picked up one of the remaining chocolate truffles from the plate on the table and placed it carefully on her tongue.*

Yes, my reference was to Honoré de Balzac, the nineteenth century French novelist, and to Alexander Calder, the twentieth century American sculptor, and, no, Faith was right, it certainly wasn't their fault that we were where *we were and, most important,* when *we were where we were. They were involved in an oblique sort of way, but...*

Saché: *Where we were at that moment wasn't so bad, really—the Loire region in the small village of Saché, seated in a warm, timbered restaurant at a table that had been pulled over next to the fire. We were drinking strong espresso and picking at plates of rich candies and cookies after having polished off a delicious five-course lunch and two bottles of wine. The question under muddled consideration was quite simple:* where would we find a room for the night? *The steady downpour, whipped into bursts by the wind, was clearly visible out the window and the nearest town with a hotel, our original destination, was still four miles up the trail. Slightly tipsy, warm and dry, too comfortable in fact, we were not in a walking mood.*

We had checked out of our hotel in Azay-le-Rideau of château fame at about nine that morning, a Sunday. The clouds had been low, a grey lid on the day, and it was drizzling lightly when we walked out of town. But we were determined to leave despite the wet because, quite frankly, we didn't want to stay another day. To hell with the weather—we would walk the short distance to Artannes-sur-l'Indre, only about eight miles away. The visit to the fairy-tale Azay château, a kaleidoscope of towers and moats right out of Fontaine, had been enchanting, but the small, busy town with its bruiser Mercedes busses spilling troop after troop of weekend tourists and its overabundance of mediocre and pricey restaurants was another matter. For almost a week previous to our arrival in Azay, we had walked through town after town, some of them touristed (after all, this

*was the Loire), but none had, until Azay, crossed the
line between the natural and the forced, between a town
with tourists and a tourist town. Ennui, an endemic
disease in places everywhere that exist* for *and subsist*
on *their visitors, had, seemingly, infected every inhabitant. We didn't just leave Azay, we fled.*

The Michelin Châteaux of the Loire *green tourist guide
stated that Calder in his later years had maintained a
studio and a home in Saché, and as we walked down a
long open slope toward the town an hour and a half
after our start , we had speculated about which place
had been his. We saw a couple of candidates—a farm a
little too grand for the circumstances here, a remodeled
barn there—but, in the end, we couldn't decide just
which one had to have been his.*

*Saché, on the south bank of the Indre river (a Loire
tributary), houses only about 750 inhabitants, and I'm
sure it's the only place of that size in the world with a
very large and massive Calder stabile-mobile set plunk
in the middle of its central square. The effect is startling.
The brash modernity of the thing and the audacity of its
colors clash unapologetically with the bland façades of
the surrounding buildings, all traditionally grey, all
traditionally bourgeois. My first impression was definitely not one of delicacy. But it did seem that the scale
was right, that once you got over what it was, its size fit
the space quite nicely. But these had been, admittedly,
hurried judgments, for as we had entered the town, the
rain had begun in earnest. It pelted as we paused briefly
on the sidewalk to peer out from under our umbrellas at
the glistening construction, the wet colors glowing as if
lit from within, almost fluorescent in contrast to the
soggy grey all around. Over our heads "Place Calder"
was written in white on the traditional blue French
street sign.*

Right on the place *was a small café, and after we had
shuffled in, shaking our umbrellas out the door and
stamping our feet, we found it crowded and smoky, full
at that Sunday hour of young boys playing or spectating a game of fussbol and men, glasses in hand, who
were, perhaps, declaring by their presence a republican
indifference to the Catholic mass which must have been
going on at that Sunday morning hour in the church
across the square. We found a space for our packs and
our folded umbrellas in a corner and then sat, all smiles*

and apologies, at the end of a long table where four red-faced men were playing an intense and, to us, incomprehensible game of cards. They began each hand in

A Calder plunk in the middle of the small village of Saché

silence, concentrating and playing deliberately until the end, when suddenly talk and laughter would accompany the slapping down, one after the other in quick succession, of the remaining cards. We ordered two coffees and settled to wait out the weather.

A half hour later, Faith, annoyed by the cigarette smoke and seldom content to sit in one place doing nothing for too long anyway, had taken her umbrella and fled out into the town to "look around." I, happy to sit in the warmth out of the rain, was left to mind the packs and watch the soccer game on the TV over the bar. But five minutes later she was back, urging me to come quickly. As we maneuvered our packs out the door, muttering our "M'sieurs" to the card players, she explained that a tour of the small local château just off the central square was about to start.

Fussbol tables are common in rural cafés as are vintage pinball machines.

The château: As châteaux go the one in Saché is modest. With its extensive grounds, fine gardens and large trees, it could be described as charming but in reality it could also be dismissed as just a small, architecturally unremarkable building hiding behind twelve-foot stone walls. It was built in the eighteenth century around the ruined vestiges of its sixteenth-century beginnings. The owners allow visitors each Sunday morning solely because Balzac enjoyed coming

here in the 1830s and '40s to write and "to escape…the bustle of Paris and the dunning of his creditors" as the green guide would have it.

On an upper floor of the château, a room that had been used by Balzac as a study has been meticulously pre-served—embalmed, really—and the inkwell, the plume pen on the desk, the open leather-bound book, the chair pushed back just so, and of course the superb view into the surrounding forest are meant to look just as they had when he last visited only months before he died in 1850.

A baker's dozen of us, slightly damp but respectful, had stood in silence in the center of that room while our guide, a comely young lady in a cashmere sweater and wool skirt, explained the details of Balzac's visits to Château Saché and enumerated the chapters of novels and stories he had written while here in his beloved retreat. The room, a sort of wax museum, and the infor-mation, exhaustive and didactic, was interesting at first in a dry, impersonal way.

But as our guide droned on and we stood shifting from foot to foot, I found myself distracted by the restricted view through a partially opened door into another room across the hall, a room with lamps, a leather armchair, magazines, a vase of flowers and a yellow toy dump-truck overturned on the parquet floor. Here was a place in this old building with its fifteen-foot ceilings, fancy plaster and impressive wood work that was still lived in! Was that really roast chicken I smelled?

But understandably we weren't given more than tan-talizing peeks at the home within the château. Visitors were tolerated there only because they paid homage to the great man, to the bookcase full of his first editions, to the illegible scribble on the pages of his original manu-scripts, to his aura. The tour took only half an hour, and once we had appreciated the study and heard the rote chronicle, our group was herded purposefully back down the halls and stairways to the entry with its benches, its cases full of more Balzac memorabilia and all the wet umbrellas, jackets and, in our case, packs that, on entering, we had been asked to shed.

Outside, the rain continued, and, while the other visitors scuttled through the wet to their cars, we had stood

facing each other under a tree, umbrella to umbrella, and considered our problem: it would be unpleasant at best to continue walking, but there was no hotel in town in which we could settle to take refuge from the weather. Therefore, we reasoned, we had *to continue on our way to Artannes-sur-l'Indre sometime but as we talked we rationalized. There was time. Perhaps if we waited, had lunch—yes, that was a good idea—the weather would change. In our family eating well is always a good substitute for less pleasant alternatives.*

Sunday lunch: *And that was how we had found ourselves, almost three hours later, sipping coffee, eating cookie after cookie and procrastinating at our table in front of the fire in a restaurant called the Auberge du* xvii *Siècle located on a corner of Place Calder.*

"Let's ask the waiter," Faith prompted. Translated, this meant that I *should ask the waiter since my French is better than hers.*

"But there aren't any hotels. Nothing in the guide. Besides, we can see that," I said with a sweeping gesture toward the square outside. But of course I did ask and of course the waiter responded that, yes, there was something, and he would be happy to phone for us if we wished. The lodging was just outside of town on the other side of the river, a chambre d'hôtes *called the Manoir de Bêcheron.*

"Teddy bears on the pillow," I said as the waiter left to telephone for our room.

"Bad wine on the sideboard. Charades in the parlor. Our new best friends in France," she responded.

We giggled.

We both harbored a general and rather intense dislike for bed-and-breakfasts but now, in desperation, we were about to try France's version, a chambre d'hôtes. *Under the circumstances we supposed that we were lucky it was available. Anything would be better than walking for an hour and a half through the heavy rain that was still pouring down outside, but, nevertheless, we were dubious, resigned to spending an uncomfortable or, at best, a strange evening and night. We both bemoaned the fact that there was no reasonable alternative.*

But we couldn't have been more wrong.

The Manoir de Bêcheron: *Our waiter's "nearby" was of course predicated on car travel, so it took us twenty wet, blustery minutes to walk to the Manoir, and, when we got there, it was hard for us to believe that we were in the right place. Ahead was a lovely stone farm complex, which embraced, off to one side, a medieval tower. It looked entirely too tasteful, entirely too grand, and only the green and yellow Gîtes de France logo on a post near the road gave us the courage to walk up the path to the door and knock. Madame, an attractive, middle-aged redhead, dressed casually in wool slacks and a sweater, opened the door immediately—she had been waiting for us—and after thirty seconds of polite greetings she showed us to our room located right off the rather stark entry hall.*

What time would we want breakfast? Yes, eight-thirty would be fine. This key was for our room and the other fit the front door. Was there anything else she could do for us? No? We had only to knock at the door at the end of the entry hall if we needed anything; otherwise she would see us at eight-thirty in the morning. Did we prefer coffee, tea or chocolate? Just walk through that same door for breakfast.

Our first French chambre d'hôte, *the Manoir de Becheron, convinced us that bed-and-breakfasts were different (and from our point of view better) than similar establishments in the United States.*

Then, with a friendly smile, she was gone.

We were left standing in our room, silent, amazed, dumbstruck.

Over against one stone wall a very large bed matched perfectly the proportions of the room, which was at least eighteen feet wide, thirty feet long and twelve feet high. There were heavy double drapes over the two casement windows, large watercolors and oils on the walls, a leather couch, easy chairs, lamps, a desk with an extravagant bouquet of tulips and two large armoires. Altogether it was an overwhelming, eclectic, yet pleasing mix.

Grand in an understated way, this room was not the work of a decorator. Full but not overly full of furniture, it exuded a lived-in feel that, in my experience, only seems to come after people have inhabited and used a space for years. Our room immediately brought to mind the glimpses I had stolen that morning into the animate part of Château Saché.

"Firm," I called as I tested the bed.

"Oh! Look at this!" Faith exclaimed from a small hallway that led off from the other side of the room.

I walked over as she pointed to her right into a small round space that contained a small fold-down desk, an overstuffed chair and, between the slit windows, curved wooden shelves filled with leather-bound books. This was the bottom part of the tower we had seen as we arrived. The bathroom off the other side of the hall was modern and as large as our whole bedroom at home. It had both a shower for me and an immense tub for Faith.

Tired, full of good food and wine, we hugged each other and laughed out loud.

Monday: *At breakfast* Madame *was, at first, as discreet as she had been the day before; pleasant but reserved, she served our breakfast at the big dining-room table and then retired to the kitchen. We ate the toasted day-old bread (the local bakery was closed on Mondays), home-made plum jam, good butter and slices of moist pound-cake in silence until* Madame

returned to ask if we wanted anything else. More alert, more social after coffee, we began to ask questions, and at our invitation, she sat with us to chat. She was interested in us—Where were we from? How far did we walk each day? How long had we been traveling?—and I was reminded again that the reserve of most French people, which some Americans interpret as unfriendliness, is in most cases only an expression of their respect for privacy, both yours and their own. We talked for twenty minutes over cups of café au lait.

This Manoir de Bêcheron, her home, had been built, she said, in the seventeenth century but the tower was from the fourteenth, two centuries older than any part of the château in town. She called the round room in the tower a boudoir. *In addition to our grand suite she rented out two other rooms, but both had been unoccupied last night. Yes, she enjoyed having guests so long as there weren't too many for too long. Our compliments on the decor, the fine linen sheets and the good breakfast were gracefully accepted.*

Later, after paying the equivalent of $60 for the two of us, we exited the Manoir into sunshine. As we strolled back down the road toward Saché and the GR, *we shook our heads at our good fortune. The* chambre d'hôtes *had been much more enjoyable than any of our hotel stays up to that point and, when the cost of breakfast was factored in, cheaper to boot. Perhaps our experiences with bed-and-breakfasts in America had no relation to what we'd find in French* chambres d'hôtes? *Certainly they had nothing to do with last night's stay!*

To say that we had been comfortable at the Manoir would be a ridiculous understatement, and any fantasies we acted out had certainly not been scripted by the owner. They were our own.

** **Note:** According to the latest guidebooks, the Manoir de Becheron no longer operates as a* chambre d'hôte.

Eating
More than just sustenance

THE A.J. LIEBLING quote in the margin of this page applies to walkers in France as well as to youths first wetting their toes in the pool of this world's pleasures.

Liebling, well known for his writings about France and its food, points out in the "Just Enough Money" chapter of his delightful book that a wealthy young person beginning an investigation of the subtleties of food and wine is unlikely to learn the relative merits of humble, inexpensive cuts of meat like heart or modest local wines in carafe because he or she can, from the start, afford to order what is supposed to be the best. On the other hand, Liebling goes on to state, the young person "without the crippling handicap of affluence" is forced to make choices—the Côtes du Rhône with pasta *or* the *vin ordinaire* with a steak but not both the steak and the Côtes du Rhône—and this financially strapped incipient gourmet will learn the relative values of different foods and wines when he or she makes those choices. The wealthy youth, able to order both the Côtes du Rhône and the steak without thinking about the cost, learns nothing.

A man who is rich in his adolescence is almost doomed to be a dilettante at table. This is not because all millionaires are stupid but because they are not impelled to experiment. In learning to eat...the customer, in order to profit, must be sensible of the cost.

– A.J. Liebling, *Between Meals*

Many foreigners who consider themselves *becs fins* (gourmets) head for France, determined to make the most of their time there by eating every meal at the best possible restaurant they can find. In a car it is tempting and all too easy for these visitors, guidebooks open for reference, to drive from one top restaurant to another, never eating a meal at a modest place serving regional dishes. The mobile food-obsessed visitor could be said to be the equivalent of Liebling's "rich" youth.

But foodies on foot in the French countryside cannot eat in France's best restaurants every night. Instead they are forced to eat at least some of the time in simple restaurants in small villages and, like Liebling's impecunious adolescent, learn that *rillettes, cassoulet, moules marinièrres, pot-au-feu* and *boudin noir*—the broad base from which French *grande cuisine* originates—can be not only delicious but also sometimes far better than an ill-conceived attempt at something fancier. Food-loving walkers will come across more than enough ambitious restaurants serving unusual

Often it is the simple meal that satisfies the most—in this case our appetizer is dry sausage, pickles and crusty bread accompanied by house wine in carafe.

and inventive food to satisfy any cravings for a sumptuous dining experience, but those same travelers will also eat, at least part of the time, in some far simpler restaurants where the goodness of the unpretentious food may surprise and delight as well.

Dining, not eating

I must admit that I am a food-obsessed traveler. Like the male moth seduced by the faint scent of the female's pheromones, I am drawn from afar by the aroma of good cooking. My profession is the preparation of food, and one of my passions is its consumption, so when I am walking in France, not just a few of my decisions on how far to walk and where to end up in the evening are based not only on the weather or how ambitious or unambitious I feel in the morning before departure, but also on what restaurant might be luring me on.

When making up my personal walking guide for a trip (see chapter 9), one of the most important factors I consider is not just *if* there is a restaurant in a particular town or village—though that's obviously important—but also what quality of food that restaurant might offer. Before I leave home I search the guidebooks and travel articles for recommendations. Then, when a restaurant in a particular town somewhere along my route specially appeals, it's not unusual for me, even days ahead, to adjust my pace so that one evening or another I end up there.

Your priorities are possibly different from mine, but even if gnawing on a frog's leg is something you'd prefer not to think about much less do, all but the truly taste-impaired will find eating in France to be one of the great joys of traveling there. The French consider time spent at table meaningful in a way that is foreign to many Anglo-Saxons, who too often dismiss mealtime as wasted time. In France even a humble pizzeria will serve the elements of the most modest meal — pâté, pizza, green salad, flan — slowly in succession and not in a hodgepodge all at once And no matter how humble the place, at least a carafe of wine, an accepted and expected part of any meal in France, will be available. Whatever else happens, you will dine.

Most of those restaurants grand enough to take reservations will book a table only once during the evening because it is assumed that you will take your time, perhaps a great deal of time, to enjoy what is prepared for you. French restaurants seldom presume to "turn" a table. Doing so might rush the first party or make the next party wait, which would certainly destroy the leisurely mood that is so integral to the French dining experience. This is the same relaxed perspective— amazing to most Americans—that allows anyone sitting in a French café nursing a single coffee or beer to linger for the better part of an afternoon at a prime table, undisturbed by hovering waiters anxious for another sale and a bigger tip. Aside from the generally high quality of the cuisine itself, it is, then, this considerate and relaxed attitude, the rule at bistrot and temple of *haute cuisine* alike, that makes eating out in France such a pleasure.

Those of you who have spent time in France and are familiar with most of the dining options will find

Eating frogs' legs is a long, sensuous process. First, it's finger food. And the legs themselves are so small—notice the pile of tiny bones—that the diner, never feeling that the last bite was enough, always ends up wanting more.

repetitive much of the information that follows. You may, however, find useful some details about certain types of eating establishments—specifically *tables d'hôtes* in *gîtes* and *chambres d'hôtes*—with which you may not be familiar if you have previously traveled only by car.

Breakfast

Though there certainly are delightful exceptions, breakfast in France is frequently a mediocre affair. More often than you might expect, it consists of nothing more than an expensive pastiche of slightly stale bread, leaden croissants, foil-wrapped butter, little plastic packets of jam and, if you're "lucky," canned juice, all served in a spartan, smoky and perhaps even windowless breakfast room of your hotel. Even the coffee, though it may look fresh-made in its small pot, is sometimes powdered. When you consider what five dollars will buy in a village diner at home and how good and reasonably priced French lunches and dinners can be, this meal, at 30 to 45 FF per person, is overpriced. Those who prefer a large meal to start the day will find that French breakfasts don't *break* the fast, they merely *crack* it. But if your habitual breakfast at home consists of only a quick cup of coffee with toast, you will not, I suppose, find inadequate the quantity of what you are served in France. Only its sometimes pedestrian quality will disappoint.

To be fair, the first meal of the day has never seemed very important to the French. They actually seem puzzled by our ability to consume, so soon after getting out of bed, bacon and eggs or—horrors!—biscuits and gravy. More logical for them is the slow start, followed, at least up until about thirty years ago, by a *casse-croûte* (break crust), a second breakfast eaten midmorning that included cold meat, cheese, bread and wine. Today only those who do hard physical work eat a *casse-croûte*. But since you too, one could say, are working hard, you should not feel at all guilty if you stop at a café or along the trail at 10 AM to eat a little something—say, half a baguette slathered with a hundred grams of pâté washed down with a big slug of red!

Interestingly, it is at both ends of the economic scale, in the *gîtes d'étape* on the bottom and in the hotels associated with France's finest restaurants at the top, where the walker may find the best breakfasts and the best value. *Gîtes,* because they cater to hungry, active people, frequently serve, for about 25 FF, ham, cheese and soft-boiled eggs in addition to the usual bread. And, because those plastic packets of fruit preserves are not just annoying but also relatively expensive on a per-serving basis, the jam or jelly usually comes from a more economical (and tasty) store-bought jar or, to save even more money, is homemade. Breakfast in a *gîte* is honest, filling and good.

In contrast, a breakfast at a hotel associated with one of France's best restaurants can be much, much more than just good. A sybaritic delight, breakfast here—taken on a tray in bed of course—is full of surprises, absolutely delicious and, despite its 100 FF plus price, an experience not to be missed. House-made jams, pastries still warm from the oven, fresh orange juice, thin slices of salty prosciutto, a perfect soft-boiled egg wrapped carefully in a little towel...it goes on and on.

You are not required to take breakfast in your hotel. If you prefer instead to go to a café down the block you are free to do so. It can be marginally less expensive to take a *grande crême* (somewhat analogous to café latte) with a couple of croissants or an order of *pain-beurre-confiture* (bread-butter-jam) at the counter or on the terrace of some busy café, and it is often much more pleasant. But if you do so, be sure to peruse your hotel bill for breakfast charges when you check out. Because it's convenient, most guests *do* take breakfast in-house, and it is often assumed by the management that you have as well.

In a *chambre d'hôtes* you will, in the evening, negotiate the time for breakfast the next morning. In a *gîte d'étape* the communal affair is offered, generally for about an hour, starting at 7 or 7:30. Up and at 'em and all that. In hotels breakfast is usually served from 7 or 7:30 until 9 or 10.

Years ago many French hotels included breakfast in the price of a room but now almost all charge extra. Remember, though, that the price of breakfast is *always* included in the room price at *chambres d'hôtes*. True to their name in translation, they are bed *and* breakfasts.

Picnics

As often as possible when I'm on the trail, I buy bread, meat, cheese, fruit and wine sometime during the morning and then, around noon, choose a pleasant, shaded spot to eat a leisurely picnic.

Buying the ingredients for a picnic does involve a bit of planning. Before you set out from your lodging in the morning, you must examine that day's route on your map and determine whether or not you will pass through a town where a picnic could be bought sometime before noon. If not, you should buy your picnic in the town where you have spent the night. The individual stores where you will do your shopping—the bakeries, the butcher shops and the grocery stores—close promptly at noon and do not open again until two hours later. If you don't plan ahead, you may end up with only a sandwich from some café or, if you will be passing through no town or village, not even that.

You will almost certainly at one time or another during your walk encounter another French institution where the ingredients of a good picnic can be had: the open-air market.

On a sunny day nothing satisfies like a picnic followed by a nap.

Almost all towns in France with more than a few thousand inhabitants and many even smaller host such a market once each week. If you are lucky enough to stay in a town the night before market day, you will awake surprised at the sudden bustle in what, the night before, had been a somnolent village. Overnight parked cars will have disappeared from the central square to be replaced in the morning by neat rows of silver-sided trucks and vans, some of which open from the side to reveal a shop counter. Awnings and umbrellas sprout over long folding tables that are used for display. By eight o'clock the town is alive as everyone, men and women alike, emerges from the houses in town and from nearby farms to shop for clothes, food and even "antiques."

For your picnic you can choose from an array of products like cheese, bread, sausage, ham, paté, fruit and wine, which often arrive directly from (or with) the producer. But even if you buy nothing, the interaction of phlegmatic villager with ebullient vendor, the expert haggling by stubborn housewives and the lively, sometimes raucous café scene are all worth an extra hour before you set off for your day on the trail. Don't hurry out of town on market day.

Open-air markets are worth a visit even if you don't buy the ingredients for a picnic.

Lunch

Traditionally in France the main meal was taken at midday, but today, with most of the population living an urban rather than rural lifestyle, that tradition is fading. It makes sense to eat a large, two-hour meal at noon if you will return afterward to the fields to prune vines or to wrestle a plow behind a horse. But the French have realized that to eat such a meal and then drive a taxi or draw up architectural plans during the rest of the working day is an unhealthful and soporific combination. Many people in France, not nearly as physically active as their peasant antecedents, are eating less and are eating the majority of what they do eat in the evening.

Though I prefer to picnic at midday when I walk, there are those cold and damp days when a hot meal can be both restorative and satisfying. My problem is that when I consume a large meal with wine in the middle of the day and then settle in afterward with an espresso, it can be not just a little bit difficult for me to get back on the trail and keep going with any determination once I get there. Even though I fit the active profile and could justify eating a big meal at noon, doing so still makes me think afterward more of bed and a nap than trail and walking.

If you do choose to eat a prepared meal at midday, you can, of course, eat a long lunch in a fancy restaurant, but when I decide to abandon the out-of-doors and eat in a warm room, I try to find a simple meal of the type still served in a few country cafés. Normally, of course, cafés do not serve meals; if they serve food at all, most limit their offerings to such items as packaged slices of pizza hot out of the microwave and cold sandwiches. Cafés are, first and foremost, drinking establishments and, secondarily, informal social clubs for the regulars. But sometimes, particularly in isolated villages with no real restaurant nearby, a café will also serve a reasonably priced lunch for the people (usually men) who come to the area each day from other villages to labor in the forests or fields. To return home at noon would be a hardship for these men, and brown-bagging is definitely not the French way, so the café fills a void by serving a simple, hearty *plat du jour* (daily special). If you arrive at the one of these cafés soon after noon and there is enough food to go around, you are quite welcome to join this group.

At these meals the diners sit together at long tables where the food is served not family style but on separate plates to each customer. Such a set meal, with little or no choice offered, might consist of a quarter of a liter of red or white wine, a first course like *assiette anglaise* (cold meats, sausages and patés), a main course like *coq au vin* or slices of roast pork with new potatoes, green salad, a portion of cheese and a dessert of flan or slice of tarte. The cost: a modest 40 to 60 FF. Portions are more than adequate, and to say that the atmosphere is convivial would be an understatement. Even if you speak French well, much of the banter—jokes, plays on words, in-the-know kidding—is incomprehensible, but the laughter is infectious. Your fellow

diners work and eat lunch together every weekday, and by joining them, you get a privileged peek into their lives.

The French Sunday lunch

The tradition of the large noon meal may be fading, but at least a seventh part of it survives, indeed thrives, in the French people's continued dedication to lunch on Sunday. This is a large, festive meal celebrated with family members and as many friends as possible, most often at home but frequently in a restaurant. Sunday in France has always been a time for gathering and feasting, and that has changed hardly at all.

The walker will notice a quickening rhythm in the villages on Sunday. The bakery, the butcher shop and the grocery are all open in the morning and busier than usual. Long lines form at the pastry shops, where the waiting shoppers fidget, impatient to pick up the cakes, puddings or *tartes* they have preordered and paid for during the week. By midmorning the cafés are crowded with men taking an *apéritif.* Between eleven and twelve o'clock the pace becomes almost frantic. You can sense the urgency, the anticipation; then when it comes, the usual noon shutdown is abrupt after all the activity. This is a real shutdown because many of the food shops, having been open all day Saturday and until noon on Sunday, will not reopen until Tuesday. Even some of the cafés close, usually for just a few hours to allow the proprietors to have *their* Sunday lunch.

But at noon on Sunday the restaurants come to life. People from the surrounding towns and cities as well

as the locals have planned ahead, have made reservations, and now they arrive in their cars, which spill friends, uncles, cousins, aunts, laughing children and excited dogs. By one o'clock on Sunday most good restaurants in France are busy, the food flowing from the kitchens, the corks popping in the crowded dining room. It's all very festive. On any other day of the week most of these restaurants would welcome the walker into their empty dining rooms at midday as a prodigal but on Sunday they display *complet* (full) signs in the window.

Unfortunately for the foot traveler who keeps to his normal routine and walks all day Sunday, many restaurants close after serving a long, busy Sunday lunch. In a small village with both the one restaurant and the one grocery shuttered, a walker may not find anything to eat at the end of the day. To avoid this situation and because I admire the tradition, my usual strategy is to join the celebration. On Friday or Saturday I research a restaurant and a hotel a good half day's walk away from my Saturday hotel and phone ahead to reserve both a room and a table for Sunday. Then, by starting early Sunday morning, I can walk for three to five hours, drop my pack, take a shower at the hotel and subsequently, as late as one-thirty, sit down in the restaurant to participate in that civilized ritual, French Sunday lunch. I would add one warning: *do* get a hotel room, for even if you aren't a wine drinker, walking is difficult at best after a three-hour lunch.

How can you expect to govern a country that has 246 kinds of cheese?
– Charles deGaulle, *Newsweek*, 1 October 1962

There are some exceptions to the Sunday let's-have-a-fête custom. Many city restaurants, which depend on a steady stream of business clients on weekdays, close on Sunday because they cannot afford to take any other day off. Paris is a gastronomic desert on Sunday. Also, a scattering of the very best restaurants all over France, full at all times anyway, close on Sunday by preference because, so the snide say, the chefs consider the clients they get then—families with children, normal people out for a treat—to be amateurs, neophyte Visigoths tracking manure and straw into gastronomic heaven.

Dinner

When planning each day's walk, the person on foot must take care to arrive in a town with both a place to sleep *and* a place to eat. As I pointed out in the last chapter, the choices for lodging are not limited to hotels; *gîtes d'étape* and *chambres d'hôtes* can be attractive alternatives. Similarly, the hungry wanderer does not necessarily need to find a restaurant at his destination; at least some *gîtes* and *chambres d'hôtes* also serve food to their guests.

Gîte d'étape: Not every *gîte d'étape* serves meals, but those that do are a wonderful bargain. If my experience has been typical, you will for no more than 60 FF enjoy a good multicourse meal, which will often include carafes of local wine, various hors-d'oeuvre—ham, sausages and vegetable salads—followed by a main course—some sort of stew or *daube*, cooked vegetables and copious starch—and, to finish, cheeses accompanied by a dessert or fruit. Meals in a *gîte d'étape* are always filling and sometimes excellent. I still salivate when I recall one such meal my wife and I consumed on a warm spring evening at the gîte in Vitrolles, which I described in the last chapter. With the rays of the June sun still streaming through the windows, we ate earthy

When you eat at the table d'hôte in a gîte you will sit down with and have the opportunity to talk to walkers from France and other European countries.

homemade dry sausage with a mustardy celery-root salad, perfectly roasted quail, a bitter *mesclun* salad, wedges of local goat and sheep's milk cheese, and a *reinette* apple baked with raisins, all washed down with a generous quantity of fruity rosé wine. Bliss. No other meal could have been better or more satisfying after that afternoon's hot, steep climb up from the valley floor.

Snacks

While you're walking it's likely that you'll build up an appetite that won't be satisfied by three squares a day. The first line of defense is a crusty sandwich from a café.

A better option if you're in the south is a slice of thin-crust pizza cooked on the truck in a wood-fired oven.

The last resort is the pastry shop. *Tuiles. Palmiers.* Mmmm.

Bon appétit!

Like the accommodations, meals are communal in a *gîte*. Everyone sits down together at whatever time has been announced, usually 7:30 or 8 PM, early by French standards but practical since most of the guests have exercised all day and will retire early.

The food is prepared by the proprietor, who, with spouse and children, will often eat dinner with the guests. Seated at the table with them, you are eating French family food, which is rarely gourmet but which is almost always balanced, copious and good in a non-commercial, honest and straightforward way. While the platters of food are passed family style around the long wooden table, there is a great deal of talk about trails, routes and, as the individuals get to know one another, home, business, politics, family...life. The mood is friendly, the group often polyglot. There is no better way to get to know the French than to plunge into the elbow-to-elbow friendliness of a *gîte d'étape*.

The *gîtes d'étape* that offer food are indicated in the *Gîtes d'étape et séjour* guide (see chapter 9) with a (TH) *table d'hôtes* (host's table) symbol. In that same guide you may also find a *demi-pension* (half-pension) price. This price includes breakfast, dinner and your bed for the night. But *demi-pension* seldom means extra savings since it's typically the sum of the individual prices for each. Even so, totals in the 130 to 210 FF per person range, all included, remain a great bargain.

Remember that *gîtes d'étape*, even in the off-season, can fill up, so it's a good idea to phone ahead to reserve a place. And because *gîtes* are situated in tiny villages or isolated farmhouses far from sources of supply, it is important to let the proprietor know in advance that you wish to eat too.

Gîtes that do not offer food are often in a village that supports a restaurant where the hungry walker can go in the evening to eat. If this is the case, the *Gîtes d'étape et séjour* guide will usually note that fact. In rare instances, however, you may be left to your own resources in an isolated *gîte d'étape* with only an improvised communal kitchen with a two-burner stove, four small battered aluminum pots and five other people who are pushing in to prepare their own soups or pastas. If I were ever faced with this prospect (not yet), I think that I would prefer to avoid the kitchen altogether and eat a cold picnic.

As mentioned in the previous chapter, *gîtes d'étape* do not take credit cards or travelers' checks. Be prepared to pay cash.

Chambres d'hôtes: Only one in eight *chambres d'hôtes* serves meals, but when you eat in a *chambre d'hôtes,* the experience mirrors the experience of staying in a *chambre d'hôtes.* Just as you are sharing a roof with a French family, the food you are served is the same that they eat, but just as your room and even your entryway are private, you are not asked to sit down to eat the meal at the same table with the family. Instead, they will take their meal around the kitchen table while you and any other guests sit down in what was once their dining room. The experience here is altogether more private—more French! And it is certainly less *sympa*, less fun, though perhaps also less demanding than that which you might have in a *gîte d'étape.*

Mealtimes are set by your host, frequently at 7:30 PM if there are children in the household. Though most meals in a *chambre d'hôtes* do not differ significantly from the meals served in a *gîte*, the cost is generally slightly higher, averaging around 80 FF per person. For this still reasonable price you will be served soup or hors d'oeuvre, a main course—a chop, a roast or stew, cooked vegetables and a starch—sometimes followed by a salad and always cheese and dessert. A carafe of wine is often included in the dinner price, but when it's not, modestly priced wine is available.

As I pointed out in the chapter on lodging, the styles of the *chambres d'hôtes* vary widely. The dining experience you will have will mirror that variety. In a modest farmhouse, for 50 FF per person you might sit on benches at a long wooden table and share a family-style meal with any other guests who might also be staying there that evening. At the other end of the scale are the grand establishments, where for as much as 200 FF per person, you and your party, seated at separate tables as in a restaurant, will be served an ambitious and elaborate meal. Only people staying at a *chambres d'hôtes* are permitted to eat there; since such establishments have at a maximum six guest rooms, you will share the meal with at most eight or twelve

Bread

An important component of any meal or picnic in France is the bread.

During the Second World War, the bread in France, so I have been told, was bad, full of weevils and made from dark, unrefined flour or worse. Once the war was over, a backlash developed that took the curious form—to us today—of making all bread as white as possible. Refined and bleached flour made into white-white loaves was what the public wanted, and it really didn't seem to matter what the bread tasted like so long as it was the right color. Beginning in the late 1940s and extending into 1980s, the typical French loaf was as bland and as light as any bread an American at that time might have used to make a peanut butter and jelly sandwich.

But in the 1970s there was a mini revolution in France led by a publicity-savvy baker in Paris named Poilâne. He made bread that tasted good and he made that bread not from just bleached white flour; aside from *baguettes* with taste, he made *pain complet* (whole wheat bread), *pain de seigle* (rye bread), *pain de compagne* (country bread from unbleached flour) and *pain au levain* (a very long-rise bread made using the sourdough principle).

It has taken years for Poilâne's methods to spread, but French breads are now almost back on track. The San Franciscan may still on occasion miss his Acme and the New Yorker his Tom Cat, but today the bread in France is often better than good and worthy of a smear of superb Normandy sweet butter.

other people when all the rooms are occupied. These other guests will not necessarily be walkers or even *sportifs*. Most who stay at *chambres d'hôtes* arrive by car.

The *Chambres et Tables d'hôtes* guide is published by the same organization that publishes the *Gîtes d'étape et de séjour* guide, and the symbol in the listing indicating that meals are served in any particular establishment, ⒯⒣, is the same for both. When no meals are offered, the text in the *Chambres d'hôtes* guide usually specifies, in meters or kilometers, the distance to the nearest restaurant. It will also be noted if kitchen facilities are available to guests. Because *chambres d'hôtes* are run much more casually than hotels and because they have so few rooms, it is always prudent to call ahead to reserve and, if food is served, to indicate that you also wish to dine there.

The family running the *chambres d'hôtes* will be unequipped to take a credit card and will be unwilling to deal with travelers' checks. Cash in French francs or, starting in 1999, euros is the medium of exchange.

Pizzerias, crêperies and restaurants: An American may find it strange that I have lumped pizzerias with restaurants, but what French pizzerias serve has little to do with the usual cheese-laden "the works" pie served in the United States. First, pizzas in France are small affairs with at most four ingredients on a thin crust and are the product not of a gas-fired "pizza oven" but of a classic wood-fired oven built of brick in the Italian style. Most important, though, pizza is only one item on a longer menu of first courses, main courses, salads and desserts, all of which are served by the establishment slowly in courses by a waitperson to the customer who is seated at a table. In other words, pizzerias in France *are* restaurants, more casual and cheaper than their grander cousins but restaurants none the less, and most of what can be said about restaurants applies equally well to pizzerias. You can order a complete meal at any sit-down pizzeria, and there is no obligation to order a pizza when you do. The walker on a tight budget will find pizzerias reliable and reasonable.

Crêperies, like pizzerias, are simple, modestly priced restaurants that specialize in one item—*crêpes* or thin pancakes. Again, the menu usually lists many items, so there is no obligation to eat *crêpes* when dining in a crêperie, though a delicious apple pancake, sprinkled with coarse sugar and redolent of calvados, may be hard to resist for dessert.

We all have the stereotype of a great French restaurant in our heads. Perhaps it's a picture of Victorian Maxim's plucked whole from the movie *Gigi* or a table at the prow of the Tour d'Argent in Paris, with its magnificent view of the Notre Dame cathedral. Monuments to grandeur such as these do still exist, particularly in Paris and other large cities, but the walker deals on a day-to-day basis with a much less fancy but still remarkable brand of restaurant: the modest establishment in small villages throughout France that serves good, uncomplicated food to both the locals and to travelers passing through.

Most towns here in the United States with a population under one thousand (and many much larger than that) have no restaurant at all, not even a café serving eggs, burgers and sandwiches, but in France it is not unusual at all for a village of that size to have at least one decent restaurant serving both lunch and dinner six or seven days a week and, if, as is often the case, the establishment is part of a hotel, a continental breakfast as well. The number of such restaurants and associated hotels is vast, and it is their ubiquity that makes it possible to walk relatively short distances and then stop for the evening.

But, as I have hinted, there is more.

As described at the beginning of this chapter, the majority of the restaurants in the small villages serve basic, wholesome food. But if you are a first-time traveler in France, what will surprise and delight is the fact that some of the very best, most renowned restaurants are also found in these villages. The automobile, a good system of four-lane autoroutes, the compactness of the country and the high density of the population have made it possible for any ambitious chef who, say, takes over his family's restaurant in a small village, to make a critical and financial success of a sophisticated establishment if he or (rarely, even today) she has the talent and is willing to work very hard. The French dining public takes food seriously and will drive quite

Looking over the menu is always an enjoyable exercise. Lacking the reality of the food, anticipatory fantasy can make every item seem innovative and delicious.

long distances by car to patronize *any* good restaurant. You, however, have only to walk. Extraordinary restaurants literally dot the landscape in France, and if you are at all lucky, your path is sure to pass by one or more such establishments where, happily, you will be as welcome as the customers arriving in their Peugeots and Mercedes.

Most restaurants in France arrange their menu entries in à la carte form—more or less extensive lists of first courses, fish courses, main courses, cheese and desserts, with each item priced separately. When you add up the separate prices for each course, a traditional French meal can be quite expensive. These same restaurants, however, almost always offer, in addition to the *carte*, one or more *menus* that propose set meals,

Franc–dollar conversion

$1 = 5 FF	then 100 FF = $20
$1 = 5.5 FF	then 100 FF = $18
$1 = 6 FF	then 100 FF = $16
$1 = 6.5 FF	then 100 FF = $15
$1 = 7 FF	then 100 FF = $14

France on Foot

complete from first course through dessert. The dishes that make up the set menus are usually drawn from the à la carte menu, but the price is *much* more reasonable than if each were ordered separately. The variety of dishes offered the diner who orders a set menu is limited or nonexistent, but the price, if the items themselves appeal, makes the lack of choice worthwhile. Often, too, the most appealing and therefore the most popular and often-ordered dishes are included on a set menu, making the choice of this alternative easier.

At a simple restaurant the cost of a set menu starts around 60 FF, and often this price will be advertised on a chalk board outside to attract the budget-minded. Inside, the same restaurant is likely to offer in addition to the 60 FF menu a whole list of more extensive and expensive set menus—80, 100 and 120 FF—to tempt the customer to spend more. Prices in a restaurant in a government ☆☆ hotel will vary greatly, depending on the place's reputation as well as the ambition and ego of its owner, but menu prices at such places usually range from 90 FF per person for the least expensive menu to 250 FF for the most expensive menu. At the top of the scale is the *menu gastronomique* or tasting menu offered by the most ambitious restaurants. These

By law menu prices are posted outside all restaurants. As a result, you should never be surprised by what is charged.

menus usually consist of six, eight or even ten small courses, which are meant to show off both the freshest of the season's ingredients and the skill of the chef. In France's best restaurants these tasting menus can be inventive masterpieces, superb in every way, but they can also cost 700 FF or more per person!

The range—50 to 700 FF— is large, but no matter how high your bill, you will have only yourself to blame if you are surprised by the expense; by law, all eating establishments in France *must* post their menus with prices outside the restaurant next to the entrance so

that prospective diners will know before they enter what is offered and how much they will have to pay for it. A happy result of this law is that the walker arriving in a town with many restaurants can window shop, can walk from restaurant to restaurant and peruse the menus before deciding where to dine.

Outside the largest cities like Paris, Lyon or Nice, where in at least one place or another a hungry person can eat at any time, restaurants in France serve dinner between 7:30 and 10 PM with "normal" seating times tending toward 7:30 to 8:30 at an unassuming restaurant in a rural village and shifting toward the later hours, 8:30 to 10, as the size of the town and/or the sophistication of the restaurant increases. Almost all French restaurants open at 7:30, but if you show up at an elegant establishment at that time, you may find that during the first hour of your meal you are dining alone in a quiet, otherwise empty room.

Menu prices in France always include both the tax and the tip, so leaving extra money for the wait staff is not required, though an extra two to five percent of your bill in cash (to assure that it goes directly into your waiter's and not the proprietor's pocket) is customary and appropriate if you have received good service.

Visa, Mastercard and, to a lesser extent, American Express and Diners Club cards are welcome at all but some very small restaurants. The majority of European diners appear to pay their bills with debit cards, using when they do so a clever cordless phone devise that is brought to the table by the waiterperson to process the cards and punch in personal access numbers. So far, I have not been able to use my ATM card in French restaurants but I do expect this to change as the digital revolution continues to sweep over the world.

Wine prices

Anyone who orders French wine with any frequency in American restaurants may be quite surprised to find that the same wine in a French restaurant may cost more than it does at home. In other words, a very good Beaujolais Morgon from a producer like Lapierre may cost $24 in a restaurant at home and be listed for the equivalent of $28 in a French restaurant. Same vintage, same bottling, just more expensive in the country where it's made than in a country an ocean away.

Something's wrong.

It's evident from the reasonable prices charged for good wines in French wine shops that French restaurant owners pay lower wholesale prices for French wine than do American restaurant owners, so the conclusion can only be that French *restaurateurs* mark up their wine prices much more than their American counterparts. And if you investigate the situation as I did, you'll find this to be true. It turns out that the French mark up their wine three and one-half to as much as five times the wholesale price, while in the United States two to two and one-half times wholesale is considered fair and reasonable by the trade.

But before we condemn the French *restaurateur* to the appropriate ring in Dante's hell, we should remember that the restaurant business is extremely competitive in France and that, while a French diner is looking for quality, he or she is also looking for good value. Consequently, food prices and particularly set menu prices are low considering how good and plentiful the food is; to attract customers most French restaurants operate on a much slimmer margin vis-à-vis their menu prices than their American counterparts.

Once when I had the opportunity to ask a French owner-chef directly about the high prices charged for wine, his answer began with an embarrassed mumble that included the words "necessary," "difficult" and "taxes." Finally, though, he admitted that the prices charged for wine make up for the low menu prices and added that, in some extreme cases, wine sales supply all of some restaurants' profit. High prices charged for wine, then, help keep the system solvent.

Eating is touch carried to the bitter end.
– Samuel Butler

If you are knowledgeable about and a lover of good wine, my suggestion is to bite the bullet whenever it seems appropriate. You're on vacation. Go ahead, order a good wine, taking care to choose a producer or vintage you would be unlikely to find in a store or restaurant at home. If you can afford it, the experience is not one you can duplicate elsewhere. On the other hand, if you are just a casual wine drinker or if you are a wine lover with a limited number of francs, then I suggest you stay with the carafe or house wines, which,

though they also may have been marked up a great deal, have started from such a low wholesale price that they are still inexpensive by our standards. Besides, with some meals there is absolutely no better liquid accompaniment than a carafe of fruity, down-the-hatch Côtes du Rhône.

A caution

You should not go to France expecting every meal to be a masterpiece. Though I would say that the average level of French restaurants is far superior to that of restaurants in the United States, that fact does not mean that you cannot be served a meal prepared with a can opener in a *gîte*, a tasteless mix of peas and carrots in a modest bistrot or even a too salty fish preparation in one of France's best restaurants. The famous restaurant that you have looked forward to for days can turn out to be inspired, each dish a surprising and delicious combination of extremely fresh ingredients that is so good it redefines the way you look at food. But another restaurant, just as highly touted, might be tired and stuck in a rut, the once-innovative menu now the product of a much-too-conservative owner and a bored group of *sous-chefs* who have cooked the same dishes for so long that they have forgotten what the food is supposed to taste like.

But it's perhaps comforting to remember that if on some rare occasion you have a very bad dining experience—a really disastrous meal when you had every right to expect better—after your trip, it is likely to be even more memorable, even more likely to be the subject of an exaggerated tale than any of your more frequent (and therefore more ordinary) superb feasts. It's the extremes in life that stick in our mind long after the everyday has faded from memory.

Sunday lunch with the soccer team

Eating lunch with a soccer team is, I fervently hope, a once-in-a-lifetime experience.

One Sunday morning in May, my wife and I were walking east near St-Rémy-de-Provence toward Cavaillon, a small city famous all over France for the

perfumed charentais melons raised nearby on the alluvial soil of the Durance river flood plain. We were hurrying. This was only our third day in France and only our second day on the trail, and earlier that morning a trace of residual jet lag had kept us in bed later than we had planned, delaying our start.

A few years previous there had been a large forest fire to the south and east along what normally would have been our route, the GR 6, so instead of walking through miles of blackened landscape, we had opted to strike off cross-country to Cavaillon using our detailed IGN blue map as a guide. There we would spend the night, rejoining the GR 6 the next day, Monday, on the far side of town. We were hurrying in hopes of reaching Cavaillon by one o'clock, an hour when we still might be able to find a good restaurant where we could relax over a traditional French Sunday lunch.

But it appeared that the lunch was not to be. Our late start, the roughness and sometimes the obscurity of the nonofficial trail, our tiredness on this our second day of walking coupled with the unseasonal heat and humidity conspired to slow our pace so that thirty minutes after twelve found us walking past scattered suburban cottages on the wrong side of the Durance River, still a full four kilometers outside of town.

We rested. There was no hurry. We would souper *(eat an evening meal), not* déjeuner *(eat a midday meal). Tall cottonwood trees along the river threw pools of cooling shade and the air smelled of slow water and stones. After our rest we strolled, more relaxed now that there was no reason to hurry.*

But then we spotted up ahead a country restaurant in the trees next to the river, and once we reached the large, sprawling clapboard building itself, we stepped onto the porch to look at the menu. The items listed were not extraordinary, but then neither were the prices. There was the muffled buzz of a crowd inside. Perhaps all those people—there were *a lot of cars—meant that the food was good? I turned then to a woman who had been standing back in the deeper shade of the porch, smoking a cigarette.*

"Pardon," I said, "can you tell me if one will eat well here?"

Facing page:
France is full of fine restaurants, from the simple to the luxurious, that will welcome the person on foot as warmly as the person arriving in an automobile.

She hesitated just a moment before answering. "Oh, yes. The food is very good. You will eat well here." I thanked her as she stubbed out her cigarette. Opening the door to go back inside, she turned to add, "And there's another reason to eat here as well. The patronne *is very nice. You will like her." A breath of cool, air-conditioned air wafted out as she closed the door behind her. The recommendation and the air decided it. We went in.*

Of course the woman on the porch was herself the patronne, *the owner, and it was she who graciously stowed our packs near the front desk and then showed us to our table at the front of the simply decorated, almost full dining room. Curiously, the restaurant and its windows faced the street, not the river. The smell of food, a mix of steamed carrots and cinnamon that reminded me of Morocco, was in the air.*

"I'm putting you here," she said as she handed us our menus, "as far away from them as I can. They're a bit noisy, but they mean no harm. I hope you won't be disturbed."

Them was a group of about twenty men seated at a long banquet table at the back of the restaurant. The folding plastic doors between the main dining room where we were seated and their room were half open to allow some natural light from the front to illuminate their table. There were no windows or, for that matter, decorations in that spartan back room, and the light from the tacky plastic ceiling fixtures was barely adequate. The men, dimly lit, were eating their main courses, and at that moment the festive hum of their laughter and conversation added a pleasant note to the quiet in our dining room. Two waitresses, apparently the whole of the wait staff, were rushing about, grim and harried as they alone served the thirty diners in front and the twenty men in the back. It was finally madame *herself who came to our table to take our order. As we discussed the choices, I remarked to her that she was right, the* patronne *was indeed* sympathique. *She laughed.*

I can't remember what our first courses were, perhaps because just as they were served a large tray with at least six tall carafes of red wine arrived at the banquet table, and the men, having polished off their main courses and the forest of carafes already on the table,

*roared their approval. The waitress carrying the wine
jumped back as soon as she set the tray down, spoke
sharply to the laughing men in front of her and then
walked away without bothering to pour. Pinches? Pats?
It was startling how quickly the volume went up as the
men began toasting with their refilled glasses. Someone
started the chorus of a drinking song and they all joined
lustily, "...DU BON VIN !"*

*No one in our dining room seemed surprised by the
noise; apparently, it had been as bad earlier before the
men got their main courses. We had arrived just as they
had begun the serious business of eating, just, that is, as
the eye of the hurricane passed overhead. Now, however, the storm had returned and some diners in the
front room were definitely not amused.*

*One older man at the table next to ours rose abruptly,
threw his napkin with a flourish onto his plate of half-
eaten chicken, stalked out into the entry hall and then
quickly returned to escort his wife away from the table.
As she left, she expressed her indignation, and I took
that opportunity to ask who or what the group was?
"Une équipe du foot," she answered, her scorn vocal as
she spat out the word "foot," a solid word-cum-expletive
that hit the ear with a clunk. The men were members of
a soccer team, and it seemed apparent to me that they
were boisterously celebrating their victory in a game
played that morning. More people left and madame
spoke quietly to the group, asking them to quiet down.
The sniggering calm lasted little more than a minute.*

*By the time we had finished our main course—I re-
member only the overcooked carrots—just ten diners
remained in the front room while the soccer team in
back had taken to drinking cognac from the bottle.
Faith and I were completely distracted as we stared
fascinated at the increasingly raucous group, which
was having a great deal of fun but was, at the same
time, out of control and drunk to the man. One thing
was different though. It did not seem that the men were
thumbing their noses at us—at all the stuffy people in
the rest of the dining room—as a group like this elsewhere might. There was no us-them animus. Instead,
they were completely self-absorbed, intent only on one
thing: having a good time. Their behavior was innocent,
not malicious, and as a result, it was hard to be too
critical. Nevertheless, I continued to stare. I had never,*

in all my time in France, seen anything like this. It was like watching a ship sink or a house burn. You couldn't take your eyes away.

At last, after two of the younger men had given mumbled speeches while standing on their chairs and after the cheers for whatever it was they said had died down, all the men stood up and waded obliviously through our room out into the hall. They were leaving.

One of the older men detached himself from the others and went table to table, jovially apologizing to the few diners left in the dining room for the ruckus they had made. When he got us, I said, "Congratulations."

"Pardon?" He seemed confused and was asking me to repeat what I had said.

"Congratulations," I said again. "You must have won." Again, he didn't seem to understand, and I wondered if somehow my French was wrong. "The game. This morning," I said, hoping to clarify.

"Ah, the game. Yes... But, this morning? Non, monsieur, *it is this afternoon that we play." Then, understanding, he roared with laughter. "We're going out* now *to play." He swept his hand toward the back room. "C'est normal, monsieur, all this was the preparation, not the celebration!"*

As he chuckled his way out the door, I translated for Faith what he had said.

Startled, all she could say was, "Well, good luck to them."

Then, though it's probably not politically correct to say so today, we both started to giggle as images of the match-to-be formed in our heads. Finally, as we described to each other imaginary events from that drunken game, we began to laugh out loud.

Madame, *who was clearing coffee cups and dessert plates from an empty table nearby, looked up, concerned when she heard us guffaw. But perceiving immediately that we, unlike so many others that day, were not upset, she shook her head ruefully in an almost motherly gesture of resignation and then, joining us, grinned broadly.*

Guidebooks
Finding meals & beds

Throughout this book I have stressed that your walk in France needn't operate on a fixed schedule and that spontaneity and impulsiveness not only *can* be but *should* be a part of your stroll through the countryside.

But your ability to be flexible will depend largely on the information you gather before you set out concerning the availability of restaurants and the various types of lodging—*gîtes, chambres d'hôtes* and hotels—along the route you propose to walk. However unplanned your itinerary or even your day on the trail may be, you *must* know that at the end of that day a bed and a meal will be at your destination. You will not have the option of picking up and leaving for the next town as you would if you were in a car.

The guidebooks you should buy

Compiling the necessary information means using guidebooks, and there are four I consider essential: the red *Michelin Hôtels-Restaurants*, the *Logis de France*, the *Chambres et Tables d'hôtes* and the *Gîtes d'étape & de séjour*. A new, updated edition of each of these appears in the spring of every year, and, while you won't miss a great deal except current pricing if you use a one-year-old guide, changes do take place so it's best to use the most current version. Each of the guides I recommend has its strengths and weaknesses, but

Other French guidebooks have tried over the years to dethrone it, notably GaultMilau, which ranks second in sales. Yet Michelin *remains the unrivaled arbiter of France's restaurant scene—largely for credibility reasons.*
— Stewart Toy,
The Wine Spectator,
30 November 1996

taken together, they cover thoroughly a wide range of eating and sleeping establishments in France.

I can hear the screams now, *But they're all in French!*

That's true, but these are organized listings, not passages of text, and all the necessary information is represented by names, symbols and numbers that anyone can understand. Armed with the instructions in English that each guide includes, you will find these books—once you have mastered the various organizing principles—easy to use.

I recommend that you use French instead of English guides because, unfortunately, the books available in English—*Fodor, Lonely Planet, Birnbaum, Rough Guides, Sawday's Guide to French Bed & Breakfasts* and the rest—are not nearly as inclusive or up to date. Those guidebooks serve the English-speaking visitor who travels by car or train quite well, but your walk will take you to small towns and villages off the beaten tourist track, and the guides in English have no reason much less the space to include these obscure locations unless some truly wonderful facility—a renowned restaurant or a particularly fine hotel—is there. The walker needs detail, which is only available from the up-to-date and comprehensive guidebooks published in French.

The guidebook you should carry

As I have hinted throughout this book, you should not carry the actual guidebooks with you when you walk in France. There are several reasons not to do this, but just one should suffice to convince you that to do so would be unwise: the four restaurant and lodging guides together weigh five and one-quarter pounds!

Do not carry the original guides with you to France.

Their weight, should *not* be used as some sort of masochistic ballast in your pack. Instead, you should extract—at home before departure—all the information in the various guides that is pertinent to your chosen route and then arrange that information into a format usable on the trail. To be succinct, I want you to assemble your *own* guidebook. Even an absurdly elaborate self-compiled guide (for instance, one with information on local wines and history made by some obsessive person like myself) weighs only half a pound. Beats the hell out of five and one-quarter.

In the rest of this chapter, I will first give you an overview of the strengths and weaknesses of each of the four guides along with some hints on how to understand and use the information in them. After that I will discuss briefly other sources of information before I tell you how to obtain the guides. Then—finally!—I will explain how to use all the many pounds of books to make your own small, lightweight extract that you will carry on the trail.

Restaurant and hotel criticism in France

French critics of the hospitality industry are a strange breed. While most of their counterparts working for newspapers, magazines and guidebooks here in the United States go to great lengths to hide their identity—by avoiding photographers who might publish their picture, by regularly using aliases when making reservations and by sometimes resorting to disguises when dining out—few in France operate anonymously. Some even seek the spotlight to such an extent that they became media stars, easily recognizable to chefs, hotel owners and the general public. The indefatigable Messrs Gault and Milau, guidebook publishers who inspected and then wrote the reviews for the hotels and restaurants they rated as the best, hosted at the same time their own national television program!

Restaurant criticism in France is particularly suspect. No restaurant reviewer in the United States who values his or her reputation would accept a free meal from any establishment that might become the subject of a published review, but in France—and, to be fair, all over Europe—such largesse on the part of restaurants is commonplace. Some restaurant reviewers not only accept free meals, they expect them.

The scenario goes like this. The critic is recognized, seated at the best table, the kitchen is alerted and then the specialties rain down. *You must try this Champagne we just found... This is a new preparation of pheasant, just a little something I cooked up today... The foie gras is so good, I thought you would enjoy it...* And at the end of this specially prepared feast the critic does not ask for a bill, nor is one presented. It's a very cozy—too cozy—relationship.

To be fair, restaurant critics in France claim that their reviews are not colored by the special treatment they receive. Negative reviews do get published in French books, newspapers and magazines, but anyone reading such a review is left to wonder whether it's the result of a bad meal or payback for a not sufficiently lavish freebie. While there are certainly many critics (the majority, no doubt) with integrity who write honestly despite what we on this side of the Atlantic might call bribery, appearances alone are enough to cast doubt on published hotel or restaurant recommendations.

The *Michelin Hôtels-Restaurants* guide

Any except those published by Michelin, that is.

The tire company prides itself on the integrity of its big red book, the *Michelin Hôtels-Restaurants* guide, which it has published almost continuously for one hundred years. The book is produced in Paris by Bernard Naegellen, who assigns his staff of approximately eighteen anonymous inspectors to stay in hotels and eat in restaurants; only Naegellen himself is anything like a public figure and even he remains unphotographed and as unknown as he can manage.

Michelin inspectors pay for every room they stay in and for every meal they eat and are regularly transferred by Naegellen from area to area to avoid even the chance of becoming familiar to the restaurants and hotels they test. And any business that advertises the fact that they are listed in the *Michelin* is immediately deleted from the next edition of the guide.

This is integrity with a capital I. The *Michelin* guide is the most respected and feared by *hôteliers* and *restaurateurs*, and the French public knows and appreciates that fact. They trust *Michelin*. You can too.

Michelin is the one French guidebook that is familiar to many Americans. Here in the United States it is known as the red guide—red to distinguish it from the many green *Michelin Tourist Guidebooks* that detail the history and sights of the various regions. In over twelve hundred pages the red guide lists the most

The *Michelin Hôtels-Restaurants or red guide has been published for one hundred years.*

hotels and the most restaurants in the most places in France of any of the guidebooks. It is also the *Michelin* that, with the new edition each March, awards one, two and three stars for culinary excellence to a small, select group of restaurants.

Michelin is justly famous for the stars it awards, but another less-well-known feature of the guide is its listing of restaurants that, to quote the guide itself, "offer good value for money and serve carefully prepared meals." Such places are marked on the maps in the guidebook with a red tire-man symbol and in the text as "**Repas**" (meal, always in red) and are often worth seeking out for the good and copious food they serve at a reasonable price.

Using *Michelin*

It's best to read this section with your *Michelin Hôtels-Restaurants* in hand. The italicized text that follows is detailed practical information about the guidebook that will be useful to those who are currently making their own guide. Those not doing so at this moment can skip ahead to the end of this section. Come back to the italicized text when you're actually planning the specifics of your trip.

The Michelin, Hôtels-Restaurants *guide is easy to use and understand. Open the book to any page and you will see very little text; almost all of the information is conveyed by symbols, numbers and the proper names of streets, cities or towns. Turn to the front of the book where you will find clear instructions in English that explain the price listings and the almost intuitive symbols. If you take the trouble to fully understand the symbols and abbreviations, you can glean a surprising amount of information from each of the entries in the body of the book.*

And looking up one of those entries in the Michelin *is as easy as looking up a word in the dictionary, since every village, town or city with a hotel or restaurant mentioned in the guide is listed alphabetically. There are no confusing sections or divisions.*

And as you can see, if the name of a town appears, then its entry will be followed by the details about the one or

---

Restaurant Stars

I sometimes hear people boast that while they were in France they ate in a four- or five-star restaurant, and the pride with which they tell their story makes it clear that they believe that they ate in not just one of France's fanciest restaurants, but also in one of France's best restaurants. But many organizations use stars to classify restaurants, not always with the same criteria or even intentions in mind.

The government tourist bureaucracy, for one, classifies restaurants in the same way that they classify their hotels—on a scale of one to five stars—and, since these rankings can be used in advertising, they cause the most confusion. Contrary to the expectations of most tourists, the government's stars are not based on the quality of the food, but rather solely on the amenities, the fanciness of the restaurant or its lack. The government, being prudent, doesn't dare jump into the viper pit of quality judgments—the pâté at Chez Jo is tastier than the pâté at Chez Michel—but as a result it's possible that a restaurant, full of crystal, fine linen and with a spectacular view over the Mediterranean, might gain a four- or five-star rating from the government yet serve mediocre or even bad food. Unfortunately government stars have nothing to do with the quality of the food.

But a guide like *Michelin* does base its judgements and star awards on the quality of the cuisine. And, while the government ranks with its one to five stars every restaurant in France, in 1998 *Michelin* saw fit to dole out only 405 single stars, 70 two stars and just 21 three stars. *Michelin,* unlike the government, is selective.

---

more restaurants or hotels located there. But if you can't find the name of a village you're looking for in the guide, then there are either no hotels or restaurants at all in the town or, almost as likely, no hotels or restaurants that the Michelin finds worthy of listing.

Turn to the two sets of maps that follow the instructions section. The first set locates in a general way towns with tranquil hotels. The second set shows the towns and cities with starred restaurants and restaurants that offer good food for a reasonable amount of money. If one of your goals when walking is to eat in some of France's best restaurants, this map will alert you to any that may lie on or near your route.

Other useful maps are included in the guide. As you have undoubtedly noticed by now, street maps for most major towns and all cities are a part of the listings. Also, two pages of the book's instructions in English are devoted to an explanation of "local maps" that appear here and there in the body of the book.

Turn to this explanation and you'll see that these maps highlight the area within a half-hour drive (twenty to thirty miles) of the featured city. They show every red-guide-listed town and village that rates any mention for a restaurant or hotel within—and usually well beyond—that limit. If a town is pictured on one of these maps, that fact is signalled in its listings by a highlight in blue type of the name of the town or city with the map. Look up the village of Fuissé. When you do, you will see that the city of Macon—in the list of towns with their distances from Fuissé just below the heading—is highlighted in blue, and when you turn to Macon you will see that Fuissé along with a host of other towns in the region are indeed included on Macon's "local map." Perusing the red guide, it appears that over three-quarters of the towns included in the Michelin are mapped in this way. You will find these "local maps" to be very useful as you carry out your prewalk research. If only Michelin mapped all of France as thoroughly.

And this is the one criticism I have of the Michelin guide. It does not include comprehensive maps detailing the location of all the villages, towns and cities in France that it lists. Admittedly, this guide does include many places, so many, in fact, that pages of maps would be required to show every entry. But other guides *with almost as many listings do manage to publish just such a map. The omission here makes it much more time consuming for you to gather information about which places along your route do and do not have* Michelin *restaurants or hotels.*

While planning your trip you will not be searching your guidebook for just one particular town whose name is known—easy when everything is listed alphabetically as it is here—but, rather, you will be trying to find which of the many, many places along your route are or are not listed. Lacking a map, anyone doing such research (you) is left with the tedious task of looking up, one by one, each and every likely prospect along the way.

One other map can make this task easier. The Michelin touring maps do underline in red all villages, towns and cities mentioned in the red guide but, since these maps are not updated every year, the reliability of the under-lines quickly becomes suspect. Don't mistake what I'm saying. The red underlines are helpful, and you will find them a handy tool when researching your walk in the Michelin, *but the underlines should also be considered potentially incomplete and somewhat unreliable unless the map has been republished within the past year.*

Prices for Michelin-*listed hotels and restaurants range from the stratospheric to the reasonable.*

Government star ratings for the listed hotels correspond to the number of towers in the house-castle symbol placed in the margin to introduce each facility. Similar-ly, the government star ratings for the listed restaurants (strictly for the amenities and not *for the quality of the food) are indicated by the number, from one to five, of crossed forks in the margin before the restaurant's name.*

Of the guides I recommend the red guide is the most useful . But over the years the quality level of the establishments it includes has crept upward so that now it includes fewer basic hotels and fewer simple restaurants than in the past. This ascent of the stand-ards is natural and understandable since the general level of the amenities offered by the restaurants and, particularly, by the hotels in France has also risen. But in practical terms for the walker the upgrading means

Guidebook glossary

For those unfamiliar with the French language, this short glossary should explain those few abbreviations, words and phrases used in the various guidebooks but not always explained in the English-language instructions.

avec ch. or avec chambres	◆ with rooms (usually associated with a restaurant listing)
sans rest. or sans restaurant	◆ without a restaurant
repas	◆ meal (usually followed by prices)
dim. or dimanche	◆ Sunday
lun. or lundi	◆ Monday
mar. or mardi	◆ Tuesday
merc. or mercredi	◆ Wednesday
jeudi	◆ Thursday
ven. or vend. or vendredi	◆ Friday
sam. or samedi	◆ Saturday
midi	◆ midday, lunchtime
déj. or déjeuner	◆ lunch
soir	◆ evening, dinnertime
dîner	◆ dinner
prévenir	◆ to notify, to reserve ahead (used as admonition)
dim. et fêtes prévenir	◆ reserve ahead on Sundays and holidays
fermé	◆ closed
sauf	◆ except
fériés or fêtes	◆ holidays
Fermé dim. soir et lundi sauf fêtes	◆ Closed Sunday evening and Monday except holidays
hs. or hors de saison	◆ out of season
vac. or vacances	◆ vacations, vacation time
vac. scol. or vacances scolaires	◆ school vacations
Fermé début mars à mi-avr., vac. scol. mai, ven. soir et sam. midi hs.	◆ Closed from the first of March to mid-April, school vacation in May and on Friday evening and Saturday noon out of season

that fewer of the listings will now be found in remote villages where a charming but old and somewhat out-of-date hotel-restaurant may survive unchanged from the 1950s.

Michelin may be the best of the guides, but its list of establishments does need some augmentation from another guide that includes places at the cheaper, more modest end of the spectrum.

The *Logis de France* guide

The *Guide des hôtels-restaurants Logis de France* is the book that fills the gap on the budget end of the price scale. Though some of its listings are duplicates of those in the *Michelin,* many are unique and these tend to be those that are missing from the *Michelin*—the older restaurants and hotels located in remote areas. These less than grand places, ignored or even rejected by *Michelin*, are important to the person on foot because they can, as you plan your trip, fill in gaps in the string of hotel-restaurants along your chosen route

The niche of the *Logis* guidebook may be modest hotels, but walkers who use this practical guide need not worry that they will be staying in *bad* hotels. The *Logis* standards, though different from *Michelin's*, nevertheless assure that any listed hotel will be clean and at the minimum, reasonably comfortable. In fact, have found most of their hotels to be charming and *very* comfortable.

Using the *Logis* guide

Again, the reader will best understand the following with a *Logis* guidebook in hand. What follows is practical how-to-use-it information. You can skip to the end of the italicized text if you are not now in the process of planning your trip.

The Logis *guide with its useful map*

Because Logis *guide includes a folding map that locates all listings, it is simplicity itself to use.*

Let's say, for example, that you are planning to walk along the GR 21 on the Normandy coast from Dieppe to Etretat. Look for the town of Etretat on the map. You will find that it does happen to have a listing, but if it didn't, you would then try Dieppe or other towns along your route until you found one that was listed. Turn to the page given on the map for the Seine–Maritime Département where Etretat is located. Here you will find a map showing Dieppe and Etretat as well as the seven other towns in between that also have Logis *hotels. Detailed listings for each facility, arranged alphabetically, follow the map.*

If you were planning a longer trip along the coast from, say, Calais to Etretat you would use the page numbers in the green arrows along the margins of the Seine–Maritime map to find the maps for the adjoining départements and subsequently the individual entries for the towns highlighted on those maps. That same information is of course plainly visible on the large folding map. It's easy to see, then, that once you locate one listed town along your route it's a simple matter to find them all.

Turn to the front part of the book. There, as in the Michelin, *you'll find complete instructions in English for using the guide, along with a detailed explanation of the various symbols. Again, place names, symbols and numbers convey all the information except the days, if any, when the establishment will be closed.*

The word logis *means lodging in French, so it is quite understandable that among the criteria for inclusion in a guide named* Logis de France *is that the establishment be, first of all, a hotel. But luckily for the walker, almost all* Logis *hotels also house a restaurant; those rare ones that don't serve food are indicated not only by a lack of a listed price for meals but also by a crossed-out knife and fork in the margin preceding the hotel's name. Look at the hotel listings. Government star classifications for each are indicated by the insertion of no stars to, in theory, five stars immediately following the name of the establishment.* Logis *hotels being what they are, I have been unable to find anywhere in the guide a hotel with more than three stars after its name.*

As I stated earlier, a few Logis *hotels are fancy and expensive establishments, but the vast majority are more basic, simple and, on average, quite a bit less expensive than the hotels* Michelin *lists.*

The *Chambres & Tables d'hôtes* guide

After the *Michelin,* the *Chambres & Tables d'hôtes* is the most important guidebook you will purchase. Unless you are walking in a heavily populated area that is absolutely peppered with hotels, you will, even if you would prefer to stay exclusively in hotels, probably be forced by circumstances to stay at least once or twice in one of these French bed-and-breakfasts sometime during your walk. And for those on a restricted budget or even for those people who can afford hotels at any time but prefer more casual and idiosyncratic lodging, this guide is an absolute necessity.

Seven thousand establishments with over twenty-one thousand rooms are listed in the 1998 *Chambres et Tables d'hôte* guide, and none are in large cities. There are no bed-and-breakfasts in Paris, Lille, Brest, Lyon,

Strasbourg, Grenoble, Bordeaux, Carcasonne, Nice or Marseille, a fact that makes their number all the more significant to the person on foot because it means that all seven thousand of these bed-and-breakfasts are located in the small villages and towns where the walker is more likely to end up at the end of a day on the trail.

Using the bed-and-breakfast guide

Again, the information in italics that follows is of interest primarily to those, guide in hand, who are in the process of putting together their own guidebook. Other readers can skip to the next section.

Open the Chambres & Tables d'hôtes *guide, and near the beginning, you will find ninety pages of départemental maps that detail the location of every town or village where a* chambre d'hôte *is located. These maps make it very easy to find all the towns along your route with one or more bed-and-breakfasts.*

Again, taking our hypothetical trip from Dieppe to Etretat, look for Etretat on the appropriate section of the Seine–Maritime map. It isn't there (in 1998), meaning that there's no bed-and-breakfast in Etretat, but Dieppe is on the map as are about twelve other towns on or near the GR 21 between Etretat and Dieppe. To find the listing for Dieppe, turn to the alphabetical list of towns located after the maps but before the main body of text. Turn to the page number you'll find there for Dieppe. This will bring you to the Dieppe listing as well as to the listings—nearby in the same section—for all the other chambres d'hôtes *between Dieppe and Etretat in the Seine–Maritime Département. Unlike the* Michelin, *every entry described on the approximately nine hundred pages of listings is mapped. As a result, locating every* chambres d'hôtes *on or near your route is simplicity itself.*

Looking at the actual Dieppe listing, you will immediately notice that, unlike the Michelin *and the* Logis, *each entry in this guide contains a paragraph of text in French. Don't panic. While this narrative includes interesting information about the site, building and amenities, the essential information—price, fanciness, telephone number, address and whether or not meals*

are served—is still clearly conveyed using symbols and other easily understood conventions, which are carefully explained in two pages of instructions in English at the front of the guide. And even if you speak no French, you should be able to glean a little information from the French text, peppered as it is with easily understood words and phrases like anglais parlé *and* restaurant à 100 metres. *But even if you find written French about as understandable as hieroglyphics, you will still find that* all the *basic information you need is easy to retrieve.*

The *Gîtes d'étape & de séjour* guide

The *Gîtes d'étape & séjour* guide is published by Gîtes de France, the same organization that publishes the *Chambres & Tables d'hôtes* guide. The *gîte* guide is a hybrid, including both *gîtes d'étape* and *gîtes de séjour*. The latter are establishments with amenities similar to those found in *gîtes d'étape*—dormitories—but unlike those establishments they seldom accept overnight guests. *Gîtes de séjour* prefer instead to house hikers and other *sportifs* for longer stays, a three-day weekend as a minimum and preferably an entire week. *Gîtes de séjour* are therefore the perfect solution for the day walker on a restricted budget. This guide contains about 1400 listings, the majority of which are *gîtes d'étape*, not *gîtes de séjour*.

Above and below are two publications, the Chambre d'hôtes *and the* Gîtes *guidebooks, from the organization Maison des Gîtes de France. New editions of each are issued every year in March.*

Using the *Gîtes* guide

Again, the italicized text is for those who are actively assembling a personal guidebook.

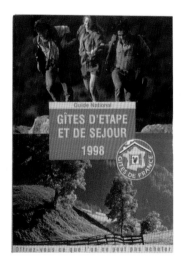

Unlike the Chambres & Tables d'hôtes *guide,* Gîtes d'étape & de séjour *does not contain* département *maps at the beginning that can be used to pinpoint the location of the various* gîtes. *Instead, all the listings are grouped by* département, *and every* département *appears in alphabetical order with, happily, no intervening regional grouping to confuse the matter. It's simply the Ain to the Val–d'Oise. Once you know the names of the* départements *you will cross on foot, it's a simple matter of turning to the proper sections of the book to find which towns in those* départements *have* gîtes d'étape. *And by this time, having worked your way through the other guides, you should already be familiar with the names of the* départements *you will cross.*

Find the section for the Seine–Maritime Département. At the beginning of that listing you will see a map of the département. *It shows the locations of the* GR *trails and all the* gîtes *including two along our hypothetical route from Dieppe to Etretat. Some of the maps of other* départements *also include the location of a few (but far from all)* chambres d'hôte *and* Logis *hotels as well. The text mimics the* chambre d'hôte *guidebook in that it uses the same symbols, layout and even paragraph of text to accompany each entry. At the front of the book you'll find explanations in English of the symbols and abbreviations used.*

Other guidebooks

GaultMillau: *GaultMilau* is the best known of the two other major guidebooks beside *Michelin* that actually attempt to rate restaurants according to their quality. While *GaultMillau* might be helpful to the person planning a walk, particularly someone who speaks and reads French well, I do not consider it a necessary purchase. First of all, it contains fewer listings than the *Michelin*, and those it does include are predominately in bigger cities and towns where the walker is less likely to go. Equally important, it is considered by many people to be less reliable. To top it all off, most of its restaurants and hotels are likely to be duplicates of those already listed in the *Michelin*. The strong point of the *GaultMillau* is its French text that describes, sometimes in flowery (some say snooty and tiresome) detail, the strengths and weaknesses of each restaurant and each hotel. If you are fluent in French and a foodie, you might wish to buy *GaultMillau*. Otherwise, forget it.

Bottin Gourmand: The other major guide that attempts to grade restaurants is the less well-known *Bottin Gourmand*. Again, this is a guide full of French text that, in a more down-to-earth way than *Gault-Millau*, attempts to detail the strengths and weaknesses of certain hotels and restaurants. Most of the listings are duplicated in the *Michelin,* and if only for this reason, I recommend that you don't spend the more than thirty dollars it costs to buy and have a copy shipped to you.

Guide du Routard, Hotels & Restos de France: This book is an entirely different animal. Because it depends almost exclusively on its French language text rather than symbols to convey information, I have not included the *Routard* in the list of books you should buy, but if you read French, I heartily recommend this book as a fine source of smaller, cheaper but good out-of-the-way places to stay and eat. I personally have not had as much experience using the *Routard* as I have the other guidebooks I mention, but those restaurants and hotels it recommends and I have patronized have been, without exception, clean, comfortable, reasonably priced and, in some undefinable way, sophisticated, fun and alive places. The guide appears to target a younger clientele than other guidebooks. In consequence, there's nothing *fade* (dull and tired) about *Routard* establishments.

Other* gîtes *guides: The day walker in search of a comfortable room in a farm or in a home in a small village should also purchase *Les Nouveaux Gîtes Ruraux,* another publication of Gîtes de France. *Gîtes ruraux* (rural *gîtes*) are exactly the same type of establishment as *chambres d'hôtes,* except that *gîtes ruraux* will only accept guests for a minimum three-day weekend stay and prefer that they stay a full week or longer. (*Gîtes ruraux* are to *chambres d'hôtes* exactly as *gîtes de séjour* are to *gîtes d'étape.* That is, *Gîtes ruraux* and *gîtes de séjour* require long stays, while *chambres d'hôtes* and *gîtes d'étape*— each exactly equivalent to their counterpart in every other way—will accept overnight stays. Is it any wonder that even the French themselves get confused by the names and accompanying hair splitting?)

If you will be traveling on a restricted budget or if you will be walking in the high mountains, you might want to supplement your *Gîtes d'étape & de séjour* guide with another guide, *Gîtes d'étape Refuges, France et frontières,* which lists thity-six hundred establishments, including *gîtes* and the more primitive alpine huts called *refuges.* This very complete if somewhat difficult to use guide includes facilities all over France but is strongest in the mountains. It even lists *gîtes* and *refuges* in Switzerland, Italy and Spain that are adjacent to the French border.

FFRP trail guides: In chapter 5 I have already discussed the FFRP trail guides and the limited lodging and restaurant information they contain. While buying the appropriate guide is far from essential when you will be traveling in heavily populated areas, if you read French at all I would recommend that you buy a copy of the guide (assuming there is one) for your trail if you will be traveling in less populated areas. As I indicated earlier, a list in table format in the front of each of these books ticks off in short form the amenities available in all the towns that are on or near the GR. This list can be helpful to anyone planning a walk on that trail and specially helpful if you will traverse remote areas where accommodations and eating establishments are fewer and farther between than normal. The FFRP guide may actually give the address of a rustic hotel not listed in any other guide or even, in some rare cases, the phone number of the person on some remote farm who just might be willing to put up a tired walker.

French tourist offices: In the appendix I have listed the tourist offiices for the various French regions. Some of these organizations publish brochures listing the hotels and restaurants in their region. These lists can be particularly helpful to the person planning a walk in a sparsely populated area with few hotels in guides like *Michelin* or *Logis de France*. Tourist offices list *all* hotels, the good with the bad, and this information can be a valuable addition to what you can find elsewhere. If you or a friend speak French, the quickest way to obtain anything from these overworked offiices is to telephone directly, inquire about their brochures and then ask them to send you the relevant ones by airmail as soon as possible. You can also write, but the information might be a long time coming.

Michelin green guides: The *Michelin, Tourist Guidebooks*, the green guides, are a series of eighteen books, eleven of which (at this writing) have English-language versions. These no-nonsense guidebooks detail the history and the tourist sights of specific regions in France. They contain no hotel or restaurant listings but do contain specific and extensive information about the geography, history and sights. To become better acquainted with more than just the hotels and restaurants in the area you will visit, I suggest that you read the green guide for your region before you go.

The reading list: In addition to the above, there are many other general books in English on the history and culture of France. If you, like me, enjoy reading in advance as much as possible about the country or area you are about to visit, you will find information about some of my favorite books on France in the reading list, starting on page 213 near the end of this book.

Buying the guides and maps you need

Once you've decided to walk in France, you'll need to obtain the maps and current copies of the tour guides I have recommended so that you can begin work on your own personal guidebook. Purchasing these materials will entail some expense and may take considerable time. Plan ahead.

The expense comes from the high price of French books in general vis-à-vis prices for the same type of books published in other countries. And then we foreigners have to add shipping charges on top of that. The time caveat is caused by the fact that I have not discovered any travel or map store in the United States that carries even the majority of these maps and guides. Many regular bookstores, of course, carry the red *Michelin* guide, and some travel and map stores also carry map 903, the translated versions of the FFRP guides and the seventeen Michelin regional 1/200,000 scale regional maps. If you can't find these resources locally, there are mail-order stores here in the United States (see appendix) where they can be obtained. But apparently the rest of the French-language guides are not, as I write, even imported into the United States. When I searched a book database for them using their ISBN numbers, I came up empty-handed. To obtain three of the guidebooks, then, you must look to Britain or, in a pinch, France.

The Elstead Map Company in England is the best source I have been able to find. At this writing, their store in Surrey carried all the primary guides I have mentioned and every one of the maps (including both the Didier Richard and the Rando éditions series) you will need to plan your trip. It's easy to place an order with Elstead by FAX or, simplest of all, by phone. They take all credit cards and ship by air, so your order should arrive in under two weeks. Shipping charges will be substantial, more than half the cost of the books themselves, but the convenience and quick service seem worth the cost. This obliging shop offers a super-express service (for approximately four dollars more) that they claim will get your order to you two to three days quicker than the ordinary air service. If you're really in a hurry, they will ship via Fed-Ex.

You can also browse an abbreviated Elstead catalog online. On their website Elstead also lists links to map companies in other countries around the world including a thirty-page state by state listing for such stores in the United States.

It may seem strange that I recommend an English store when right across the Channel is the country where all the guides and maps are produced, but with one exception it's difficult to order maps or guidebooks by phone from France without going through a byzantine ritual reminiscent of earlier times when paper money—suspicious stuff!—first supplemented coins as a means of exchange. *A credit card over the phone? Impossible!* In France the FFRP store in Paris carries all the guides I recommend, but to order from their antiquated marketing arm entailed a painfully tedious and ludicrous procedure involving months of time, multiple letters, certified bank checks, etc. (In 1998 the FFRP moved to a new, more up-to-date facility; the younger members of the staff promise that procedures will change soon.) The very modern, bustling IGN store in Paris also carries all the guides, but at this writing they also seem unwilling to bother with foreigners who might telephone speaking English and offering a credit card in payment.

The one exception is the Maison des Gîtes de France, located in a brightly lit store at 59, rue Saint–Lazare in Paris' ninth arrondissement. The store is owned and run by the publishers of the *gîte* and *chambre d'hôtes* guidebooks. Many of the items stocked are targeted at the person on foot, and the management, in stark contrast to the responses I received from the other organizations, is willing to please.

But for the reader who speaks no French and even for those who do, using Elstead as your source is still the simplest and easiest way to obtain the pretrip materials you will need to plan a walking trip in France. You must use France as your source only if you want to buy FFRP guides or any of the other more obscure French-language guides I mentioned above, which are not available in England. To obtain FFRP guides, you should

Elstead	
☎	44 1252 703472
FAX	44 1252 703971
online	www.elstead.co.uk/

Gîtes de France	
☎	33 1 49.70.75.75
FAX	33 1 49.70.75.76

US mapstore list	
online	www.maptrade.org

first phone the Maison des Gîtes de France (every time I have called, the person answering was able to speak good if not completely fluent English) and ask that the current Topo-guides catalog be air mailed to you. This publication is free, and the store will send it without charge. The catalog lists all the current FFRP trail guides, and once you've made your choice, it's an easy matter to FAX or phone in your order using your credit card. Be sure to stress that you want your order shipped by air; their usual shipping method is by ship, which takes at least a month.

Summary

The procedure, then, is this. Obtain IGN map 903 from an American travel shop. Then, once you have decided to actually go on a walk and where, obtain your red *Michelin Hôtels-Restaurants* guidebook and the relevant Michelin touring maps from a local book store or by mail order. At the same time, phone or FAX abroad to obtain *Logis de France, Chambres & Tables d'hôtes, Gîtes d'étape & de séjour* and any specialty maps that may exist for your chosen GR. If you think you might need an FFRP guide, phone the Maison des Gîtes de France to obtain a free catalog. When everything is gathered together, well in advance if possible, you are ready to extract the information you will need to make up your own lightweight guidebook.

Your "fee"

One of the negative aspects of walking in France with an adventure-travel company is the large amount of money such firms charge for a week or ten days in the countryside. While it's true that their clients usually stay in deluxe lodgings and eat well, a substantial portion of the money still goes to pay the guide's salary, to support the infrastructure of the company and to supply a profit for the owners. By walking on your own, you will avoid these costs, but as I indicated in the first chapter, you still must pay a "fee", and this will consist of the time you spend assembling your own guidebook. This task will probably take you at least four hours, and if you are planning a long walk, you may have to spend as long as ten hours. But when you consider how much adventure-travel companies would charge to guide you on your trip, this relatively small amount of time will seem a great bargain.

Making your own guidebook

Making your own guide is a process that can only
begin after you have consulted map 903 with your
traveling companions—friends, your spouse, your
significant other, your entire family, whomever—and
decided, say, that you're going to walk for twelve days
on the GR 6 from Gordes to Sisteron in the Luberon or
for four days on the GRs 7 and 76 between Dijon and
Beaune in Burgundy. To repeat, whatever route you've
chosen, the next step is to gather the four primary
guides and the relevant regional Michelin touring
maps. (You already have 903.) To avoid rushing, start
making your guide as far in advance as possible.

The process

What follows are the specific instructions for making
your own guide. If you are not now ready to start, you
can skim or skip this material and return to it later
when you're ready to begin.

*Spread out the Michelin touring map that covers the
terrain of the proposed walk. On this map you will
mark every place along your route that has a* chambre
d'hôtes, gîte, *hotel, restaurant or, as is usually the case,
an establishment that provides both food and shelter.*

*But first, to discover which villages and towns are on or
near your chosen GR, you must locate that route on the
Michelin map and then highlight it with a transparent
Magic Marker. Michelin traces out the GR paths, but
they are not marked prominently. However, with map
903 open nearby for reference, finding and highlighting
your route is not a difficult task.*

*While you're highlighting the trail, you may notice on
map 903 that there is a choice of paths along the way, a
fork in the trail that offers an alternate path to your final
destination. The GR 60 that parallels for a time the GR
6 in the Massif Central and the GRs 76 and 76A that
dart out and back to the GR 7 in Burgundy are such
trails. Be sure to highlight each alternative along your
route because you will want to research hotels and
restaurants along that trail as well. Being prepared to
take either route will postpone the decision of which one
to take until you are actually on your walk and con-*

When you compile your personal guidebook, finding and marking your route on the appropriate Michelin map is your first task. Then you must find in the guidebooks the restaurants and hotels along that route, mark them in the books with a pencil tick, bookmark them with a slip of paper and finally highlight the towns where they are located with a Magic Marker on the map. Here I am using the Michelin Atlas Routier *book rather than one of the sixteen folding maps.*

fronted with that decision. Don't eliminate choices until you have to. Allow yourself as much freedom on the trail as possible.

Once the primary GR and all possible alternates are highlighted, you can begin the task—tedious or exciting depending on your temperament—of locating in your guidebooks the hotels and restaurants that lie along or near that route.

On the map, starting with your point of departure, work your way down through the villages and towns, looking up each likely place to see if they are in the Michelin. *Many of the listings in this guide will be in towns that are already underlined on the map in red, a fact that makes the book easier to use, but I'll repeat: if your map is older you should also check other towns and villages along your route for listings that may have been added to the guidebook since the map was published.*

As you find towns with accommodations and restaurants you should bookmark with a piece of paper and mark with a pencil tick the actual listing in the guide. At the same time, highlight that town's name with a transparent marker on the map. By doing this you'll end up with not only a physical reference in the book but also a visual reference on the map that will make it clear if there are wide gaps that might require further assiduous searching or an extra long day of hiking. After Michelin *find the hotels and restaurants listed in the* Logis, Chambres d'hôtes *and* Gîtes d'étape *guides. Again, bookmark, mark with a pencil tick and highlight every entry you find. Do the same for all alternate routes.*

When searching don't confine yourself to just those towns and villages right on the GR. *Look away from the trail. I have stayed in hotels as much as four kilometers off my route and four kilometers translates to almost an inch on a Michelin touring map. As you search, the map will fill with highlights indicating the towns with hotels and restaurants, and the books, sprouting torn pieces of paper, will look as if they're being used as references for a term paper, which in a certain sense they are.*

Once you have found and marked all the restaurants and hotels along your route, you are ready to assemble your guide. You can do one of several things to transfer the information you have amassed, and the choice you make depends in part on how elaborate a guide you wish to make.

The simplest homemade guide would consist of a handwritten list of the towns arranged sequentially in the order you will pass through them, accompanied in each case by the name, price range, days of closure, number of rooms and phone number of each establishment in each town. Keyboarding this information into a computer instead of writing everything out by hand could be quicker and definitely would make arranging the material easier. This method is particularly suited for short trips that require only a limited amount of information.

But, if you will be walking for a week or more, keyboarding or copying the necessary information by hand could become tiresome. In this case I recommend that you photocopy each of the bookmarked pages in every one of the guidebooks. After you've finished this task the next step is to scissor out the relevant entries (the ones with the pencil ticks next to them) from the copies and to arrange and physically paste all those bits of paper, again sequentially town by town, onto blank pages. This method, by including the entire entry, assures you that

Once you have copied each page with a listing from each guidebook, you then must cut out those individual listings from the copies, organize all those small slips of paper and then paste them onto blank pages, which, once they're assembled, will again be run through the copier.

you'll have all *the information. It also allows you to make a more elaborate guidebook that could include whatever other information—history, copies of city maps from* Michelin, *etc—that you think might prove useful.*

Defacing an actual book by attacking it with scissors seems to me to be an extreme measure, even if that book is only a guide that will be out of date next year. But you could *avoid the copying step by cutting out the references directly from the books.* Ouch!

Either way, once you have the pages assembled, you should return to the machine where you will photocopy the pasted-up pages (double-sided, if you really want to cut down on the weight). Punch holes in the resulting copies, then collect them together in a light cardboard binder. By making a second or even third copy during the last run through the machine, you can produce guidebooks for others in your party.

Alternately, it might be possible for those readers comfortable with page-layout software to scan the relevant pages from the guidebooks into a computer, then crop and arrange the information electronically in the page-layout program before printing finished pages. This method, it seems to me, could prove to be the quickest, but a powerful computer would be needed to hold and manipulate all those images.

Whatever method you use, you'll end up with the information you need in condensed form, which means that you'll carry a guide that weighs ounces, not pounds. Your personal guidebook and, for a quick visual reference, the original Michelin map you marked up (or a color copy of the relevant portions of that map trimmed and mounted in your guidebook) will give you everything you'll need to find rooms and meals on the trail.

Making your own guidebook will be the most time-consuming trip-related task you will accomplish before you leave, but once you're on the trail in France, you'll realize that your "fee" was a great bargain. Your care and thoroughness at home will pay big dividends on the trail. If you know that along your route for any particular day there are, say, four and not just two different towns with places to stay within your walking range, then any contingency or diversion—a lazy picnic with naps, unexpected rain or a small museum so captivating you spend three hours looking over the

A carefully assembled homemade guidebook will, by showing all the options, give you maximum freedom during your walk.

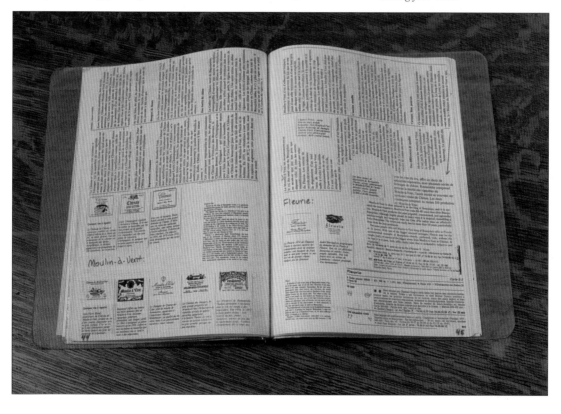

collection—will only call for an adjustment in plans, not panic. The more complete your information, the freer you will be.

I enjoy making guidebooks for my walks because as I find the establishments along the route I can begin to imagine my trip—its shape, rhythm and pace. If it turns out that I'll pass near a restaurant with *Michelin* stars, I can even then start figuring how to end up spending an evening in the town where it's located.

Some say that half the pleasure of a trip lies in the planning and anticipation. I think fifty percent is stretching it a bit, but there is still much to be said for the walks you take in your head.

Last Details
Cost, packing & travel

"But how could you afford it? Wasn't it just outrageously expensive?"

This from friends who had just returned from their first trip to France, during which they had spent four days in Paris in a "modest" $200-a-night hotel and eaten bistrot meals, none of which cost less than $120 for the two of them. At a café along the Champs Elysées they had been charged $12 for a cup of coffee and were still in shock. Listening to my wife and me discuss a recent walking trip, they found it incredible that we had spent almost three weeks in the same country where they felt in their gut they had been overcharged.

Like Tokyo, New York or Rome, a large city like Paris can be an extraordinarily expensive place to visit, in fact so much more expensive than what any small-town visitor is used to paying at home that it's easy to believe the locals are taking advantage even though the prices are, probably, only the going rate. People whose only experience of France is a stay in Paris often ask how anyone could afford to travel in such an expensive country. My answer is to point out that prices in the rural areas are lower. Just as Albany or Hartford are considerably cheaper than New York City, towns like Tours or Colmar are much less costly than Paris.

All right, I'll be walking outside the cities where it's not so expensive, but exactly how much will this trip cost?

Take half the clothes and twice the money.
    – Rule of travel

Money

Money

If France is indicative of what will happen elsewhere, the era of the traveler's check is coming to an end.

Back in the 1950s cash—carried as traveler's checks—was about the only way to pay for anything in France unless you patronized the fanciest restaurants, hotels or shops, which just *might* accept an American Express card. Later, as VISA and Mastercard became popular and accepted everywhere, the amount of money the tourist needed in traveler's checks went down but, because portable cash was still sometimes necessary, didn't disappear. Now however, that last use for traveler's checks has, for all practical purposes, been superseded by the appearance everywhere of *points d'argent* (ATMS).

With a PIN number and your credit card or even sometimes your ATM card, you can withdraw money anytime in any town or village that in the past might have had a branch bank. Banking has definitely gone electronic in France, and it's now hard to find an actual teller outside the largest towns.

Having said all this, I have to admit that I still carry two hundred dollars in traveler's checks when I walk in France. Perhaps because I'm older, I don't trust completely the electronic manipulation of money. I find it easy to imagine a situation in which none of my credit cards work and I'm stuck in the middle of the Auvergne without cash or credit, so I carry the checks as insurance, money that I could use while I was getting the electronic mess straightened out. Needless to say, I have not cashed a traveler's check on either of my last two trips to France.

Good question, and though I'd like to give a definitive answer, I must instead weasel and respond that it all depends. And in truth, of course, it does depend. It depends on your tastes, on your budget and sometimes even on where you choose to walk.

Costs

On our last long-distance walking trip, when the franc was around five to the dollar, my wife and I spent, exclusive of air, train and bus fare, almost one hundred dollars or 500 FF a day for each of us. That was for everything on our walk, including one very expensive meal in a *Michelin* two-star restaurant, five other quite expensive meals and a not modest amount of better-than-average wine at meals and while picnicking. (We were, after all, walking through wine country.)

It's difficult to pin down what is typical. But so long as you understand that many variables can modify my estimates, the expenses for the two of us on a typical day almost anywhere in France might run as follows:

- Drinks, snacks at rest stops & pre-dinner   100 FF
- Picnic lunch with wine   70 FF
- IGN map, *Herald Tribune* newspaper   56 FF
- Restaurant, two 120 FF menus, tip   250 FF
- Wine, coffee   130 FF
- ☆☆ Hotel and breakfast   340 FF

946 FF

Of course, a more expensive meal, a fine bottle of wine, a fancier hotel or, worse, a combination of these factors (better?) could quickly add half again or more to this total, but the comfort that the above level of expenditure buys is more than adequate for us and would, I believe, satisfy most people. The hotel would not offer a pool, but the room would have a large double or, for just a bit more money, two single beds, a TV (though not the satellite hookup to CNN that you would find in a ☆☆☆ hotel) and a full modern bath. The meal at this price would include a first course, main course, cheese and dessert, and one of those courses would be a regional or house specialty like trout, salmon, lamb, duck or guinea hen. The 100 FF bottle of wine with dinner would be local or, in the north, a bottle or a large carafe of good-quality Côtes du Rhône or Beaujolais. You may have noticed that the entire cost for this day's walking adds up to less than our acquaintances' "modest" $200 Paris hotel!

Two walkers on a restricted budget could easily reduce the above figure:

♦ Water, beer and snacks at rest stops	70 FF
♦ Picnic lunch	50 FF
♦ Map	46 FF
♦ Two *table d'hôtes* dinners with wine	160 FF
♦ *Chambre d'hôtes* including breakfast	220 FF
	546 FF

Here I have omitted the wine (30 FF) with lunch, the newspaper (10FF) and have assumed that the *table d'hôtes* dinner included a quarter-liter carafe of wine for each person. Since *chambre d'hôtes* rooms are in private homes, your room here could actually be larger and more comfortable than the more expensive ☆☆ hotel in the previous accounting. It would probably lack a TV, but some French bed-and-breakfasts do have pools.

Two walkers on an extremely tight budget could reduce expenses even further:

♦ Two liters water from grocery	16 FF
♦ Picnic lunch	30 FF
♦ Map	46 FF
♦ Two *table d'hôtes* dinners with wine	100 FF
♦ Beds in *gîte d'étape* and breakfast	170 FF
	362 FF

Totals like this bring back memories of the earliest editions of Frommer's *Europe on $5 a Day*. We're not far off if you adjust for inflation. And, yes, at least in some areas, a day of walking in France for this modest amount of money is not impossible, but at the same time it might be difficult to maintain this low level of expenditure over a long period of time. *Gîtes d'étape* are more common in mountainous regions but are often few and far between elsewhere. In consequence, the frugal traveler will likely have to spend at least some nights in more expensive *chambres d'hôtes* or hotels. To be safe then, I would add 50 FF per person per day, making the minimum total for two 460 FF.

No matter what your target budget is, expenses will

Franc–dollar conversion		
$1 = 5 FF	then	100 FF = $20
$1 = 5.5 FF	then	100 FF = $18
$1 = 6 FF	then	100 FF = $16
$1 = 6.5 FF	then	100 FF = $15
$1 = 7 FF	then	100 FF = $14

vary up and down each day as you spend one night in a plain bed-and-breakfast and the next in a fancier ☆☆☆ hotel. You might eat a simple 60 FF menu featuring *boeuf bourguignon* one night and a 225 FF menu with *foie gras* the next. Also, prices for the same type of accommodation and meal vary from place to place; certain fashionable spots like the Luberon region in Provence or some towns on the Normandy coast seem to extract a premium from the traveler, a *supplément,* as it were, just for the privilege of being there. Also, as I pointed out in chapter 7, in any lodging other than a *gîte d'étape,* the single traveler will pay more for his bed on a per person basis than will each person in a couple. To quote the travel brochures, *Prices are based on double occupancy.*

During the day, everyone will walk the same path, everyone will have the same experience. Out there on the trail you could call it a socialist world where the amount of money in pocket doesn't matter. The differences come in the evening, when the tired walker chooses lodging and a meal, and the diversity in costs at that time—above and beyond the minimum I have detailed above—is seldom determined by the hard and fast requirements of a particular situation but rather, quite naturally, by individual preferences and—the ultimate triumph of capitalism—by the fatness of the walker's wallet.

How much will it cost?

What's the French for fiddle-de-dee?
— Lewis Carroll
Alice in Woderland

The answer to the question is that your walking vacation, exclusive of transportation, will cost you whatever you can afford to spend above the minimum figure of 230 FF per person per day. As I indicated earlier, my wife and I spend on average 500 FF per day per person, a budget that allows us to stay in a mix of *chambres d'hôtes,* ☆☆ and ☆☆☆ hotels. We eat and drink well most days and sometimes, when the occasion presents itself, eat and drink very well indeed. But *you* could spend half that or, by trying extremely hard, twice that amount.

What clothes should you bring?

The type and quantity of clothes I recommend you bring on your trip are based on my own and my wife's experiences and preferences; what you ultimately pack is, of course, up to you, but I do urge you to limit what you bring to an absolute minimum. I once saw an admonition in a traveler's bookstore that instructed anyone setting out on a trip to carefully lay out all the clothes he or she thinks necessary on the bed, immediately put half of them back in the closet and *then* begin to pare down the remainder. Not bad advice when you consider that everything will be carried on your back.

The list that follows may strike you as being absurdly minimal, but I assure you that everything you will *really* need is included. In fact, my daughter and her husband, who have walked in France, believe that my list includes *too many* clothes. Yes, you will have to wash some clothing in your room every evening and, yes, at the end of your trip you will probably be so sick of the clothes you wore day after day that you may never want to see them again, but, by packing only the items on the list that follows (or less), the pack you end up carrying will weigh somewhere around a reasonable and (believe me) comfortable eighteen pounds. Vary my recommendations if you absolutely must, but remember that every item you add will increase the weight on your back

One thing should be made immediately clear: normal dress in restaurants outside Paris is surprisingly casual. Even in a deluxe *Michelin* three-star located in a small town, you will see French men wearing nothing more formal than a cotton turtleneck with a sweater and women in skirts. This means that men definitely do not need to carry a sports jacket and that women can leave the tailored suit and the elaborate dress in the closet at home.

Notes on the choices

Skirts: Years ago, a woman with whom I was bicycling through rural France was, out of the blue, called a *putain* (whore) by a fat, dour Frenchman wearing an outraged look, decent black and, as many country people still did at that time, a beret. I can still picture him there by the side of the road, one hand on his cane, the other curled into a fist and raised in the air to emphasize his displeasure at the fact that my traveling companion wore Bermuda shorts, indecent and improper attire for a woman as far he was concerned. Today, with images of naked women on roadside

> ### *Learning some French*
>
> Once you're outside Paris you will find that people are very willing to help you *if* you make even a small effort to speak French. Country residents, unlike their city cousins, are tolerant, friendly and likely to go to great lengths to understand and fulfill your needs. Just learning a few phrases before you leave on your trip—*s'il vous plait, merci, bonjour, un-deux-trois-quatre...*—will pay big dividends.
>
> If you speak no French at all, I would recommend that you buy a French language tape to play at home while you prepare dinner or in the car while you commute. Even if you learn only the bare basics from the tape, you will unconsciously become habituated to the rhythm and pace of the language, making it easier to separate and understand individual French words (there are many English cognates) when you walk in France.

Packing list

Men:
- 2 pairs cotton chino pants for trail
- 1 pair wool worsted pants for "good"
- 3 long-sleeve cotton shirts: 2 for walking, 1 for "good"
- 1 cotton turtleneck
- 1 lightweight wool sweater
- 3 cotton T-shirts or undershirts
- 3 pairs undershorts
- 1 necktie
- lightweight shoes for evening wear, *or* shoe polish

Women:
- 2 pairs cotton pants *or* 1 pair pants and 1 cotton skirt for trail
- 2 cotton shirts for walking
- 1 light cotton turtleneck
- 1 lightweight "good" skirt
- 1 black scoop-neck T shirt, blouse or equivalent for evening
- 1 pair tights or pantyhose
- 1 sweater
- 2 bras
- 3 pairs underpants
- 1 pair foldable shoes for evening
- inexpensive jewelry

Both men and women:
- 1 web belt
- handkerchiefs
- 2 hats: 1 cotton, 1 straw purchased there
- 2 sets socks: 2 lightweight, 2 medium-weight hiker's
- 1 pair boots
- sunblock
- toilet articles
- light, compact, water-repellent windbreaker
- umbrella
  > *or* in flatlands
- 1 lightweight hooded poncho
  > *or* definitely in the mountains
- 1 set lightweight waterproof jacket and pants
- sarong
- picnic knife
- sunglasses
- small, lightweight flashlight
- books
- handkerchiefs
- toilet articles

Optional :
- compact, water-repellent shell pants
- wool cap, gloves for mountain walking
- shorts
- bathing suit
- camera and film
- 1 cotton or silk sleeping-bag liner (see page 124)

One per couple:
- Ziplock bag of detergent
- insect repellent

One per group:
- first-aid kit (see page 108)
- maps and homemade guidebook
- walking stick (see page 110)
- compass

billboards promoting perfume or soap, and scores of Germans and Scandinavians visiting France wearing short shorts, the *paysans* now tolerate short pants. But even so, both men and women walkers will get a better reception in rural France if they wear more conservative attire such as long pants and skirts. Many women actually prefer to walk in a skirt, which in hot weather is cooler than pants. Equally important, wearing this tentlike garment affords a woman more privacy when during the walk she finds it necessary to pee behind a bush in the woods.

Colors: As in New York, San Francisco and other large cities, a dark color—black in particular—seems to be the preferred shade for clothing. Bright colors and bold patterns are not, at least at this writing, "cool". If you want to blend in with the French, dress somberly.

Web belt: I recommend a web belt because it's not only lighter but also thinner than a leather belt. A pack's wide waist strap, when it's cinched up, can press very tightly into your hips, and a thick leather belt with its hard edges under that waist band can dig painfully into your skin. Web belts are too thin and flexible to chafe.

Sarong: In our heads Faith and I keep a list we facetiously call the "Rules of Travel," and high up on that list is the admonition: *Always bring your sarong along.* No, this is not frivolous nonsense. It's practical advice, particularly for the walker. Since carrying less weight is the important consideration, it stands to reason that if an item in your pack can serve more than one purpose, your burden will weigh less in the end. And the sarong, a light cotton cloth approximately six feet long and two and one-half feet wide for men and three and one-half feet wide for women, is a veritable chameleon, the ultimate in multi-use magic. It is, first and foremost, a bathrobe. When the only hotel in town is an older one, clean and charming but out of date with the bath down the hall from your room, the sarong serves as a handy cover to get you to the shower and back. Conversely, in luxe hotels with a swimming pool, that same sarong can supply a bit of modesty over your bikini after a dip. It's a towel and it's a light blanket. It's a garment: on a spring evening after the sun has set, it can serve as a stylish wrap or shawl for a woman on the cool walk back to the hotel from a restaurant. It is—

and this is the last use I can think of—also a service-able ground-cloth for picnics. Spread before you settle, it keeps you off the dirt and the picnic separated, at least temporarily, from the ants. As if all this were not enough to recommend the sarong, it is also light (ap-proximately eight ounces) and not at all bulky (it rolls into a tube three inches wide and eight inches long). If you don't already have a sarong, buy or make one and bring it along on your walk.

Overpants: If you get cold easily, you should consider packing the lightweight shell overpants, which I have listed as optional. Like your windbreaker, they are not worn to keep you dry but to keep you warm. Once I am walking at a good pace, my legs don't get cold even when my pants are wet so I omit the shell pants, but your metabolism may differ from mine.

Waterproof clothing: At the risk of repeating myself once too often, if you plan to walk in the French high country, I urge you to purchase and use a set of water-proof outerwear. Hypothermia is a life-threatening condition, which, to put it mildly, you will want to avoid on your vacation.

Men's shoes: Because I have found over the years that carrying a light pack with the minimum of clothing greatly increases my enjoyment on the trail, I have become a fanatic about eliminating unnecessary items before I leave. One of the heaviest items a man can carry is an extra pair of shoes for evening wear. Men's dress shoes, even loafers, are heavy and bulky—the lightest pair weighs one and one quarter pounds, to me an unacceptable percentage of the eighteen to twenty pounds I normally carry. I have tried various solutions to this problem—fancy soleless black leather slippers for one—but the best solution I have found so far is to carry no extra shoes at all and to wear instead my leather-toed walking boots in the evening. To make the boots presentable in even the most formal restaurant I carry a small plastic bottle of shoe polish and a cloth in a Ziploc bag to buff up the toes before dinner. Women who want to avoid the punk look should probably not appear in boots and skirt, but fortunately women's dress shoes are light and not bulky, if well chosen.

The wash: Obviously, with so few sets of underwear and socks, one set must be washed every day. In the hotel room after walking, I wear my socks and under-wear right into the shower, shed them and wash them there, stomping and scrubbing with my feet as I rinse off soap and shampoo from my body. Of course, if this seems a bit bizarre (as it does to Faith, who laughs and shakes her head), you may want to choose another method. If you take a day of rest, most towns large enough to have a commercial center have self-service laundries.

More caveats

Weight: The byword is *light* because it means less weight in your pack *and* quick-drying of those items that you will need to wash in the hotel sink (or shower). For example, bluejeans are heavy, bulky and slow to dry when wet, but chino pants and skirts, made from a material like poplin or madras, are just the opposite—light, compact and quick to dry. Similarly, cotton seersucker shirts are more practical on a walking trip than are shirts made of a material like corduroy.

Warmth out of doors, when you need it, should not come from just one or two heavier items of clothing but from layers of clothing that can be removed or added as needed. On a hot day you may walk in a T-shirt and shirt. When the days are colder, you add layers until, on the coldest day, you may put on a T-shirt, turtleneck, shirt, sweater and windbreaker. Thin layers are adjustable; a single warm piece of clothing like a down jacket is either on or off. There's no in-between.

Evening wear: Even though normal dress in country restaurants is casual, the clothing you carry for wear in the evening should look as good as possible. Casual does not mean unstylish or sloppy.

For my sojourns to a fancy restaurant I carry a pair of lightweight worsted wool pants (wonderfully wrinkle-resistant) as well as a necktie to wear with a shirt, but the tie is really an unnecessary though lightweight extra if you are carrying a turtle neck. Faith carries inexpensive costume jewelry, which she uses to em-bellish one of the permutations of skirt and black scoop-neck T-shirt she wears in the evening. As I have explained, I do not carry extra shoes for after-walk wear, but use, instead, my boots buffed up as necessary with shoe polish and a rag. Faith carries a pair of

> **Walking alone**
>
> When I was eight or nine years old, I read a book that began by describing a man who, for weeks, walked alone, unseen and unheard, through the woods and hills of Germany. The time was World War II and the hero was a spy with Leatherstocking skills, a man of stealth who was able to move carefully but quickly through the countryside gath-ering intelligence without being observed by the Nazis. The image of that man alone in the woods has remained with me throughout my life, lurking at the back of my mind as the ideal and, yes, the most exciting way to travel. But the truth of the matter is—now that I have actually had the chance over the years to travel alone on foot, by bicycle and in a car—I find traveling with-out companionship incom-plete. It lacks the necessary element, at least for me, of sharing the experience.
>
> Certainly it's possible to walk in France alone, but I feel the experience is richer if others accompany you. On the trail a companion will see things you miss, perhaps know the iden-tities of birds and flowers along the trail or have a surprising knowledge of the history of the local region. And, most im-portant, in the evening you will not have to eat alone. Instead you will have someone to talk to, someone with whom you can share the experiences of the day as well as a bottle of wine.

lightweight, slip-on flat shoes; women should avoid shoes with high heels because, aside from the unnecessary bulk and weight, they can be awkward when strolling from hotel to restaurant on cobbled streets.

Toilet articles: If you're to carry a light pack, you must pare weight from your toiletries. The principle is simple: take only enough toothpaste, only enough shampoo, only enough of anything consumable to last until the end of your walk. Carry a *small* if not *tiny* tube of toothpaste. At home before you leave, pour just enough shampoo into a plastic squeeze bottle. Rather than bring a full-size bar of soap from home, pick up and carry with you one of the small bars supplied by hotels all over Europe. Bring a stick deodorant rather than a heavier liquid roll-on. Bring creams, oils or lotions in small light plastic jars, tubes and squeeze bottles (available in specialized travel stores). Lightweight also extends to the nonconsumable items you carry. If a comb will do instead of a brush, bring the comb. If you need the brush, carry a light one.

Part of woman's toilet kit is her makeup, and the items each woman needs are obviously a personal matter. But whatever is brought should be packed whenever possible in small, light plastic jars, tubes and squeeze bottles. Bring only what you will need for the duration of your trip.

A carelessly assembled toilet kit can weigh as much as four pounds, whereas a carefully assembled one weighs less than two pounds. Mine weighs in at one pound.

Extras: It's hard to cut down on the clothes and toilet articles you bring, but it's often even harder to cut down on other items, things like books and cameras, which, if you're not careful, can make up as much as half the weight of your pack. If you want to reduce the weight you carry (and please believe me, you do), then you must cull the extras as ruthlessly as you will cut back the amount of clothing you bring.

For example, a professional photographer like my wife, Faith, will, of course, carry at least two thirty-five millimeter camera bodies, three or four lenses, twenty rolls of film and even a tripod, all of which will add at least four and perhaps as much as seven pounds to her pack. It's understandable that the professional

Facing page:
A walking vacation in France combines exercise with pleasure. You may sweat and become deliciously tired while walking through the beautiful and fascinating countryside during the day, but in the evening you will eat and drink well and, later, sleep in a comfortable bed.

considers the burden worthwhile, but do *you* really
need to carry all that equipment if selling pictures is
not the way you make your living? Wouldn't one of the
modern and lightweight automatic cameras with an
adjustable lens serve your purposes just as well? Think
about the weight difference.

Because you will be walking in rural France where few
book stores carry any English-language books (perhaps
only a hard-back edition of *The Complete Sherlock
Holmes* along with two obscure Anthony Trollope
novels in Penguin paperback), you will need to carry
with you all the reading material you will use to fill
those relaxing hours before sleep or to help pass a lazy,
rainy afternoon in the café down the street from your
hotel.

If your favorite leisure reading consists of a good murder mystery, a complex sci-fi yarn or a sentimental
romance novel, then buying lightweight paperback
books to carry on your trip will not be a problem.
However, if your tastes, like mine, also range farther
afield into nonfiction and literature, then your choices,
for *lightweight* books are more limited. To assure that
I'll have enough reading matter, months before my trip
I start collecting and setting aside books chosen not
only for their content but also for their read-to-weight
ratio. To go into my pack a book must be, ideally, over
five hundred pages long, densely printed, light *and*
interesting.

Incidentally, one of the reasons this book has been
printed on heavy, large-sized paper is to discourage you
from taking it with you on your walking trip. This is
not a trail guide; it contains only how-to information
to be used and absorbed *before* you leave. Like the
Michelin and all the other guidebooks, this book is too
heavy to carry. *Don't take it with you!*

*On a long journey even a straw
weighs heavy.*
— Spanish proverb

Extras will creep in. Perhaps you are a student of
wildflowers and want to bring a field guide to help you
identify the blooms you'll see along the trail. Or birds
are your passion, and you want to bring field glasses as
well as a guidebook. Items like this will add greatly to
your enjoyment of the trip and are certainly worth the
extra weight, but they will only fit comfortably in your
pack if you have chosen every other item with a very
sharp eye on both weight and bulk. Bring extras that

will enhance your trip but be reasonable. I know a person who, to avoid a wrenching disconnect from the world, walked with his laptop computer—five pounds four ounces plus charger—stowed away inside his pack.

Packing up

So, everything—clothes, equipment, books, toilet kit and too many other items as well—is laid out on your bed. You've read my carping about weight, but still you're indecisive. Right in front of you are all the things you know you'll need as well as many items that you feel deep down that you *may* need, and you're tempted to bring them all. Weight be damned.

I can only repeat, *resist!*

And it might help you to do so if you remember that you will be walking in civilized, modern France, not some third-world backwater where men can only get a shave by visiting outdoor barbers who wield dull straight razors. You can buy plastic razors as well as toothpaste, deodorant, shampoo, Tampax and nail polish in any French *droguerie* or *pharmacie*. Indeed, any item you may have left behind on purpose or inadvertently can be replaced easily with a simple visit to the appropriate French store.

So if there's any question in your mind about whether to bring or leave an article, *leave it.* Perhaps you will find after you start your walk that you do need that item left behind on the bed, but if that's the case, you *can* buy a substitute. However, it's more likely that after a few days on the trail you'll be looking for a cardboard box to make a package of all the superfluous items you did bring and now want to mail back home.

Stay away from heavy, bulky clothes. Be light. Take care to eliminate the ounces that quickly add up to pounds. Leave home with some extra room in your pack for small purchases along the way. Your walk will be much more enjoyable if you do.

How do you get there?

Because most flights from the United States arrive in Europe in the morning, I usually plan to skip a stay in

Paris after my arrival and push on instead to the place where I will start my walk. Staying in Paris is such a different experience from walking in the countryside that I hesitate to combine the two. Besides, I'm anxious to *walk*.

Once I have made my plane reservations and have picked out my starting point, I select a hotel there from my *Michelin* or *Logis de France*, then phone or FAX ahead to make a reservation for my first night. Even though I have only the vaguest idea where I might be staying two or three nights after my arrival, I do want to know well in advance of my departure that I will have a hotel room reserved for me on my first night in France. The run from my home on the West Coast of the United States to the village where I will start my walk crosses nine time zones and is usually an exhausting twenty-four hour marathon involving at least four changes of the plane to plane to train to bus type. Sleepy, tired and disoriented, I have found that being expected by a hotel is a comfortable way to end a very long day.

Everyone can figure out how to get to Paris, but after that the first-time visitor may have some difficulty getting to that hotel in the city or small village where the walk will start. While I won't attempt to tell you in detail how to use French public transport system— other guidebooks can do that—I will outline some strategies that will be of use to the person on foot attempting to reach the starting point of a long walk.

The major cities like Lyon, Nice, Strasbourg, Clermont-Ferrand, Marseille, Lille and Bordeaux and some small cities like Avignon, Perpignan, Brest, Grenoble–Valence and Nantes are served by air from either of the two major Paris airports. Domestic service is more frequent from the older Orly airport, but quite a number of flights also depart from Charles de Gaulle. No matter which airport you land in, your travel agent can arrange ongoing flights on the government airline or on one of the privately owned airlines that are sprouting (and fading) at a great rate.

But if the French domestic schedule doesn't mesh with your arrival time, you may want to take one of the efficient French trains or, even better, one of the superb two-hundred-fifty-kilometers-per-hour-plus *trains de grande vitesse* (trains of great speed or TGV).

While governments in the United States argue about the feasibility of running subways from our cities to the airports that serve them, France has not only constructed a branch of their efficient urban subway, the RER, from Paris to Charles de Gaulle, but it has also opened a TGV station right in the airport with direct high-speed train service to the north, the west, the southwest and the south of France. Without leaving the airport, you can actually hop a TGV for Avignon, Lille or Bordeaux right after you clear customs. Anyone arriving at Orly will have a more difficult time connecting with the TGV, since they will have to take a bus, taxi or subway to the proper train station within Paris.

Now that the TGV is operating to so many cities, few places in France are more than five hours from Paris, city center to city center. To obtain the TGV schedule and to make a reservation, you or your travel agent can call Rail Europe. This private travel agency is owned by the Swiss and French railroads. It serves as the representative in the United States and Canada for almost all the European railway companies and in particular, of course, for the French railway system, the SNCF.

If your final destination is near Paris or if the TGV does not pass anywhere near where you are going, then your remaining option is to take a conventional train from one of the Paris hub stations. Again, Rail Europe can tell you which towns have rail service, what station in Paris serves your destination and how frequently and when trains depart for that town. They will also sell you a ticket. However, if you arrive in France without a ticket, once you reach the proper station it's a simple matter to read the schedule and then purchase one. Many French ticket agents speak some English. The people in the *Information–Renseignements* booth always do.

Rail Europe	
☎	800 438-7245
Canada	800 361-7245
FAX	800 432-1329
Online	www.raileurope.com

If the starting point for your walk is served by air or rail transport, once you have completed that part of your journey you have just to find your hotel and collapse. But if your final destination is a smaller village outside of town, you still have one more lap to go, and that lap will probably be taken by *car* (a bus that serves towns and villages along a predetermined route). The bus station is called the *gare routière,* and its location is

Left luggage

I have assumed throughout this book that you will leave home, travel to the starting point of your walk, amble and then immediately travel home again. But some walkers may want to extend their holiday and doing so may involve bringing another suitcase full of clothes more suited to, say, a week in Paris. The question is, of course, where can you leave the suitcase while you walk?

In the old days the *consigne* (baggage-check area of a train station) would store suitcases for days or weeks for a minimal per-day charge. However, today metal storage lockers seem to be the rule in most train stations, and the coins used to lock one of these buys only twenty-four hours of storage. Past that limit your bag will be removed and extraordinary fees will begin to accrue. Similarly the rare manned *consigne* operates like the lockers: reasonable for twenty-four hours and outrageous after that.

An alternative is to leave the suitcase at the hotel where you start your walk. Most French hotels will store luggage for a customer, particularly if that customer makes a reservation for a room on the day when the stored items will be picked up. Also, if, while you're traveling to your starting point, you should happen to pass through a town at or close to your planned finish, you could also make a reservation at a hotel there and ask them to keep your luggage.

But short of bringing no extra suitcase at all and continuing to live out of your pack after your walk—not impractical unless you are planning to spend time in Paris—I know of no completely satisfactory solution to the problem.

marked on *Michelin* red guide city maps with—quite logically—a picture of a bus. Once you have located the *gare routière* (often near or at the train station), ask the clerk in the office which bus to take and when it will depart. The clerk will sell you the proper ticket. If the office is closed, schedules for the various private bus companies are posted outside the station building, and a ticket can be bought from the bus driver. If you are confused and if your smattering of French has abandoned you, simply repeat to other travelers the name of the village you wish to reach. Someone will undoubtedly speak some English, and even if no one does, you will be directed to the proper place to catch your bus.

Buses serving larger towns leave quite frequently, particularly early and late in the day, and all but a few express buses also serve the smaller towns along the route to that larger town. Even the most obscure village off the main roads should have at least two buses a day, one in the morning and one in the evening. However, it might prove difficult to reach a really remote place. Thus when you are planning your trip, I advise you to choose as your first destination a larger town or a village on a main highway. It will have more frequent bus service than a small isolated village.

The first day

The best cure for jet lag is exercise. So once you're in France, it's best to walk at least a short distance—not too much, never more than twelve miles and preferably less—on the first full day after your arrival. To make this possible I advise you to start out from a town with a hotel that's located about six to ten miles from the next town with a hotel. No matter how wiped out I may feel after my first night in France, I have found that I feel much better the following evening if I have walked for at least a short distance during the day. Napping and lolling about in the hotel does me no good. It simply delays the cure.

Attitude adjustment

Now that you've read how you can organize and take a walking trip in France on your own, I want to remind you of what I said in the beginning: a walking vacation in France has very little to do with a backpacking vacation in the United States. Ultimately, it is not the difference in gear and equipment but the difference in attitude that is important. The French think a little differently from the way we do, and it is their approach to life—tolerant, seldom didactic and with plenty of room for *joie de vivre*—that I urge you to consider and adopt.

At an internet address, www.urec.cnrs.fr/France/web.html, that purports to list all the online sites that originate in France, there is clickable category named *Sports et loisirs* (sports and leisure). Here displayed in alphabetical order are, the last time I looked, 354 entries, and the curious web-surfer can peruse such sites as the *Marathon de Reims, Bridge, Tour de France, Echecs* (chess), *Scoutisme français, le Gazette du surf* (ocean not electronic), *Snowboardnet* and *Benji 33*, a site that details information on *le saut a l'élastique* (bungee jumping).

These categories conjure up a good sweat, either physical or mental. But scattered like uninvited guests among these sport and leisure listings are such addresses as *le Chocolat, le Scotch malt whiskey society, Fromage de France* (cheeses of France), *le Champagne* (yes, the wine, not the region) and even *Passion cuisine—recettes de cuisine et de cocktails!* Cocktails? Cheese? Chocolate? Sports activities, leisure activities? Well, at least for the French, the answer is a very definite *"Oui!"*

When advertising for new members in a health club, the French are more likely to trumpet the quality of the cuisine in the snack bar than the quality of the equipment in the exercise room. *After all, anyone can install all those Nautilus machines, but who else has our pâté?* For the French the stomach is as important as the abs any day—balance! moderation!

Many Americans, particularly those who habitually finish their punishing morning jog by stoically eating unflavored, nonfat yogurt consecrated with wheat germ and washed down with two glasses of holy spring water, find heretical the French idea of mixing exercise with such pleasurable activities as eating a slice of pork pâté and drinking half a bottle of Beaujolais before lunch. Our pesky Puritan heritage, coupled with our tendency—admirable in some situations—to go one hundred percent all-the-way with what we do dictates a separation of pleasure from those things we deem to be "good for us." Moderation and compromise are not common American virtues, particularly when exercise is involved.

But the more relaxed, user-friendly French approach to exercise has a great deal to recommend it, particularly when you're on vacation. And by now I'm sure you realize that it is this tolerant French approach that this book advocates and champions.

To return one last time to that hypothetical back-packer, it certainly would be possible to hike in France with all the accoutrements and attitudes that the long-distance walker carries in the States—heavy pack weighed down with tent, sleeping bag and cooking gear along with an even heavier determination to avoid all things civilized. But I maintain that a mountain range in the United States and not the French country-side is the better place for such an activity. It is the backpacker attitude in particular that should not be brought to France. After all, the purpose of a visit to a foreign country is not just to see the scenery but also to interact with the people and to experience, not avoid, the culture.

If *your* ideal vacation would combine a dose of both exercise and self-indulgence, then I heartily recommend a walking holiday in France. As you know after reading this book, with a bit of preparation, you can—with your family or a few friends—plan and carry out such a trip on your own without the expensive and ultimately restrictive help of an adventure-travel company.

And if while you walk you let your whims as well as your maps guide you, if you allow yourself to be seduced by the quiet as well as the active moments, if you allow yourself a modicum of the sybaritic as well as the athletic, if, in other words, you adopt the relaxed French attitude, you will experience this intriguing country in a much more profound and much more enjoyable way than you might on a frantic, more conventional vacation dictated by fixed itineraries and inflexible schedules.

When you walk your chosen part of the vast off-road trail system, you'll be forced to take what comes at a slow pace. By doing so, you are certain to come to know France in a way that will fascinate, entertain and, ultimately, satisfy you deeply.

"Marchez, donc!"

Reading List
Personal, selective & annotated

Books about walking

Most of the books about walking in France familiar to me chronicle specific day walks and give at most only cursory information concerning long-distance walks. The three books listed below that do address point-to-point travel on foot are, unfortunately, out of print. To find them, check your library or visit the used-book stores.

Booth, Frank. *The Independent Walker's Guide to France*. Brooklyn, NY: Interlink Books, 1996.
This book details thirty-five day-walks in sixteen areas.

Hunter, Rob. *Walking in France*. 1982. Reprint, Sparkford, Yeovil, England: Oxford Illustrated Press, 1987.
A thorough guide to French long-distance walking paths. Though the detailed information is fifteen years old, much of it is still useful today. Out of print.

Hunter, Rob and David Wickers. *Classic Walks in France*. Sparkford, Yeovil, England: Oxford Illustrated Press, 1985.
Twenty long walks, each from one to three weeks in length, are outlined and described in this book. Unfortunately, it is out of print.

Lasdun, James and Pia Davis. *Walking and Eating in Tuscany and Umbria*. New York: Penguin Books USA, 1997.

While this book is about day walks in Italy, the attitude of the authors—that eating and comfort can and should be a part of any walking vacation—appealed to me immediately. The book is a fine read and tempts me to walk more than I have in Italy.

Lieberman, Marcia R. *Walking the Alpine Parks of France and Northwest Italy.* Seattle, WA: The Mountaineers, 1994.
A detailed and thorough guide for day walkers. Four of the five areas discussed are in France. Anyone wishing to day walk in the Alps should read this book.

Lipton, Chet and Carolee. *Walking Easy in the French Alps.* Oakland, CA: Gateway Books, 1995.
A book describing day walks from five towns in the French Alps.

Neillands, Robin Hunter. *Walking Through France, From the Channel to the Camargue.* 1988. Reprint, Leatherhead, Surrey, England: Ashford, Buchan & Enright, 1994.
An amusing and informative account of a walk across France in the early 1970s, a time when the trail system was much less developed than today.

Nicolson, Adam. *Long Walks in France.* New York: Harmony Books/Crown, 1983.
This literate book is my favorite of all the walking books. It describes in detail nine long walks in nine different regions. Nicolson knows France and its history well. He is a keen observer with a sharp tongue who writes beautifully. The photographs by Charlie Waite are excellent. Out of print.

History and culture

The more you read about France before you visit, the greater your appreciation and understanding will be for what you see and experience. I specially recommend Tindall's book to anyone walking the French countryside.

Carles, Emilie, as told to Robert Destanque. *A Life of Her Own, The Transformation of a Countrywoman in Twentieth-Century France.* 1977. Translated by Avriel. H. Goldberger. 1991. Reprint, New York: Penguin Books USA, 1992.

A fascinating and well-written autobiography by an intelligent and idealistic woman who, between her birth in 1900 and her death in 1979, changed from a traditional submissive housewife to a political activist. The story that this strong individual from the Alps tells revolves around the central event of her life, the First World War.

Caro, Ina. *The Road From the Past, Traveling Through History in France.* New York: Nan A. Talese/Doubleday, 1994.
Caro takes you on her own personal journey from Provence to Paris. A history book masquerading as a travelog.

Daley, Robert. *Portraits of France.* New York: Little, Brown and Company, 1991.
Daley explores France by relating in great detail specific events, each of which takes place in a different region. The stories give the reader close-up glimpses of the country and the people.

Durrell, Lawrence. *Caesar's Vast Ghost, Aspects of Provence.* New York: Arcade/Little, Brown and Company, 1990. Also published in paperback, without the photographs, as *Provence.* New York: Arcade Publishing, 1990.
Durrell concentrates his intelligence and talent on a part of France he knows intimately and likes a great deal. The hardcover edition contains evocative photographs by Harry Peccinotti.

Kaplan, Alice. *French Lessons.* Chicago: University of Chicago Press, 1993.
At its base, this book is personal in nature. But Kaplan's well-told story of her years spent learning the subtleties and quirks of the language reveals almost as much about the French as it does about her.

Osborne, Lawrence. *Paris Dreambook, An Unconventional Guide to the Splendor and Squalor of the City.* Reprint, New York: Vintage/Random House, 1992.
The seamy side of Paris in the tradition of Orwell's *Down and Out in Paris and London.* The book for those who want more than the superficial.

Gay sprightly land of mirth and social ease,
Pleas'd with thyself, whom all the world can please.
— Goldsmith, *The Traveler*

Schama, Simon. *Citizens, A Chronicle of the French Revolution.* New York: Alfred A. Knopf, 1989.

This scholarly work on the French revolution is a beautifully written, thorough and exciting account of the most important single event in French history.

Tindall, Gillian. *Celestine, Voices From a French Village*. New York, Henry Holt and Company, 1995. Tindall chronicles the changes that take place in a small French village between 1844 and 1933, the life span of the real-life heroine, Celestine. The changes were profound. The people of the area were uprooted from what can only be called medieval times and, in less than a hundred years, deposited abruptly in what is recognizably the modern world. Tindall's writing pleases as much as her information.

Food and wine

As a chef and a confirmed Francophile, I quite naturally read more than most people do about French food and wine. Though the subject may seem narrow and restricted, it nevertheless provides those who are interested with yet another wide-open window that looks in on French character and sensibilities.

Echikson, William. *Burgundy Stars, A Year in the Life of a Great French Restaurant*. New York: Little, Brown and Company, 1995.
For those fascinated by France's renowned restaurants, this is a day-by-day look into what it took for chef Bernard Loiseau, owner of the restaurant La Côte d'Or in Saulieu west of Dijon, to scratch his way up from two to three *Michelin* stars.

Liebling, A.J. *Between Meals, An Appetite for Paris*. 1959. Reprint, with a foreword by James Salter, San Francisco: North Point Press, 1986.
Even though this book was written in 1959, *Between Meals* remains the best and—at the same time—funniest treatise on French food written in English. Liebling was a sagacious and unapologetic gourmet-gourmand with a take-no-prisoners approach to eating.

Lynch, Kermit. *Adventures on the Wine Route, A Wine Buyer's Tour of France*. New York: Farrar, Straus and Giroux, 1988.
Anyone with slightest interest in French wine should read this jargon-free story of Lynch's quest for quality.

France on Foot

Lynch visits most of the major wine regions, and the tales he tells breathe life into both the wines and the people who make them.

Point, Fernand. *Ma Gastronomie.* 1969. Translated by Frank and Patricia Kulla, with a foreword by Joseph Wechsberg, Wilton, CN: Lyceum Books, 1974.
Point is the father of post-war French cuisine. Bocuse, the Troisgros brothers, Alain Chapel, as well as four other *Michelin* three-star chefs were trained in his restaurant, La Pyramide, in Vienne just south of Lyon. Though *Ma Gastronomie* is also a cookbook, the amusing tales and the penetrating comments on food and its preparation are at the heart of this idiosyncratic but delightful memoir. Out of print.

Root, Waverly. *The Food of France.* 1958. Reprint, New York: Vintage/Random House, 1977.
Anyone interested in the various regional cuisines of France should read Root's humorous gastronomic travelogue. Though almost all the recommended restaurants have disappeared, the strong opinions remain pertinent today. Out of print.

Fiction

There are too many well-known writers of fiction about France and the French to attempt to recommend them all. Balzac, Camus, Stendahl, Zola...the list could go on and on. They are familiar, and it would serve no purpose at all to list the names of their books here. But you may not know the three less well-known authors I describe below whom I hope you will also consider reading. Their writing, always intelligent and sometimes witty, appeals to me personally. I think you will like them too.

John **Berger** is an expatriate Englishman who has lived in France for over thirty years. Among his many fine works is the trilogy, *Into Their Labours,* which chronicles the years of disruption and change that the arrival of modern ways brings to a small village in the French Alps. The three books are *Pig Earth* (New York: Pantheon, 1980), *Once in Europa* (New York: Pantheon, 1987) and *Lilac and Flag* (New York: Vintage International/Random House, 1996). Berger has the uncanny ability to cut right to the emotional heart of his characters.

The second author I recommend to you is Jean **Giono**. Born in the Haute Provence town of Manosque in 1895, he championed and wrote about his natal area until his death in 1970. His writings sometimes border on the mystical, yet, paradoxically, they are always firmly anchored in the often grim and uncompromising details of the natural world. To start I recommend *The Song of the World* (1934; translated by Henri Fluchère and Geoffrey Myers; San Francisco: North Point Press, 1981). *Harvest* (1930; reprint; translated by Henri Fluchère and Geoffrey Myers; San Francisco: North Point Press, 1983) and *Joy of Man's Desiring* (1935; reprint; translated by Katharine Allen Clarke; San Francisco: North Point Press, 1980) are in the same vein. His great adventure novel *The Horseman on the Roof* (1951; reprint; translated by Jonathan Griffen; San Francisco: North Point Press, 1982) was made into a movie in 1996.

French cinematographer Marcel **Pagnol** also wrote three books, all of which have themselves been made into movies by others. The books, *My Father's Glory and My Mother's Castle, Memories of Childhood* (1960; reprint; translated by Rita Barisse with a foreword by Alice Waters; San Francisco: North Point Press, 1986), *Jean de Florette* and *Manon of the Springs* (both 1962; reprints; both in one volume; translated by W. E. van Heyningen; San Francisco: North Point Press, 1988), are superb evocations of less complicated times in southern France. Those who have seen any of Pagnol's own movies will know what to expect: poignant humor combined with profound truth.

Appendix

Sources & resources

Maps, guidebooks, equipment and travel

Below is a map which gives the key for the Michelin Carte Routière et Touristique series of maps. Numbered from 230 to 245 these sixteen maps cover all of France. They can be obtained locally or through either of the sources below.

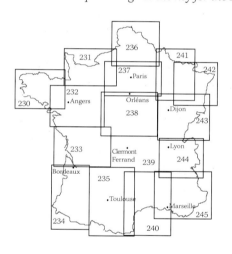

IGN Map 903 – France Grande Randonnée

Michelin France: Carte Routière et Touristique 1/200,000 regional maps

Michelin Hotels-Restaurants guidebook isbn (1998): 2-06-064089-x

If possible, buy this book and the maps at your local travel, map or bookstore. See **www.maptrade.org** for the store nearest you. If local purchase is impractical, order from either of the following sources:

Adventurous Traveler Bookstore
PO Box 1468
Williston, VT 05495
☎   800 282-3963
FAX   802 860-6776
www.adventuretraveler.com

Maplink
25 East Mason Street
Santa Barbara, CA 93101
☎   805 965-4402
FAX   800 627-7768

Guide des hôtels-restaurants Logis de France – the *Logis* guide

The walker should buy these guidebooks by phone, FAX, or mail from the Elstead Map Company in England:

Chambres & Tables d'hôtes – the bed-and-breakfast guide

Elstead Map
PO Box 52ELSTEAD
Godalming Surrey
GU8 6JJ England
☎   44 1252 703472
FAX   44 1252 703971
www.elstead.co.uk/

Gîtes d'étape & de séjour - the *gîte* guide

McCarta walking guide translations (if desired)

All but the McCarta guidebooks are also available from French sources. See below.

Topo-guides des Sentiers de Grande Randonnée - FFRP trail guides in French

Obtain a current catalog of the approximately 150 FFRP guidebooks by phoning Gîtes de France. (When telephoning from overseas *do not* dial the number 0, which I have put in parentheses. However, if you dial the number from within France, omit the country code, 33, but *do* dial the 0.)

Gîtes de France
59, rue Saint Lazare
75439 Paris
☎   33 (0)1 49 70 75 75
FAX   33 (0)1 42 81 28 53
metro: Trinité

After receiving the catalog, order the desired guides by phone or FAX. Be sure to specify that your order be shipped by air. Surface mail takes over a month. (There is a generic order form at the end of this book.) Trail guides can also be purchased in Paris at the IGN map store and at the FFRP store and headquarters:

Fédération Française de la Randonnée Pédestre
14, rue Riquet
75019 Paris
metro: Riquet

Espace IGN
107, rue La Boétie
75008, Paris
metro: Franklin Roosevelt

All of the blue maps are available (as are all the other French-language guidebooks and maps mentioned in this book) at the impressive IGN store in Paris. Blue maps are normally purchased from local newspaper and tobacco shops as you walk.

IGN 1/25,000 *série bleue* (blue maps)

Call the appropriate Regional Tourist Office listed below to request the current hotel information for that region. Stress that the information should be sent by airmail. When writing, address your correspondence to the "Comité régional de tourisme."

Regional hotel listings

Alsace
5, place de la République
67000 Strasbourg
☎ 33 (0)3 88 32 99 00

Aquitaine
21-23, rue de Grassi
33000 Bordeaux
☎ 33 (0)5 45 44 48 02

Auvergne
43, av Julien
63011 Clermont-Ferrand
☎ 33 (0)4 73 93 04 03

Bourgogne
12, bd Debrosse
21000 Dijon
☎ 33 (0)3 80 50 10 20

Bretagne
74 bis, rue de Paris
35069 Rennes Cedex
☎ 33 (0)2 99 28 44 30

Centre Val-de-Loire
9, rue de St-Pierre, Lentin
45041 Orléans Cedex 1
☎ 33 (0)2 38 54 95 42

Champagne-Ardennes
5, rue de Jéricho
51037 Châlons-sur-Marne Cedex
☎ 33 (0)3 26 64 35 92

Corsica
22, cours Grandval, BP 19
20176 Ajaccio Cedex
☎ 33 (0)4 95 51 00 22

Dauphiné (central Alps)
14, rue de la République, BP 227
38019 Grenoble
☎ 33 (0)4 76 54 34 36

Franche-Comté (Jura)
9, rue de Pontarlier
25000 Besançon
☎ 33 (0)3 81 83 50 47

Ile-de-France
73–75, rue de Cambronne
75015 Paris
☎ 33 (0)1 47 83 73 96

Languedoc-Roussillon
20, rue de la République
34000 Montpellier
☎ 33 (0)4 67 92 67 92

Limousin
27, bd de la Corderie
87000 Limoges
☎ 33 (0)5 15 45 18 80

Lorraine
1, place Gabriel-Hocquard
17036 Metz Cedex 1
☎ 33 (0)3 87 33 60 00

Midi-Pyrénées
12, rue Salambo, BP 2166
31200 Toulouse
☎ 33 (0)5 61 47 11 12

Nord, Pas-de-Calais
26, place Rihour
59800 Lille
☎ 33 (0)3 20 60 60 60

Normandie
46, av Foch
27000 Evreux
☎ 33 (0)2 32 31 05 89

Pays de la Loire (lower Loire)
Place du Commerce
44000 Nantes
☎ 33 (0)2 40 48 24 20

Picardie
11, av Albert–1er, BP 2816
80026 Amiens Cedex
☎ 33 (0)3 22 97 37 37

Poitou–Charentes
2, rue Sainte–Opportune, BP 56
86002 Poitiers Cedex
☎ 33 (0)5 49 88 38 94

Provence–Alps–Côte–d'Azur
2, rue Henri–Barbusse
13241 Marseille Cedex 01
☎ 33 (0)4 91 38 38 00

Riviera–Côte-d'Azur
55, promenade des Anglais
06000 Nice
☎ 33 (0)4 93 44 50 59

Rhône Valley
5, place de la Baleine
69005 Lyon
☎ 33 (0)4 78 42 50 04

Savoie Mont-Blanc
9, bd Wilson
73100 Aix-les-Bains
☎ 33 (0)4 19 88 23 41

Online resources about France

As the internet grows and develops, online addresses seem as ephemeral as the breeze. These sites may have already changed by the time you read this.

www.francelink.com
www.france.diplomatie.fr/
www.franceway.com/
www.urec.fr/france/webindex.cgi

Online Equipment information

General information as well as reviews of packs, boots, etc. are available at the first two websites below. At this writing I can find only three stores, REI, LL Bean and Campmor, that maintain substantial catalogs online.

www.gorp.com
www.gearfinder.com/

www.rei.com
www.llbean.com
www.campmor.com

Travel information and reservations on French railways

Rail Europe is partially owned by the French government Railway system, the SNCF.

Rail Europe:
☎   800 438-7245
Canada: 800 361-7245
FAX: 800 432-1329
www.raileurope.com

Index

A Walker's Vocabulary

On this and the next three pages I have assembled a walkers' vocabulary for those on foot who speak little or no French. It is designed to be cut out and combined into a sixteen-page booklet that can be carried on the trail in your shirt pocket. Cut along the dotted lines (*if* this is your book) and then carefully fold each of the four double pages in half. Arrange the pages in the proper order and then staple the booklet together. *Voila!*

France on Foot
la France à Pied

A walker's vocabulary

Compiled by
Bruce LeFavour

BASICS

Excuse me: pardon – par-doh_n
Hello: bonjour – bohn-jewr
Please: s'il vous plaît – seal voo play
Thank you: merci – mare-see
We're on foot: Nous sommes à pied –
    New sohm ah pee-A
You're very kind: Vous est très gentil –
    voo-zette tray jehn-tee

SOME HANDY PHRASES

Where is...? Ou est...? – oo A
How many kilometers to...?
Combien de kilometres à...? –
    comb-ee-ehn duh kee-lo-meh-tr_uh ah
Is it near here? Est-ce près d'ici? –
    Ess pray dee-see
We are lost: Nous nous sommes perdus –
    new new sohm pair-doo
We're looking for... Nous cherchons... –
    new share-shoh_n

EMERGENCIES

Help! Au secours! – oh suh-coor
Doctor: le médecin – may-duh-sah_n
Hospital: l'hôpital – oh-pee-tahl
We need a doctor: Il nous faut un médecin
    eel new foe uh_n may-duh-sah_n

1

14

NATURAL LANDMARKS

Bank of river: la rive – reeve
Beach: la plage – plahje
Cave: la grotte – grow-t
Canyon: le cañon – can-yo_n
Cliff: la falaise – fah-laze
Forest: la fôret – for-A
Glacier: le glacier – glah-see-A
Gorge: la gorge – gor-j
Hill: la colline – koe-lean
Lake: le lac – lah_c
Mountain: la montagne – moan-tyne
Oak tree: le chêne – shenn
Ocean: l'océan – oh-say-ah_n
Pass (in mountains): le col – coal
Peak (of mountain): le pic – peak
Pine tree: le pin – pah_n
Plain: la plaine – playn
Pond: l'étang – A-tahng
Ridge: la crête – kret
River: la rivière – ree-vee-air
Sea: la mer – mare
Stream: le ruisseau – roo-ee-sew
Summit: le sommet – som-may
Swamp: le marais – mah-ray
Tree: l'arbre – arb_r
Valley: la vallée – vah-lay
Waterfall: la cascade – kass-cod

EQUIPMENT

Bandage: le pansement – pahn-suh-meh_n
Boots: les bottes – boat
Laces: les lacets – lah-say
Compass: la boussole – boo-sole
Flashlight: la lampe de poche –
    lahmp duh poash
Batteries: les piles – peel
Glasses: les lunettes – loo-net
Sun glasses: lunettes de soleil –
    loo-net duh so-lay
Hat: le chapeau – shah-poe
Straw hat: chapeau de paille – ... duh pie
Knife: le couteau – koo-tow
Map: la carte – cart
IGN blue map: carte bleue IGN –
    cart bluh ee jay en
Pack: le sac a dos – sahk ah doe
Poncho: poncho
Socks: les chaussettes – show-set
Strap: la courroie – coor-wha
Sun screen: la crème solaire – krem so-lare
Umbrella: la parapluie – pa-rah-ploo-ee
Walking shoes: les chaussures de marche –
    show-sir duh marsh
Walking stick: une canne – kahn
Waterproof jacket: l'imperméable –
    ahm-pair-may-ab_luh

12

CONTENTS

PRONUNCIATION: As an aid to those who are totally unfamiliar with French I have included an approximation of the pronunciation for each entry. Pronounce "A" as in A, B, C... and the letter "J" as in judge. Final consonants are silent or (as indicated by the smaller type) almost so. To get a feel for the sounds listen to French language tapes in your car or at home before you leave. When in France don't be afraid to make mistakes. Speak out!

France on Foot

What's the French for "the blind leading the blind?"

postcard sent after his first day walking in France

—Dwight Garner,

STUFF IN THE PACK

Belt: la ceinture – sahn-toor
Binoculars: les jumelles – jew-mell
Books: les livres – lee-v_{ruh}
Camera: l'appareil photo –
ahp-pah-ray foe-tow
Film: la pellicule – pel-lee-cool
Guide: la guide – geed
Hair brush: la brosse – brosse
Makeup: le maquillage – mah-kee-yaje
Notebook: le carnet – kar-nay
Pants: les pantalons – pahn-tah-loan
Panty hose: les collants – koe-lahn
Pen: un stylo – stee-low
Pencil: un crayon – kray-oh_n
Shampoo: le shampooing – shampooing
Shirt: la chemise – shuh-meeze
Shoes: les chaussures – show-soor
Skirt: la jupe – joop
Sweater: le pull – pool
Tooth brush: la brosse aux dentss –
bross oh dah_n
Toothpaste: le dentifrice – dehn-tee-freece
Turtle neck: le col montant –
coal mohn-tahn

13

MANMADE LANDMARKS

Barn: la grange – grawnje
Bridge: le pont – poh_n
Building: le bâtiment – bah-tee-meh_n
Canal: le canal – ka-nahl
Castle: le château – shah-tow
Cemetery: la cimetière – see-meh-tee-air
Church: l'église –A-glize
City Hall (village): la marie – mare-ee
City Hall (city): l'hôtel de ville – ...duh veal
Crossroad: le carrefour – car-foor
Ditch: le fossé – foe-say
Factory: l'usine – oo-zeen
Farm: la ferme – fairm
Fence: la clôture – clow-ture
Field: le champ – shahn
Garden: le jardin – jahr-dah_n
Gate: la barrière – bah-ree-air
Highway: la route – root
House: la maison – may-zoh_n
Orchard: le verger – vair-jay
Park: le parc – par
Road: la route – root
Ruins: les ruines – roo-een
School: l'école – A-coal
Station (train, bus): la gare – garr
Steeple: le clocher – cloe-shay
Telephone pole: le poteau – poe-toe

2

Windjacket: le blouson – blue-zoh_n
Whistle: le sifflet – seef-flay

Toilet: la toilette – twah-let
View: la vue – voo
A room that looks over the ocean:
une chambre qui donne sur la mer –
oon shawm-b_{ruh} key doan sir lah mare

General: en général – ohn jay-nay-ral
ATM: point argent – pwan tar-jah_n
Is there an ATM in town?
Es-ce-qu'il-y-a une ... en ville? –
Ess-_{suh}-keel-yah oon ... ehn veal

Bank: la banque – bawn-k
Bus station (long distance): la gare des cars –
gar day day car

Phone booth: la cabine téléphonique –
cah-bean tay-lay-phone-eek

Phone card: la télécarte – tay-lay-cart
Post office: la poste – post
Air mail: par avion – par ah-vee-oh_n
Package: un paquet – pah-kay
Post card: la carte postale – cart pos-tahl
Stamp: une timbre – tam-b_{ruh}
To the US: aux Etats Unis –
oh-zaye-ta-zoo-nee

Train station: la gare – gar
Traveler's check: cheque des voyageurs –
sheck day voy-a-jur

to cash (a check): toucher – too-shay

11

PICNICS

Picnic: pique-nique – peek-neek
How much does it cost? Ça fait combien? – sah fay com-be-ehn

Bakery: la boulangerie – boo-lahn-juh-ree
Bread: le pain – pahn
Long loaf: une baguette – bah-get
Rye bread: pain du seigle – ... dew say-gluh
Whole-wheat: pain complet – ...com-play

Butcher: la boucherie – boo-share-ree
Cheese: le fromage – fro-mahj
Ham: le jambon – jahm-bohn
Made here: fait à la maison – fet-ah la may-zohn
Pâté (country): pâté de campagne – pah-tay duh cahm-pine-yuh
Sausage: le saucisson – saw-see-sohn
Dry sausage: saucisson sec – ... seck

Grocery: l'épicerie – A-pee-suh-ree
Apple: une pomme – pohm
Chocolate: le chocolat – sho-ko-lat
Tomato: la tomate – toe-maht
Wine, red & white: Vin rouge et blanc – vihn rooje A blahn
Yoghurt: yaourt – yah-oort

WEATHER (CONT.)

Breeze: la brise – breeze
Clouds: les nuages – new-ahje
Cloudy: couvert – koo-ver
Cold: froid – fwah
  It's cold out: Il fait froid – eel fay fwah
Dry: sec – seck
Dust: la poussière – poo-see-yaihr
Fog: la brouillard – broo-ee-yar
Hail: la grêle – grell
Hot: chaud – show
Mistral – mee-strall
Mud: la boue – boo
Rain: la pluie – ploo-ee
  It's raining: Il pleut – eel pluh
  It's going to rain: Il va pleuvoir – eel vah pluh-vwar
Shower: une averse – ah-vairse
Snow: la neige – nehje
Storm (long): une tempête – tohm-pet
Storm (short): un orage – oh-rahj
Sun: le soleil – so-lay
Thunderstorm: un orage – oh-rahj
Tramontane – tra-mohn-tahne
Weather: le temps – tehm
Weather forecast: la météo – may-tay-oh
Wet: mouillé – moo-yay
Wind: le vent – vehn

Water: l'eau (cont.)
Without bubbles: sans gaz – sahn gahz
Large bottle (liter): grande bouteille – grawnd boo-tay-yuh

Brand names: Badoit, Perrier, Evian
bah-dwah, pear-ree-A, A-vee-ahn

Café Food: la nourriture – noor-ree-toor
Croque-monsieur – croak muh-see-uhr
Peanuts: cacahuètes – ka-ka-hwet
Sandwich: le sandwich – sand-weech
Ham/butter: ... jambon-beurre –
    sand-weech jam-bohn-bur

IN TOWN

Restaurant: le restaurant – res-tow-rahn
Full (all tables taken): complet – koam-play
Menu: le menu – meh-new
I would like the 60 FF menu.
Je prendrais le menu à 60 francs. –
juh prawn-dray ... ah swah-sahnt frawnk
to reserve: réserver – ray-zare-vay
I would like to reserve a table for two.
Je voudrais reserver une table pour deux.
juh voo-dray ... oon tah-bluh pore duh
We're two (for dinner etc): Nous sommes
deux. – new soam duh
Wine list: carte des vins – cart day vihn

DIRECTIONS (CONT.)

By: côte à côte – coat ah coat
Down below: en bas – ehn bah
Far: loin – luh-wahn
Is it far? Est-ce loin? – Ess luh-wahn
Here: ici – ee-see
Higher: plus haut – ploo oh
Inside: dedans – duh-dahn
Left: gauche – go-shh
Lower: plus bas – ploo bah
Near: près – pray
Is it near here? Est-ce près d'ici?
    Ess pray dee-see
Very near: tout près – too pray
Next to (buildings): à côté – ah koe-tay
Next to (road, etc): au bord – oh bore
On the other side: au delà – oh duh-lah
Outside: en dehors – ehn door
It's outside town: C'est en dehors de la
    ville – Say ehn door duh la veal
Right: droite – dwat
Straight ahead: tout droit – too dwah
Go straight ahead: Allez tout droit
    Ah-lay too dwah
There: là – lah
Up above: en haut – ehn oh
Where? ou – oo
Where is...? ou est...? – oo A

AT THE CAFE

I would like... je voudrais... – juh voo-dray

The bill, please: L'addition, syp –
lah-dee-see-ohn seal voo play

Toilet (water closet): WC – doo-bluh vay say

Where is the rest room, please?
La VC, svp? – lah vay say seal voo play

Drinks: les boissons – bwa-sohn

Beer: la bière – be-air

Draft beer: la pression – press-ee-ohn

Glass of draft: un demi – deh-mee

A glass of beer for me, please: Un demi
pour mois – uhn deh-mee poor mwah

Coffee: un café – kah-fay

Espresso: café express – kah-fay eh-spress

Espresso/rich milk: café crème – ... krem

Hot chocolate: un chocolat – show-ko-lah

Tea: le thé – tay

Tea w/lemon: thé avec citron –
tay ah-veck see-trohn

Tea w/rum: grog au rhum – grawg oh rum

Lemonade (fresh): citron pressé –
see-trohn preh-say

Water: l'eau – oh

Bottled: en bouteille – ehn boo-tay-yuh

Sparkling water: eau gazeuse – ...gahz-uhz

Still water: eau plat – oh plah

A FEW VERBS

to arrive: arriver – are-ree-vay

to cross: traverser – trah-vehr-say

to find: trouver – true-vay

to follow: suivre – sweeve-ruh

to go: aller – ah-lay

to go down: descendre – duh-sehn-druh

to go up: monter – mohn-tay

to leave: quitter – key-tay

to look for: chercher – share-shay

to stop: s'arrêter – sah-ret-tay

to stroll: se promener – suh pro-meh-nay

to take (a route): prendre – prawn-druh

to walk: marcher – mar-shay

WEATHER

Weather: le temps – tehm

Good weather: beau temps – bow tehm

Bad weather: mauvais temps – mo-vay tehm

It's nice out: Il fait beau – eel fay bow

The weather is miserable: Il ne fait pas beau

The weather will be good tomorrow:
Il va faire beau demain –
eel vah fair bow duh-mahn

Weather forecast: la météo – may-tay-oh

Do you know the forecast? Connaissez-vous
la météo Kohn-nay-say voo lah may-tay-o

IN TOWN (CONT.)

Hotel: hôtel – oh-tell

Bathtub: le bain – bahn

A room with a tub: une chambre avec bain
oon shawm-bruh ah-veck bahn

Bed: le lit – lee

Bill (hotel): la note – note

Blanket: la couverture – koo-vair-toor

Credit card: carte de crédit –
cart duh cray-dee

Do you take...? Acceptez-vous les...? –
ack-sep-tay-voo lay cart duh cray-dee

Noise: bruit – broo-ee

Pillow: l'oreiller – oh-ree-yay

Price: le prix – pree

The price of a room: ... d'une chambre –
luh pree doon shawm-bruh

to reserve: réserver – ray-zare-vay

I have a reservation: J'ai réserver – jay ...

Room: une chambre – shawmbruh

Room w/two beds: ... avec deux lits –
oon shawm-bruh ah-veck duh lee

Room w/one big bed: ... avec grand lit –
oon shawm-bruh ah-veck grawn lee

Sheet (bed): le drap – drah

Shower: la douche – doosh

Telephone: téléphone – tay-lay-fone

Television: télévision – tay-lay-vi-zee-ohn

Tower: la tour – toor

Town: la ville – veal

Trail (wide): le chemin – shuh-mehn

Trail: le sentier – sehn-tea-A

Trail (narrow): la trace – trahss

Village: le village – veel-lahj

Vineyard: le vignoble – veen-yo-bluh

Water tower: le château d'eau – ...dough

Way: la voie – vwah

Wind mill: moulin à vent –
moo-lahn ah vahn

DIRECTIONS

North: nord – nor

East: est – est

South: sud – suhd

West: ouest – west

To the right: à droite – ah dwaht

To the left: à gauche – ah go-shh

Straight ahead: tout droit – too dwah

Across from: en face – ehn fahss

After: après – ah-pray

At: à – ah

Above: au dessus de – oh duh-sue duh

Before: avant – ah-vahn

Below: en contrebas – ehn kohn-truh-bah

Beyond: au delà de – oh duh-lah duh

The form below is an all-purpose one. It can be used to order—from a variety of domestic sources—some of the required maps and guidebooks. It (or a photocopy) may also be used to order by FAX those guidebooks and maps only available overseas from Elstead and Gîtes de France. The phone/FAX numbers and addresses for the various stores and organizations, both domestic and foreign, can be found in the appendix on pages 219-222.

If you can't find this book in your local bookstore, copies may be ordered for $24.95 from the publisher, Attis Press, by FAX (VISA or MASTERCARD only) at 707 963-6089 or by mail at PO Box 209, Saint Helena, CA 94574-0209, USA. For domestic orders from Attis please add a $4.00 shipping (Priority Mail) and handling charge. For orders from another country, the shipping plus $1.00 handling will be added to your credit-card charge. For orders shipped to a California address, add the required 7.75% sales tax ($1.93 per book). Please include payment (credit card only from outside the USA) with your order.

Company you are ordering from: _____

Ordered by: Ship to (if different):

name: _____   name: _____

street: _____   street: _____

apt #, PO Box: _____   apt #, PO Box: _____

city: _____   city: _____

state: ____ zip: _____ country: ____   state: ____ zip: _____ country: ____

telephone (for questions or problems only): (____) _____

# copies	item	price each	total
	France on Foot (ISBN 0-9663448-0-4)		
	IGN map 903, Sentiers de Grande Randonnée		
	Carte Routière et touristique, Michelin Touring map #		
	Carte Routière et touristique, Michelin Touring map #		
	Michelin Hôtels-Restaurants—the Michelin "Red Guide"		
	Le Guide des hôtels-restaurants Logis de France—the Logis guidebook		
	Chambres et Tables d'hôtes—the bed-and-breakfast guidebook		
	Gîtes d'étape et de séjour—the gîtes guidebook		

ship via: surface ☐ air ☐ express service ☐ _____

subtotal	
shipping	
sales tax	
TOTAL	

check enclosed ☐

Signature (card orders) _____

Credit Card: VISA ☐ MASTERCARD ☐ AMERICAN EXPRESS ☐ other _____ ☐

Card # ☐☐☐☐☐☐☐☐☐☐☐☐☐☐☐☐ expires: ☐☐ ☐☐

Book design by the author.
Cover concept: Sandra McHenry Design, San Francisco.
Typefaces: Kepler and Kepler Expert, Adobe Systems, Inc.,
set 11.6/13.
Printed in Hong Kong, China.